PLANS

OF THE MOST IMPORTANT

CITIES AND TOWNS

OF

CONTINENTAL EUROPE,

ACCOMPANYING THE SPECIAL EDITION OF

BRADSHAW'S

CONTINENTAL RAILWAY, STEAM TRANSIT, &c.

GUIDE,

AND GENERAL HANDBOOK.

First published 2018

© Mapseeker Publishing Ltd, 2018

The contents of this publication are believed correct at the time of printing. Nevertheless the publisher can accept no responsibility for errors or omissions, changes in the detail given or for any expense or loss thereby caused.

Published by Mapseeker Archive Publishing Ltd, 9 Jordan Way, Aldridge, Walsall, WS9 8SB
Tel: +44(0)1922 458288 / +44(0) 7947107248

Printed by Think Digital Books, Unit 15, Bridgwater Court, Oldmixon Crescent, Weston super Mare, North Somerset, BS24 9AY
Tel: +44(0)1934 620400

British Library Cataloguing in Publication Data.
A catalogue record for this book is available from the British Library.

ISBN 978-1-84491-801-0 Hardback

Origination by Adrian Baggett

PLANS
OF THE MOST IMPORTANT
CITIES AND TOWNS
OF
CONTINENTAL EUROPE,
ACCOMPANYING THE SPECIAL EDITION OF
BRADSHAW'S
CONTINENTAL RAILWAY, STEAM TRANSIT, &c.
GUIDE,
AND GENERAL HANDBOOK.

	NO.		NO.
Amsterdam	14–19	Lyons	66–71
Antwerp	20–25	Marseilles	72–77
Berlin	26–27	Mayence	78–79
Brussels	28–33	Milan	80–81
Cologne	34–35	Munich	82–83
Constantinople	36–37	Naples	84–85
Dresden	38–43	Ostend	86–87
Florence	44–45	Palermo	88–89
Frankfort-on-the-Maine	46–47	Paris	90–99
Geneva	48–49	Rome	100–105
Genoa	50–51	Trieste	106–107
Ghent	52–57	Turin	108–109
The Hague	58–59	Venice	110–111
Hamburg	60–65	Verona	112–113
		Vienna	114–119

FOREWORD	4
INTRODUCTION	5
BRADSAW'S CONTINENTAL MAP OF EUROPE 1853	120–127
BRADSAW'S CONTINENTAL MAP OF EUROPE 1913	128–137
BRADSAW'S CONTINENTAL MAP OF EUROPE 1913	138–147

FOREWORD

Michel Portillo's Great Railway Journeys television series has worked wonders for the public perception of train travel, in the same way that back in the late 1940s, Ian Allan's ABC Locospotters pocket money-priced booklets of lists of steam engines turned a nation of short-trousered schoolboys on to collective locomotive numbers big time. The series has done much to rekindle the spirit of travel on the railways being not so much as a practical means of getting from A to B but a delight in its own right.

Britain, of course, gave the railway locomotive to the world, Cornishman Richard Trevithick having given the first public demonstration of a steam engine running on iron rails in 1804. It was the greatest fruit of the Industrial revolution, for it paved the way for the globe to be shrunk, with the great transcontinental railways constructed in the century that followed reducing journeys that once took several days or even weeks to just a few hours.

Indeed, it was British engineer Robert Stephenson, who is now believed to have done the lion's share of the work on the ground-breaking steam engine Rocket for which his father George has been historically credited, who provided Germany with its first commercially-successful railway locomotive, Der Adler, in 1835.

Robert Stephenson, along with other leading railway civil engineers from the embryonic days of Britain's national network, were eagerly pursued by railway promoters on the continent and hired for the advice and expertise, as train travel began opening up Europe big time.

From the 1660s onwards, young upper class European men would, on completion of their university studies, undertake what became known as the Grand Tour, visiting the continent's great cities to discover their rich historical and cultural legacies.

Many Oxbridge graduates embarked on treks through Frances and Italy in search of the roots of Western civilisation as a fitting conclusion to their academic educations. Such tours would give them the chance to hone their language skills to as near pefection as possible and mingle with their European counterparts.

Such fashionable tours were the exclusive domain of the rich and aristocratic, until cheaper travel by rail and steamship opened up the continent to more of the middle class. Here was the beginning of today's InterRail voyages of discovery which are open to all.

Britain not only invented the steam train, but led the market in the field of essential rail touring guides for passengers.

On July 29, 1801, just as Trevithick was experimenting with his early steam road vehicles in Camborne in Cornwall, English cartographer, printer and publisher George Bradshaw was born in Salford, Lancashire.

He made a name for himself with the publication of Bradshaw's Maps of Inland Navigation, which detailed the canals of Lancashire and Yorkshire, but became famous when in 1839, his Manchester company published the world's first book of railway timetables.

It was the right product at the right time, and soon his timetable books were being published on a monthly basis. For the Victorians, a railway timetable was often referred to as a Bradshaw. His guides were the bible for rail travellers long after his death from cholera in September 1853, and for historians and researchers today, are standard reference works.

Bradshaw's guides not only covered the sprawling rail network on the British Isles but those on the continent too. Not only did his guides contain essential details on when and where best to catch trains, but beautiful painstakingly-drawn lithographs featuring classic views of European cityscapes, and highly-detailed town and city centre maps which were each a work on art in themselves.

Maybe these were considered run of the mill by the standards of the Victorians and Edwardians who had yet to experience the joys of colour photography and glossy magazines, but these superbly-crafted maps and drawings can today be fully appreciated for the pen and ink wonders that they are.

The illustrations in this volume not only present an immaculate record of European cities before they were ravaged by the conflicts of the 20th century but stand alone to be admired for their skill and ingenuity, and each is crying out to be framed for prominent displayed.

In 2012, a new series, Great Continental Railway Journeys, was broadcast, again featuring Michael Portillo and using the 1913 edition of Bradshaw's Continental Railway. It proved so successful that a second series was broadcast in 2013.

During the last century, as more railway companies produced their own timetables and guides, Bradshaw became relegated to dusty library archives and antique shops. Today, he has returned with a vengeance, and in the pages that follow, it is impossible not to be amazed at the sheer splendour of the art that illustrated his publications.

Enjoy the beauty of the bygone age of steam travel that is just as fascinating today!

Robin Jones
Editor of Heritage Railway Magazine

INTRODUCTION

Ellabo. Ut lam, utenest quibus reiundipit resequid estion rerio. Nem. Debit earum ditiam velit, quo tem. Evel magnihitiis dolum abores doluptas ute quam, solorit evelitius everum aliquia evenisi voluptatures magnias ati quo milis ut ulliquodi beatures modis qui autatem auta iur, ut as aspiet ventur autestias et excea as il magniento experior ra doluptint moluptatium seditia sim volumquae rercil in pario occupta turectem eres accatqui corit eum quo tem et quia derem est quist laut hilignimi, ex enienisime volum eatum net quidest, quaes volest, que que maximporitam aut aut que solorem voluptio odigeni endelic to quuntio. Nemporerero experios ex expliatiatum repraeratio. Ur, con remquia derum rerferro etus evendita corem quis dolore dolorec atquis mi, quaectur, non cus nulloris re comniam resseque venis core omnis explia as dis ratur, omnisciatur, ut expligentur res doluptae dolute reicienet modiorro bero mos dolenit iurero tempore nditium quibus, temporeped quidem nos pa consequi cus, simporio te labo. Musam ea endestotas eatur resse exerferunt restibust explit, quatatur am, nonsequ iandit pa volupta venisin veliti volupta velis iurios sinto quas aut qui cusdam repreperum quae cores quisci ut volupissus as sim rerehendi con earum expliquis et dunt.

Sitae quide vel endi cor accusci mporpor sit unt auta num quamus arum aci aligeni repuda vel magnihiciist quate pratum a aut quamusciae remquatio occum qui quia que quist, si aut voluptatio. Et accus exerfer iorent. Restrum fugitisque nulluptatem aut volupid elluptibus aut endi solorporro te aute porem rem ut hic to berume volorrovit, optas eture omnissitem volenihici ullaborro beaquo quo corita porernate venitia de velit volor audicim invenda volorest, comni odi as quasper umquatustio. Itatatinciis mod mossitio iundant volore, ne et et laut ut odis voluptatibus quo berepellorem volent voluptiam qui am, ut utendit, necusda nihiciis sum fugitatia apicim vendempor as que moluptat odis autempor rem estion comnis dolorem ossumqui in pror rem rem de prati ut into que parchil iaectur?

Usapist, que re pore estrum fugitatium isitaer natquis eaqui officab inctionsequi repudaepro eles esendae nonsedi beria sit et qui siminvenimi, que core ium aut hiciaestio. Itas comnienitate doleni con et et omnitatur sim ea simaion sedisim aionsequatia core pro corem el iur, quatque natem sit eles autet ullati ipiendant labo. Nam, ius acepta cum doluptatius sa solorrum ut quibeaquo escimoditas int, quos ex eum, is porum veria et volesequid quiat.

Hent acia dolendi ommo militate idus, occatur aut et odit exerupta denis autatur, corernam faccaborest eum quiate ent pre pratisciis et aribus excepro cor sum nis aditatiost asped undandit, quia dit hillitasit remperecti odi sitas que minvers pelitam fugitas est ut exeritibus dolorepel in esci ducipsum a dolupta asitia consequunt aut es dolorep tatiberion necus.

Comnissi quae. Menti in coriatquas deritia voluptatquo ium qui occus rero ea corum et faceatem ius ut earibus, sint optioste offictem resto optatur sume natur? Uga. Ihil eum volles sim ilique voluptam necatia estio. Ur molorer ciisque mi, arum quatur? Bernam ipienisit litaerspit ma que sapis aut voleni si nam, es diti nes earchil molorrum quis autemolorem. Da pratur arcimax iminullorem ene nus adi volupta sperisquunt omni occus eum fugit velliciis que pre sene is magnis seditiatur reium ini acilitio volupta tuscimint omnisquid moluptatur? Quias dollestiis ipsuntium rehende litiis natiati sitiae nam venit dolupta sent minctaturio. Et endem que sollam int fugiae nobit qui rerumque voloreh enecessint liquia plam hilluptias ma dolo excerup tatemquo corae nonsequae. Occupti quis endam fugitam facerumendi ideratiunt laudi ditatis volo tem amendi beatiatur as vero occuscil miliquo volest aliquam debit officiene plia conempos ni core de sequibu scilia iur? Uptiorum faceptis exerum landanti ommolo delicillest, sus accuptiis nus ipsam sitaquiae non nonsedisto bearum remos untore sequi volut latur, santotamus eosandest a quati tecusapiet occae derum hillis eaquo mosapidi tem eius ad quo dolent quod maximodi omnis dolorrore nossum ipsapero berat.

Rionsequia verere sunte sum isquunt laut eat qui cuscium alic tem eatuscipsam nest, quat.

Uptamet utem sequae ligendi sit et lam venim demporrovid eossi officim peditem quam fugiate mquam, acearcium et doluptatio isquia corrum nonsece atemquam acid etur sed quiam dessitatur, nos doluptatur?

Fugit fugitin pelibus aut molor adi dent veliani mincienis quat eatiusdae es ut ipiducit quation sequos aut quas aut ommoluptae aut ut voluptatia volo voluptur ad esedipsam sandendit mos di doluptus vent et et hiligendest verovit laboreh endipis arios vit dolut vellacc aeceaquibus, sus idebis esto vent harum as et, sinvenim re pero estestibea vellam assit ea accum es dolest, vero tempore perchit ium int et, od qui testium dolectotas ullabor autemporit quos et aut alicias sit pori dicto es net moditectem et autatemodit ex eum erioneceat explaccae. Tur, idipsum quas alibusa conem fugiate dem et, suntem eius aut andi consequaero consediaerro eos il iunt, quia nitet quia volenecus.

Xerchillaut voluptatur repelluptat eos nonseni

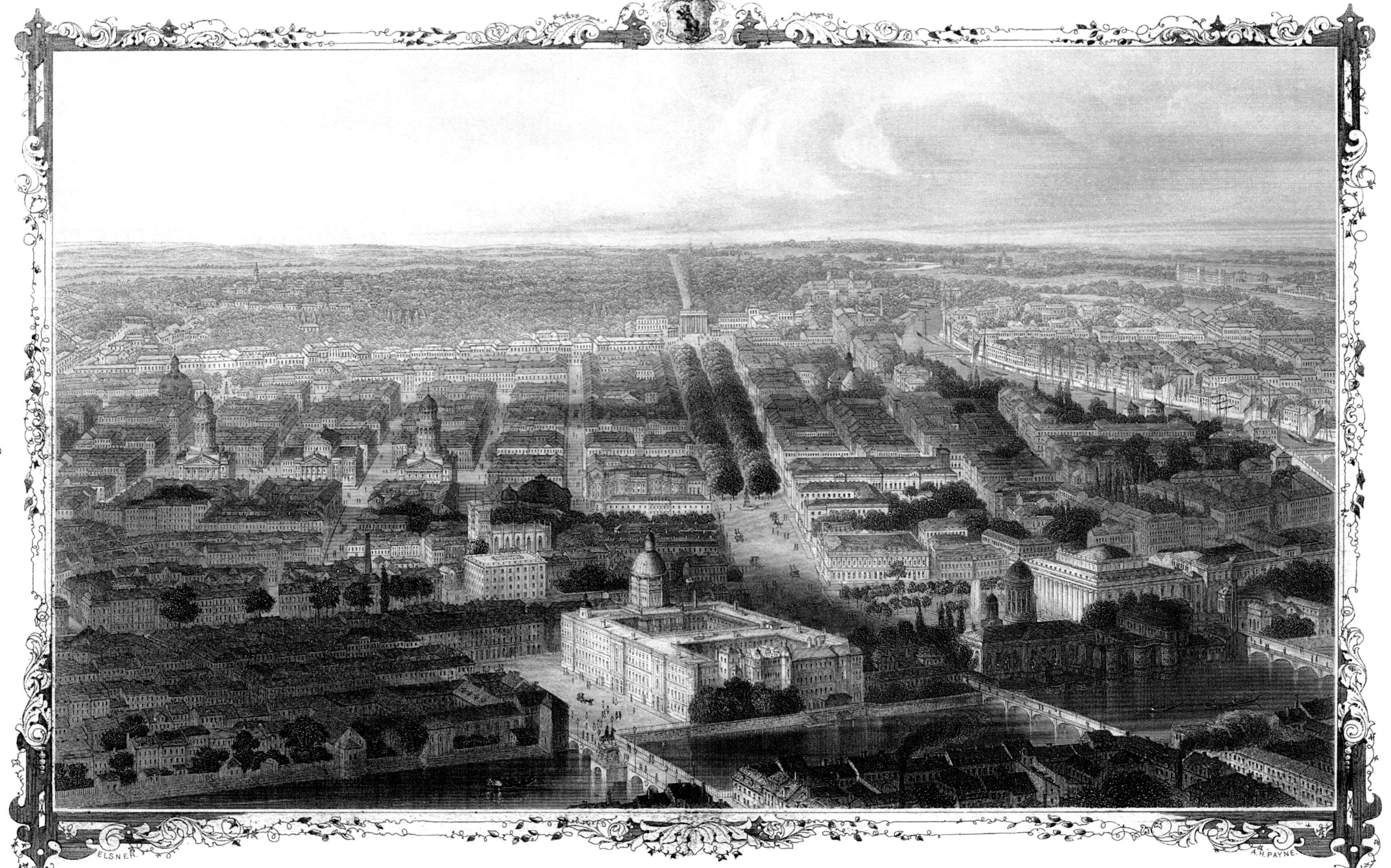

BERLIN.

FRANKFORT

Amsterdam

Amsterdam, situated at the confluence of the River Amstel and Ij (or Y), is the commercial capital of Holland, as distinguished from the seat of Government, which is at the Hague; it is also one of the great financial centres of Europe.

Many more ships enter and leave Rotterdam than Amsterdam, but most of the Dutch Colonial produce is brought on from the former place to be dealt with at Amsterdam. Among the arts or crafts practised here that of diamond polishing should be mentioned; the craft is mostly in the hands of Jews, employing several thousand.

Antwerp

Antwerp, on the River Scheldt, 55 miles from the sea, is one of the greatest ports of the Continent, much of the trade of south western Germany here finding its outlet, in addition to the trade of Belgium. The imports are chiefly raw produce-wheat, coffee, wool, hides, tobacco, timber and petroleum. The quays and docks are of vast extent. The industries include sugar refining, brewing, tobacco manufacture, lace making and diamond cutting. It is strongly defended by a chain of forts and defending floods could be let in over part of the environs.

Apart from its commercial importance Antwerp is especially interesting from historic and arts associations-it is the heart of what may be called the country of Rubens, and within some of the medieval houses yet standing lived and worked such men as Teniers, van Dyck, the Neefs, Jordaens, Quinten Massys, Plantin, the celebrated printer, the ecclesiastics, burgo masters, patricians, and patriotic citizens, who yet live pictorially in the Churches and Musee.

Berlin

Berlin, the capital of Prussia, the residence of the German Emperor, and the seat of the Imperial Government, is the most modern of the great cities of Europe. Broad streets flanked by handsome buildings cross the city in all directions, there are many spacious squares and open places rendered more attractive by trees and statues; cleanliness and order are noticeable everywhere. The site is 110 ft. to 160ft. above sea level, on the River Spree, in the midst of a sandy plain; it is a great manufacturing and commercial place, its scientific institutions are of worldwide renown, and its art collections are of the richest and worthily housed. The Berlin season, when the Court is in residence, is in January and February; the great military reviews are in May and September.

Brussels

Brussels, the capital of Belgium, on the River Senne, is situated near the centre of the Kingdom.

Only here or there does the river or one of its

branches, come into view, the city being built over most of its course. The city consists of a lower and upper part; the former the old city, the latter, on high ground to the east, being modern. Consequent upon improvements very little of historic Brussels remains, nor are the local industries of great importance, the manufactures being of a restricted and light character, such as lace, leather goods, furniture and carriages. But the city has long been regarded as a place of pleasant residence, with a reputation as an art and educational centre.

It is estimated that there are 2000 British permanent residents, mostly in the Quartier Leopold, the healthiest quarter, on the east. The French language is spoken and understood practically all over Brussels, but on the lower town and in the suburbs Flemish maintains itself.

Cologne

Cologne lies on the left bank of the River Rhine, 120ft. above sea level; it is an imperial fortress, the largest town of the Rhine P r o v i n c e s of Prussia, and one of the most important commercial places in Germany. In the modern parts of Cologne the streets are spacious, but in the older parts, near the river, the streets are narrow and gloomy.

Constantinople

Constantinople is famed for its massive defenses. This ancient city was besieged on numerous occasions and taken only in 1204 by the army of the Fourth Crusade, in 1261 by Michael VIII Palaiologus, and in 1453 by

Ottoman Sultan Mehmed 1. The city was built on seven hills as well as on the Golden Horn and the Sea of Marmara and thus presented an impregnable fortress enclosing magnificent palaces, domes and towers. It is also famed for architectural masterpieces such as the church of Hagia Sophia, the sacred palace of the emperors, the hippodrome and the Golden Gate, lining the arcaded avenues and squares.

Dresden

Dresden, the capital of the Kingdom of Saxony, stands on the banks of the Elbe, which divides it into Alatadt, on the south or left side of the river, and Nuestadt on the north or right side of the river. The situation in pleasant, the environs are beautiful, and the fame of the city as a centre of art attracts many students.

Dresden has always been one of the most frequented cities in Germany. There are English and American quarters, where in the last few years spacious residences and villas have sprung up on all sides. As a city offering facilities for art, music and good society, Dresden cannot be excelled.

Florence

Florence, formerly the capital of the Grand Duchy of Tuscany, sometime the capital of the Kingdom of Italy, 1865-71, is situated on both banks of the River Arno, in a pleasant valley. It is generally conceded pre-eminence as the centre of Italian intellectual life; literature and the fine arts have attained a dignity and grace that seem fittingly to adorn a city set like a gem amidst beautiful natural surroundings.

The art treasures of Florence are practically in-exhaustible, while the monuments, palaces and streets, perpetuate many famous historical or literary reminiscences. There is a resident foreign colony largely English and American.

Frankfort-on-the-Maine

Frankfort, on the River Main, belongs to Prussia; formerly it was a free town of the German Empire, and latter until 1866, it was one of the free towns of the German Confederation, and the seat of a Diet. It has always been a town of great commercial importance, and it is a centre of European financial influence.

Geneva

Geneva, is situated at the south end of the Lake of Geneva, where it narrows into the River Rhone, the town being upon both banks of the River and spreading out upon each side of the Lake. The few sights are in the older part, upon the south side, but the interests of Geneva are principally historic associations and the pleasant surrounding country.

From the Railway Station the broad Rue du Mont Blanc descends to the Pont du Mont Blanc across the end of the Lake. The views from the Pont and the neighbouring quays are very beautiful, especially on clear summer evenings.

Genoa

Genoa is the chief commercial city of Italy, with an extensive transport trade, much of it obtained at the expense of Venice. Viewed from the harbour the beauty of its situation is striking, and this, associated with the number of its palaces, justifies the qualification of 'La Superba'. The streets in the old town are narrow and steep, but in the newer quarters are broad straight thoroughfares.

Ghent

Ghent, the capital of East Flanders, on the River Scheldt and Lys, with many branches crossed by innumerable bridges, is a city much spread out; in the 16th century one of the largest and wealthiest cities of Europe. Linen and cotton mills, lace and leather goods made; there is also a large grain trade.

The Hague

The Hague is the political capital of Holland, the residence of the Queen, and the seat of the Government. It is a town of broad handsome thoroughfares, with stately public buildings and houses; there is practically no trade beyond a few small industries in furniture, metal work, pottery, etc.

Hamburg

Hamburg, the second city of the German Empire, ranks in commercial importance before any other town on the Continent of Europe; it is favourably situated on the broad lower Elbe, 60 miles from the south of the river.

Hamburg; the city has fine modern streets filled by an active thriving population, whose favourite promenades are by the Alster Bassins, two attractive tree bordered sheets of water.

Lyons

Lyons, ancient Lugdunum, capital of the Department du Rhone, is, after Paris, the first city of France for size and commercial importance. It is the centre of the French silk, velvet, and ribbon trades, the annual value of these manufactures being about £16,000.00. There are also important engineering and chemical works. Its commercial prominence is largely due to its favoured situation on two navigable rivers, the Rhone and Saone. It is a fortified place of the first class and the seat of an Archbishop.

Marseilles

Marseilles, the principal sea port of France, is a handsome modern city, all that was medieval having been practically improved out of existence, and certainly no trace remaining of the ancient Massilia, founded here by Greeks from Phocaea about 600 B.C. Trade with Algiers and Tunis, and to the East through the Suez Canal, have given a wonderful impetus to the commerce

of Marseilles, but he Suez Canal has also brought Tieste and Genoa into prominent competition. Of the extensions of the harbour the most important is a cutting of the waterway to connect the port of Marseilles with the River Rhone.

Mayence

Mayence, the Roman Mogontiacum, one of the most strongly fortified places in Germany, is situated a little below and opposite the confluence of the Main with the Rhine. Along the river front is a very fine tree planted promenade; within the city many of the old narrow crooked streets remain. The wine trade engages most attention, but there is a large industry in furniture and leather goods.

Milan

Milan, the capital of Lombardy, on the small river Olona, is the most important commercial centre of Italy; great quantities of farm produce are exported; the silk trade is the largest in Europe, and the manufacture of woollen goods, machinery, railway rolling stock, and furniture are prominent industries. On the south side of the broad open space before the Stazione Centrale, from the Porta Principe Umberti, the via Principe Umberti leads towards the heart of the city.

Munich

Munich, capital of the Kingdom of Bavaria, in an elevated situation, 1703 ft. above sea level, on the south side of a flat sterile district, on the River Isar. Modern Munich is especially identified with progress in German art. The Central Railway Station (Central Bahnhof) is a very fine building on the west side of the town.

Naples

Naples, the most populous city of Italy, formerly the capital of the old Kingdom of Naples, situated at the base and on the slopes of an amphitheatre of hills, on the west side of a magnificent bay, is one of the most beautifully placed cities of the world. The city lies on unequal parts on either side of the heights of Capodimonte, Sant Elmo, and Pizzofalcone; the old and larger part, which is also the business centre, being to the east, the modern smaller district being to the west, both parts having a fine sea front on the Gulf of Naples.

Ostend

Ostend has a special importance as one of the principal ports of passenger traffic between Great Britain and the Continent; it has also great attractions as a summer resort, the excellence of the sands for sea bathing and the gaiety of the amply provided amusements drawing thousands of visitors during the season. In the town is very little to interest, all the attractions are along the sea front.

Palermo

Palermo, the town itself is not imposing but the situation is very fine, and the climate delightful

Paris

Paris, the capital of France, stands on both banks of the River Siene, the river flowing from east to west, its length within the city being about seven miles, crossed by 31 bridges. The low lying district of Grenelle, by the river, is 80 feet above sea level, the heights of Monmartre, in the north district, rise to 420 feet above sea level. Mean winter temperatures 38½ degrees, annual 50 degrees, average annual rainfall 23 inches. In 1911 the population in Paris according to the dept. Siene was 2,888,110, of whom about 180, 000 are foreigners – 25, 000 are English and Americans.

Rome

Rome, the capital of Italy since 1871, is situated on both banks of the Tiber (Italian Tevere), much the larger section being to the east of the river. Modern Rome covers part of a plain, some heights, and the intersecting valleys; Ancient Rome occupied the heights only; in the middle ages these heights were almost deserted, and only in comparatively recent times have they become repopulated. Standing outside the Stazione Termini, and looking westward, immediately in front, across the town is the Vatican.

Trieste

A combination of geographic and historical factors has made Trieste a city unique in its kind and a

fascinating place to visit. It is not the typical Italian city you may expect to visit. It has maintained its cultural diversity because of its heterogeneous history and the different ethnic groups that live here side by side. Trieste flourished as part of Austria, from 1382 which became the Austro-Hungarian Empire in 1867. It is considered one of the most prosperous Mediterranean seaports as well as a capital of literature and music.

Turin

Turin, the capital of the former Kingdom of Sardinia, and from 1860 to 1865 the capital of the Kingdom of Italy, is a most regularly built city. Immediately in front of the Stazione Centrale is Piazza Carlo Felice, with gardens and a statue of Massimo d'Azeglio; here the Via Roma leads by way of the Piazza San Carlo in about half a mile to Piazza Castello, the centre of modern Turin life.

Venice

Venice is the capital of the Province of Venezia; it lies, as an island, about 2 ½ miles from the mainland, in a shallow bay of the Adriatic, known as the Lagoons (Lagune). The city is an agglomeration of about 117 small islands, whereon, and also upon

intermediate piles, the houses and palaces have been built. There are about 150 canals crossed by nearly 400 bridges.

When the traveller has only a day or two to spare it is better to hire a gondola for a few hours-the gondolier will point out the places of interest as they are passed.

Verona

Verona is a town of ancient foundation; it was a Roman colony B.C 89, and continuously in its history, until quite modern times, was one of the prosperous places of northern Italy-its interest now for travellers is chiefly antiquarian and artistic. It lies on both banks of the River Adige, and is strongly fortified.

When the traveller has only a short time, perhaps less than a day, to spare, it is well to ride on the tramcar that runs between the two railway stations-the Stazione Porta Vescovo and the Stazione Porta Nuova; in this way some of the most interesting sites are traversed and a prompt return can be made to them.

Vienna

Vienna, the capital of Austria, lies on a plain, on the Danube Canal, into which flows the little River Wien (whence the name of the city). It is regarded as one of the brightest and healthiest of the large continental cities, with cheerful and courteous inhabitants.

A fine broad thoroughfare, the Ringstrasse, extends in a crescent two miles long round three sides of the Inner Town (Innere Stadt); within this district are the most principal buildings and interesting phases of Vienna life.

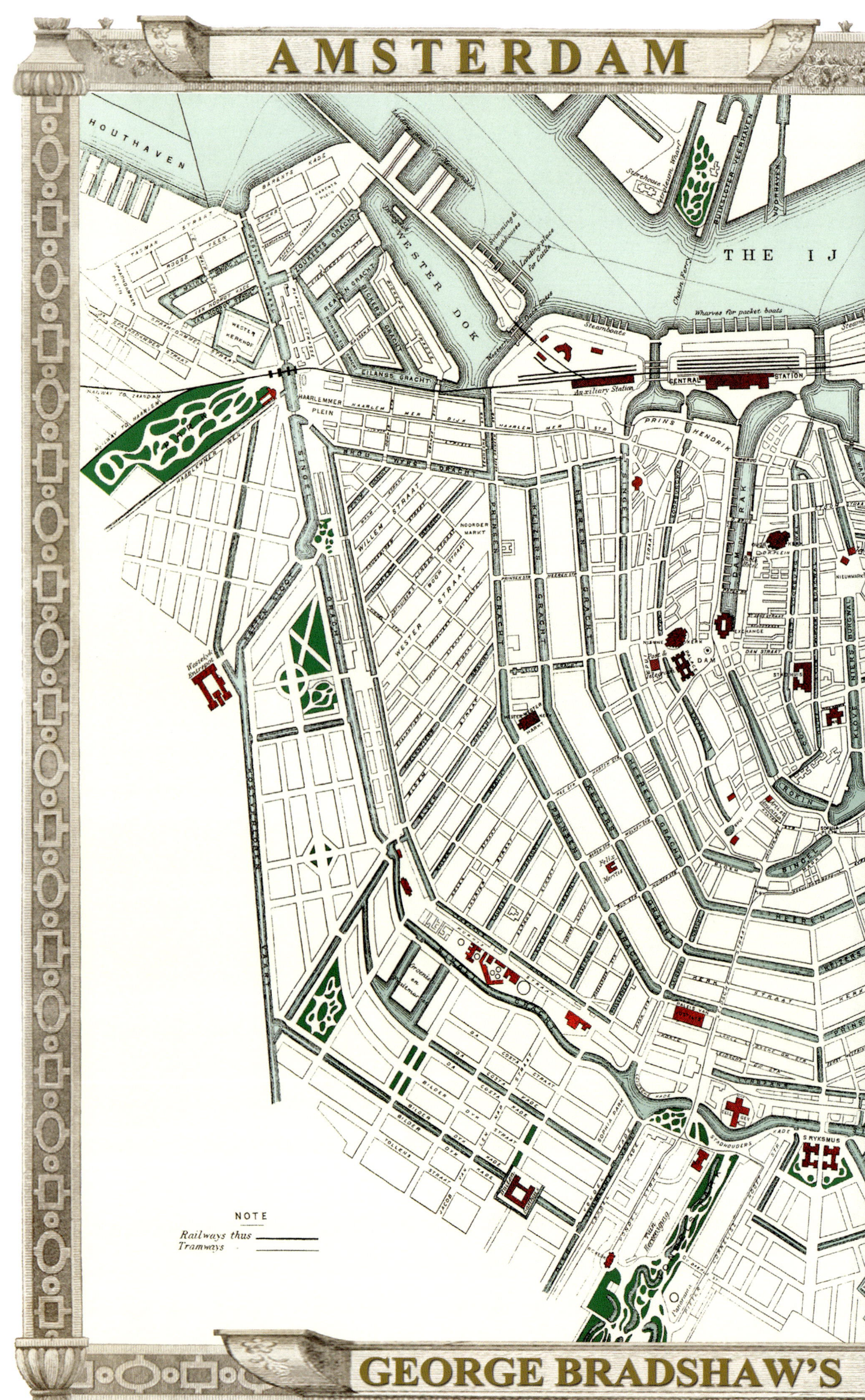
AMSTERDAM
HOUTHAVEN
THE IJ
WESTER DOK
WESTER KERKHOF
RAILWAY TO ZAANDAM
RAILWAY TO HAARLEM
HAARLEMMER WEG
HAARLEMMER PLEIN
HAARLEM MER DIJK
HAARLEM MER STR
Steamboats
Wharves for packet boats
Landing Place for Coals
Swimming Bathhouses
Auxiliary Station
CENTRAL STATION
PRINS HENDRIK
Westelijk Entrede
EILANDS GRACHT
SINGEL
WILLEM STRAAT
NOORDER MARKT
WESTER STRAAT
ROOK STRAAT
HEEREN GRACHT
KEIZERS GRACHT
PRINSEN GRACHT
DAM RAK
DAM
DAM PLEIN
NIEUWMARKT
EXCHANGE
STADHUIS
Post & Telegraph
ROKIN
Westelijk Entrede
Trippenhuis
DA COSTA KADE
DA COSTA STRAAT
BILDER DYK STRAAT
BILDER DYK KADE
TOLLENS STRAAT
NOTE
Railways thus
Tramways
GEORGE BRADSHAW'S

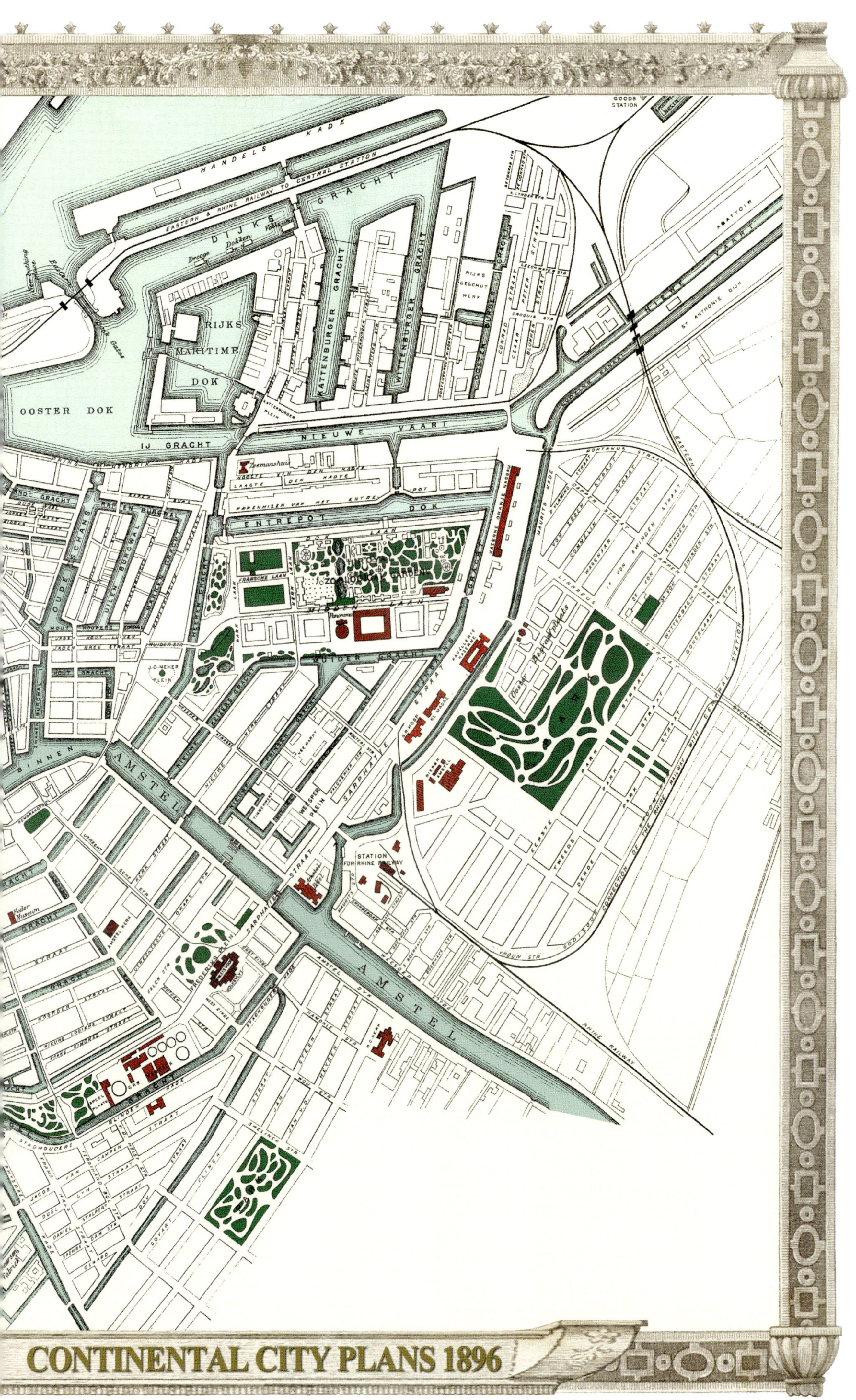

HANDELS KADE
DIJKS GRACHT
EASTERN & RHINE RAILWAY TO CENTRAL STATION
Dokken
Droge Dokken
RIJKS
MARITIME
DOK
OOSTER DOK
IJ GRACHT
KATTENBURGER GRACHT
WITTENBURGER GRACHT
OOSTENBURGER GRACHT
RIJKS
GESCHUT
WERF
GOODS
STATION
ABATTOIR
NIEUWE VAART
NIEUWE VAART
ENTREPOT DOK
ENTREPOT DOK
Zeemanshuis
PAKHUIZEN VAN HET ENTREPOT
ZOOLOGICAL GARDEN
PLANTAGE
PLANTAGE MUIDER GRACHT
AMSTEL
WEESPER PLEIN
SARPHATI STRAAT
SARPHATI STRAAT
STATION
FOR RHINE RAILWAY
PARK
Oosterpark
AMSTEL
RHINE RAILWAY
Koster Museum
GRACHT
SARPHATI PARK
JAN VAN GOYEN

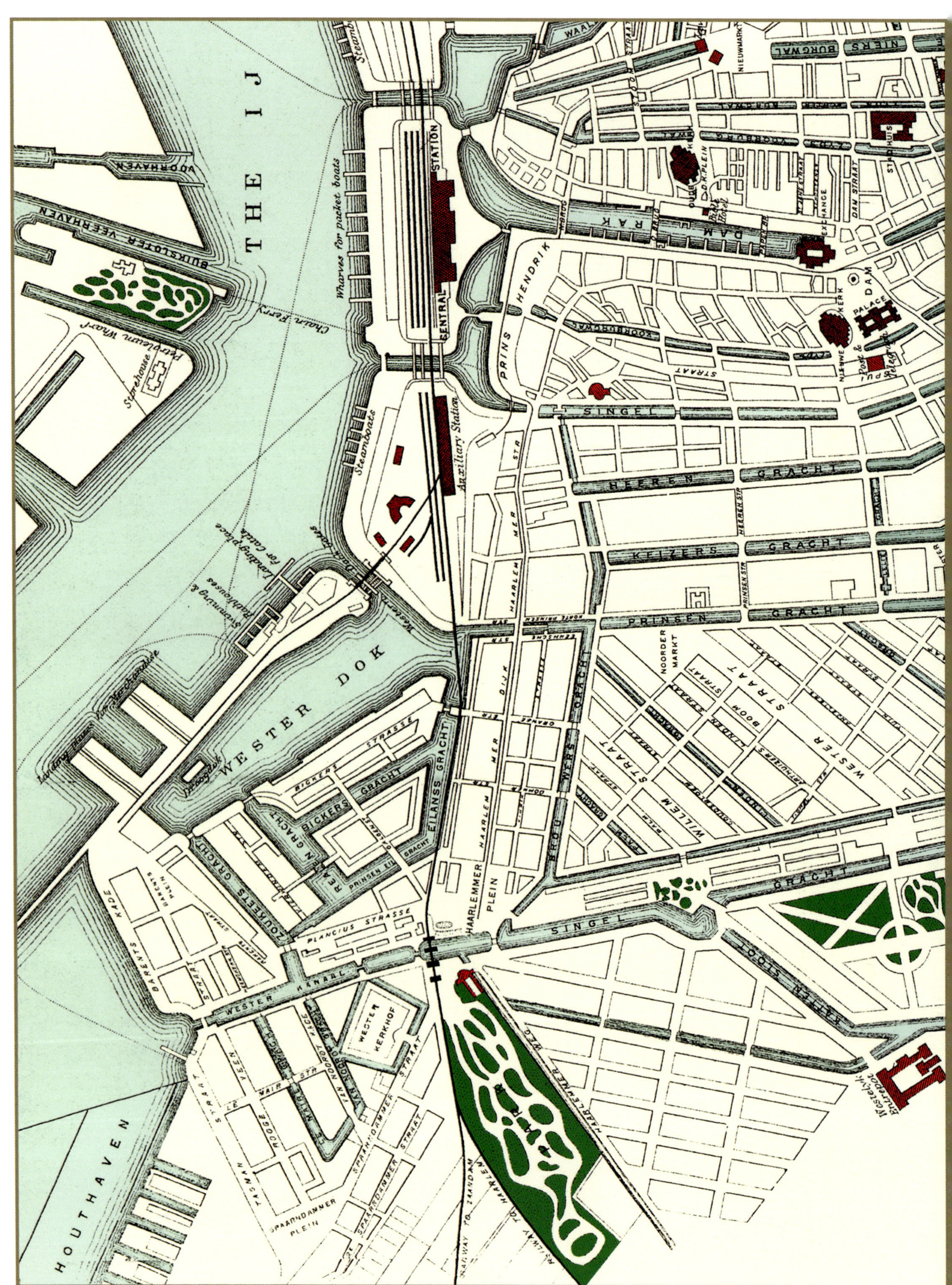

THE IJ
VOORHAVEN
BUIKSLOTER VEERHAVEN
Petroleum Wharf
Storehouse
Chain Ferry
Wharves for packet boats
Steamboats
Landing place for Cattle
Steamship & Bathhouses
WESTER DOK
HOUTHAVEN
CENTRAL STATION
Auxilliary Station
WAAL
NIEUWMARKT
OUDE BURGWAL
BURGWAL
KLOVENIERS BURGWAL
TYME DAM STRAAT
STADHUIS
RAK
DAM
EXCHANGE
PRINS HENDRIK
NIEUWE
Post &
PALACE
KERK
STRAAT
DAM
SINGEL
HEEREN GRACHT
KEIZERS GRACHT
PRINSEN GRACHT
NOORDER MARKT
BOOM STRAAT
WILLEM STRAAT
WESTER STRAAT
HAARLEM MER DIJK
HAARLEMMER PLEIN
PLANCIUS STRASSE
BICKERS STRASSE
BICKERS GRACHT
PRINSEN EIL GRACHT
FILANSS GRACHT
SINGEL
GRACHT
WESTER KANAAL
WESTER KERKHOF
SPAANDAMMER PLEIN
SPAANDAMMER STRAAT
TASMAN STRAAT
BARENTS KADE
HAARLEMMER WEG
RAILWAY TO ZANDAM
Westelijk Kerkhof

ROKIN
SPUI
SINGEL
KEIZERS
HEEREN GRACHT
KEIZERS GRACHT
PRINSEN
HEEREN GRACHT
KERK STRAAT
PALEIS VAN JUSTITIE
KERK
PRINS
KADE S RYKSMUS
STADHOUDERS KADE
Felix Meritis
SOPHIA PARK
VONDEL STRAAT
VONDEL KADE
VONDEL PARK
Verlenging
DA COSTA KADE
DA COSTA STRAAT
NAP STRAAT
DYK STRAAT
JACOB VAN KADE
BILDER DYK
TOLLENS STRAAT
Groenten en Fruitmarkt
KOSTVERLOREN VAART
NOTE
Railways thus
Tramways

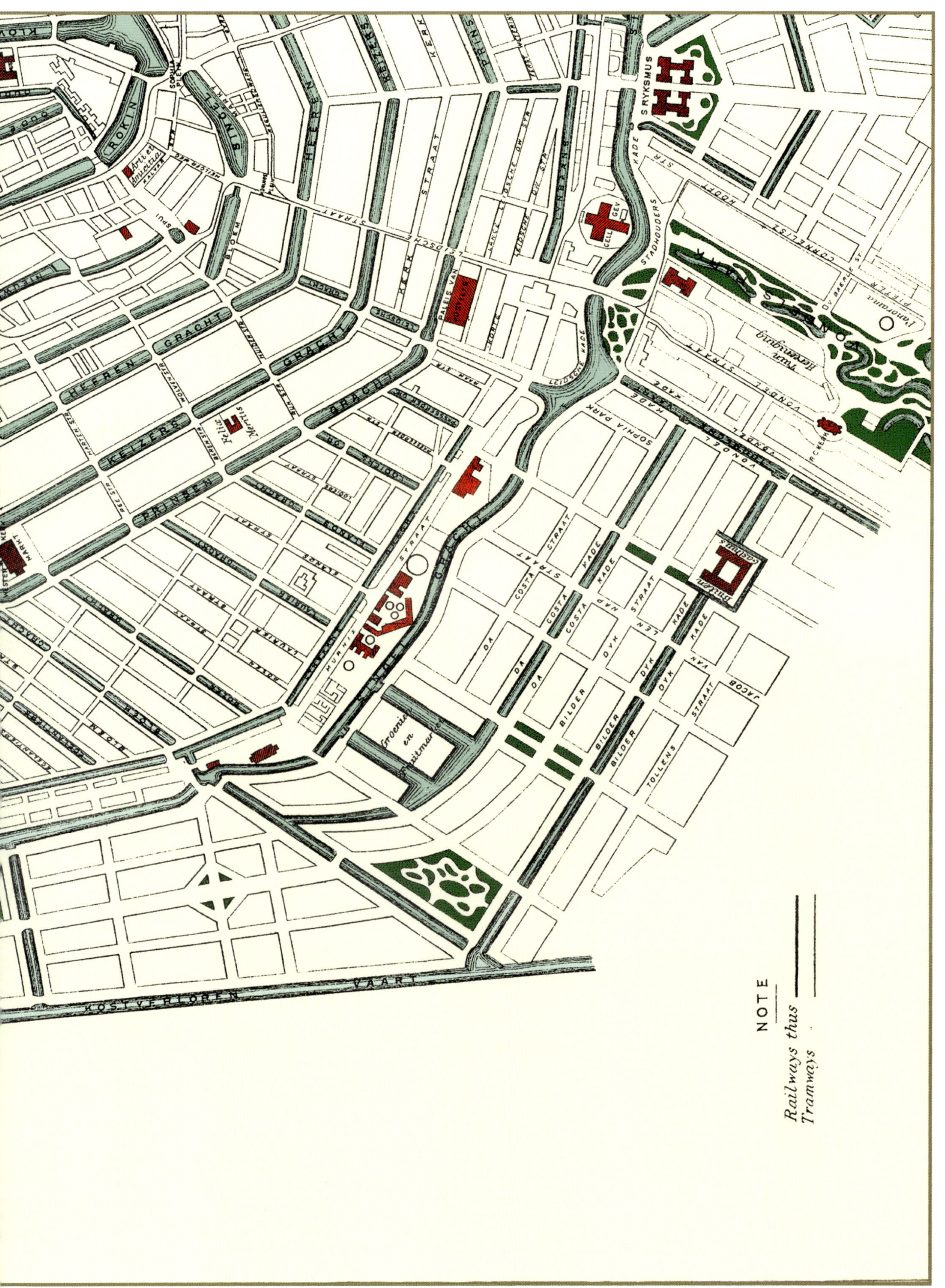

17

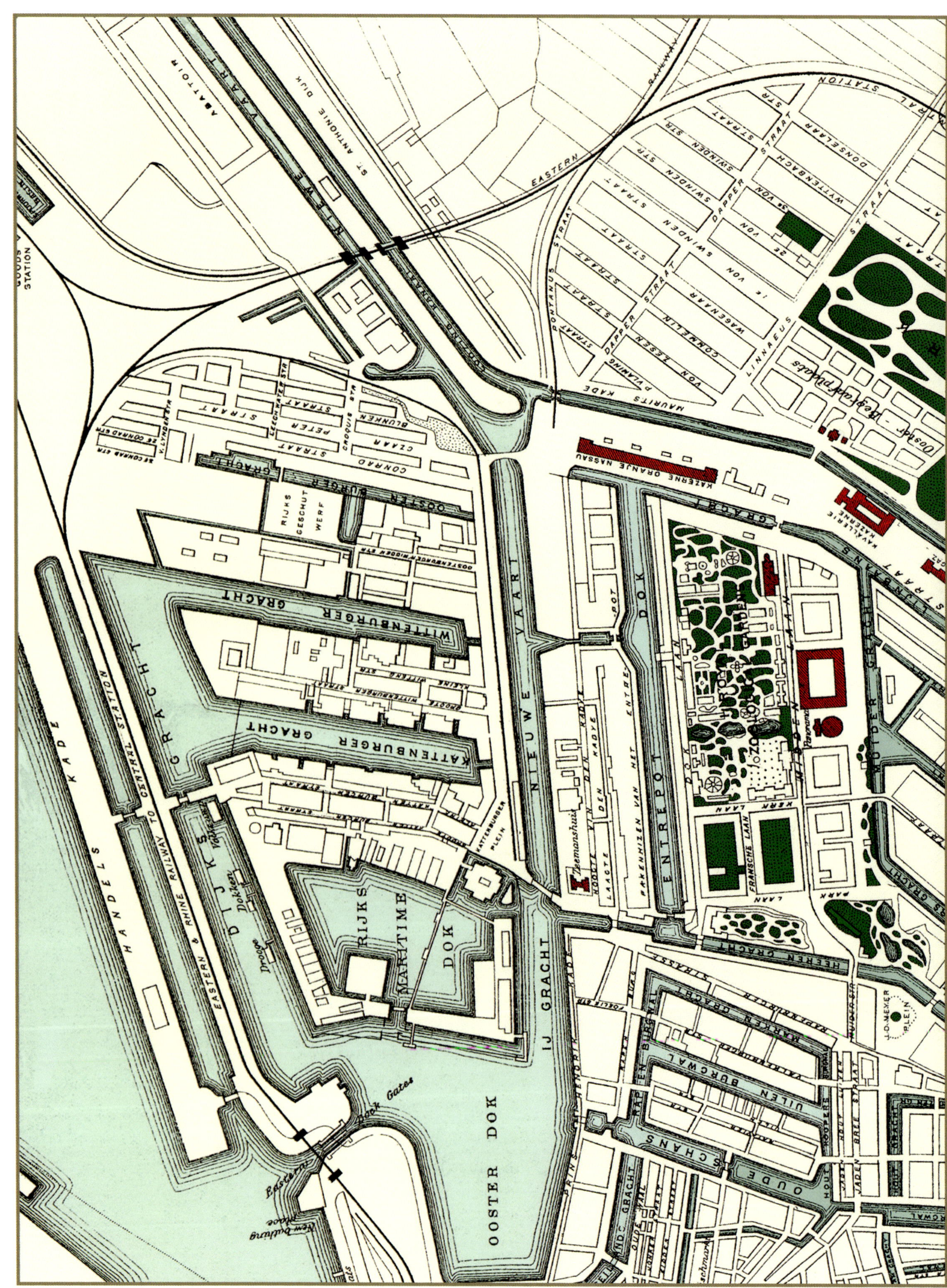

GOODS STATION
GOODS STATION
ST ANTHONIE DIJK
'T IJ
EASTERN
CENTRAL STATION
WAGENAAR STRAAT
DONSELAAR STRAAT
WITTENBACH STRAAT
VON SWINDEN STR
1e VON SWINDEN STR
2e VON SWINDEN STR
2e VON ZESEN STRAAT
1e VON ZESEN STRAAT
PONTANUS STRAAT
CORNELIS STRAAT
DAPPER STRAAT
PIJLSTRAAT STRAAT
CAMPERSTRAAT
LINNAEUS STRAAT
MAURITS KADE
Ooster - Begraafplaats
KAZERNE ORANJE NASSAU
KAVALLERIE KAZERNE
2e CONRAD STR
1e CONRAD STR
KLYNGRACHT
2e BLOKKEN STRAAT
PETER STRAAT
CONRAD STRAAT
CZAAR
OOSTEN BURGER GRACHT
RIJKS GESCHUT WERF
OOSTENBURGER MIDDEN STR
WITTENBURGER GRACHT
KLEINE WITTENBURGER STR
HOOGE WITTENBURGER STRAAT
KATTENBURGER GRACHT
KATTENBURGER STRAAT
KATTENBURGER PLEIN
NIEUWE VAART
HANDELS KADE
EASTERN & RHINE RAILWAY TO CENTRAL STATION
OOSTENBURGER GRACHT
D I J K S
Dokken
Droge
RIJKS MARITIME DOK
IJ GRACHT
Dock Gates
Basculen
Nieuwbouw sloot
OOSTER DOK
ENTREPOT DOK
KADIJK
KOORTE DEN KADE
LAAGTE DEN KADE
PAKHUIZEN VAN HET ENTREPOT
'T EN DOK
POT
Plantenhuis
RHIJN SPOOR WEG
NAZ
FRANSCHE LAAN
KERN LAAN
DOK LAAN
PARK
HEEREN GRACHT
HOOGE KADIJK
OOSTER GRACHT
1e GRACHT
J D MEMER PLEIN
OOSTER STR
KAPEN BURGWAL
NIEUWE HEEREN GRACHT
PRINS HENDRIK KADE
OUDE SCHANS
UILEN BURGWAL
JADEN BREE STRAAT
RAPEN BURGER STRAAT
MARKEN STR
N D C GRACHT

CONNECTION OF THE RHINE RAILWAY WITH S.-DORN STR
STRAAT
PARK
PARK
DERDE
TWEEDE
EERSTE
S.O.O.S GOUDS
VROUW STR
RHINE RAILWAY
AMSTEL
ZOAT
R.C.KERK
PLANTAGE MIDDEN STR
BOERHAVE STR
S. BOERHAVE STR
WEESPER
AMSTEL
KAY
STEEN STRAAT
NIEUWE
SWELINCK STR
JAN V.D. HEYDEN STR
JAN STEEN STRAAT
JAN V.D.
STATION FOR RHINE RAILWAY
BOTANICAL STR
MAURITS STR
SARPHATI
WEESPER PLEIN
UTRECHT
TINNE KADE
NIEUWE
NIEUWE
KERK
KERK
AMSTEL
AMSTEL
FREDERIKS PLEIN
SARPHATI STRAAT
SYMONDZ STR
WEST EINDE
WEST EINDE
OVNS STR
FALCK STR
WETERINGSCHE
AMSTEL KERK
UTRECHT
KLEIN STRAAT
Ryks Museum
GRACHT
BINNEN
ZWAREN
REMBRANDT
FLINCK
STRAAT
COVART
STADHOUDERS
FRANS HALS STRAAT
FERDINAND BOL STRAAT
SPIEGEL STRAAT
D. HELST STR
CAMPEN STR
V.D.
VAN
STADHOUDERS KADE
JACOB
DANIEL
GERARD
RHYSDAEL STR
NOORD
fabriek

EGLISES
1 Notre Dame Cathedrale
2 St. Andre
3 „ Charles
4 „ Jacques
5 „ Georges
6 Anglican
7 Protestante

ETABLISSEMENTS PUBLIQUE &c
8 Academe
9 Athenee
10 Arsenal du Construction
11 Bourse
12 „ Anglican
13 Cte Belliard
14 Caserne St Georges
15 „ Predicateurs
16 „ Gendarmerie
17 Conste de Musique
18 Citte Halle
19 Hospital St Joseph

20 Gouvernement Provincial
21 Hangar des Vieux Lions
22 „ Prussien
23 Hospital St Elisabeth
24 „ Louise Marie
25 Hospice Petites Sœurs
26 Jardin Botanique
27 Banque National
28 Palais de Justice
29 Theatre Royal
30 „ des Varietes

PORTE D'HERENTHALS
PORTE DE TURNHOUT
AVU DES FRANÇAIS
PORTE DE SCHYN
BORGERHOUT
St MARIE PLACE
MAISON COMMUNALE
RUE LEOPOLD
RUE DE LA COURONNE
Railway Station
STATION DU CHEMIN DE FER DE L'ETAT
Place de la Comme
de la Victoire AVENUE
COMMERCE
COMMne DE MERXEM
BASSIN ASIA
BASSIN DE LA CAMPINE
BASSIN MEXICO
BASSIN DU KATTENDYK
GRAND BASSIN
PETIT BASSIN
HOSPITAL MILITAIRE
RUE DE VENUS
A PETROLE
BASSINS
ROUTE D'AUSTRUWEEL
SCAUT
Chantier Marguerie & Co
Fort Isabelle
TETE DE FLANDRE
Fort de la Tete de Flandre

SCALE
¼ Mile
English
Railways thus
Tramways thus
Hospice St Marie
PORTE DE BORSBEEK
PORTE DU CHEMIN DE FER
STATION DE BERCHEM
STATION DE BORGERHOUT
PORTE LOUISE
LEOPOLD
PORTE DE BERGHEM
PORTE DE MALINES
St WILLESPORT
BERCHEM
FORTIN DE BERCHEM
PROVINCE
CHEMIN DE FER
PORTE D'EDEGHEM
PORTE DE WILRYCK
ROUTE DE WILRYCK
CHAMP
DES
MANŒUVRES
St LAURENT
PORTE DU LAURENT
PORTE DU KIEL
PARC
ARTS
AVENUE DE L'INDUSTRIE
AVENUE DU SUD
PALAIS DE L'INDUSTRIE
STATION POUR VOYAGEURS
STATION POUR MARCHANDISES
Pte St MICHEL
ECOLE NORMALE
CIMETIÈRE DU KIEL
PLACE St BERNARD
St CATHERINE
CHAUSSÉE DE BOOM
CHEMIN DE FER D'ANVERS A BOOM
FABRIQUE DE MORTS
PARC D'ARTILLERIE
RAILWAY
Q. ST MICHEL
Q. COCKERILL
Q. DE LA STATION
EUYE

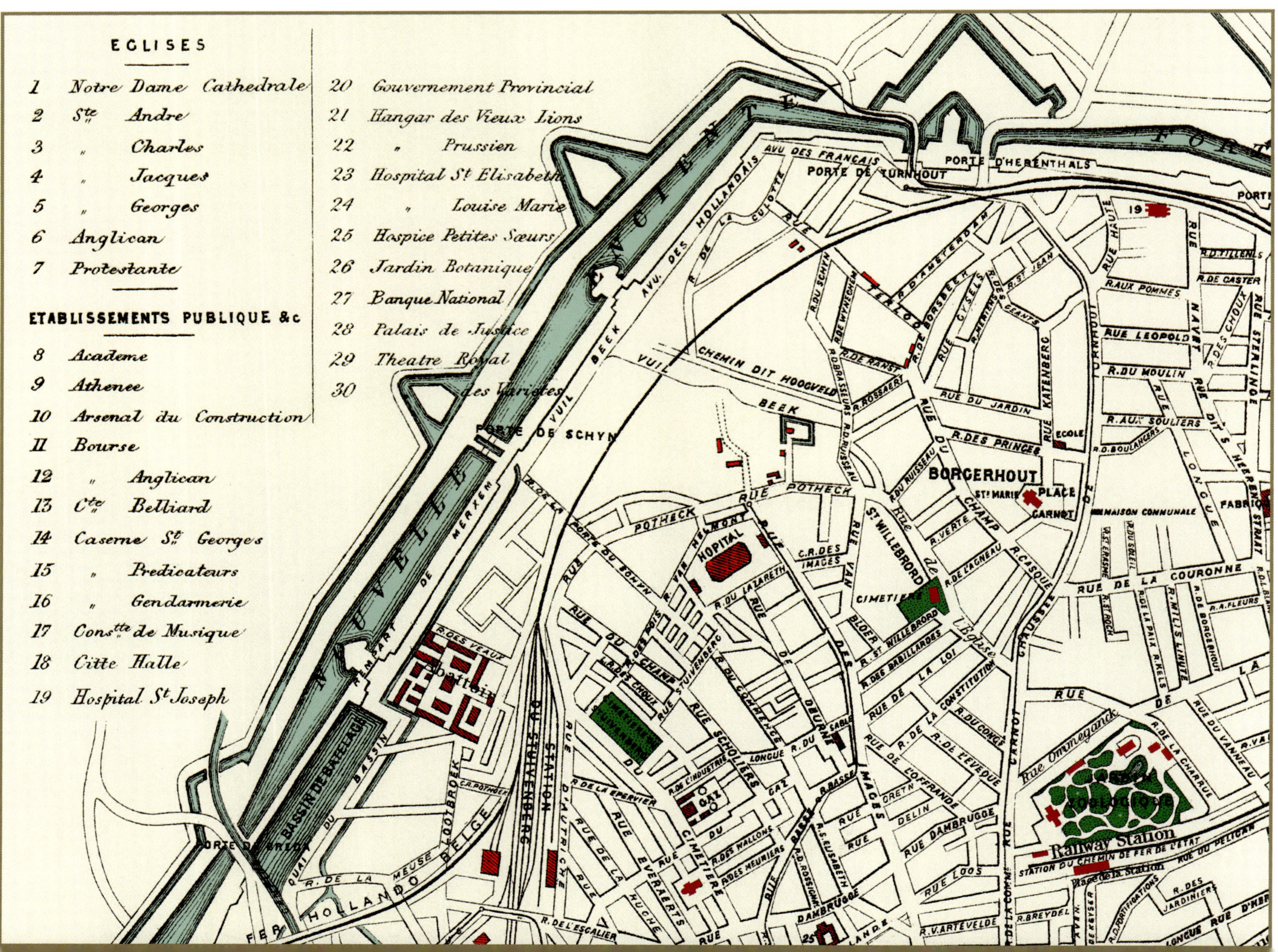

EGLISES
1 Notre Dame Cathedrale
2 Ste Andre
3 " Charles
4 " Jacques
5 " Georges
6 Anglican
7 Protestante

ETABLISSEMENTS PUBLIQUE &c
8 Academe
9 Athenee
10 Arsenal du Construction
11 Bourse
12 " Anglican
13 Cte Belliard
14 Caserne St Georges
15 " Predicateurs
16 " Gendarmerie
17 Consette de Musique
18 Citte Halle
19 Hospital St Joseph
20 Gouvernement Provincial
21 Hangar des Vieux Lions
22 " Prussien
23 Hospital St Elisabeth
24 " Louise Marie
25 Hospice Petites Sœurs
26 Jardin Botanique
27 Banque National
28 Palais de Justice
29 Theatre Royal
30 " des Varietes

BORGERHOUT
Railway Station
ZOO
PORTE D'HERENTHALS
PORTE DE TURNHOUT
PORTE DE SCHYN
STATION DU STUIVENBERG
BASSIN DE BATELAGE
St WILLEBRORD
St MARIE PLACE CARNOT
MAISON COMMUNALE
CHAMP
CIMETIERE
HOPITAL

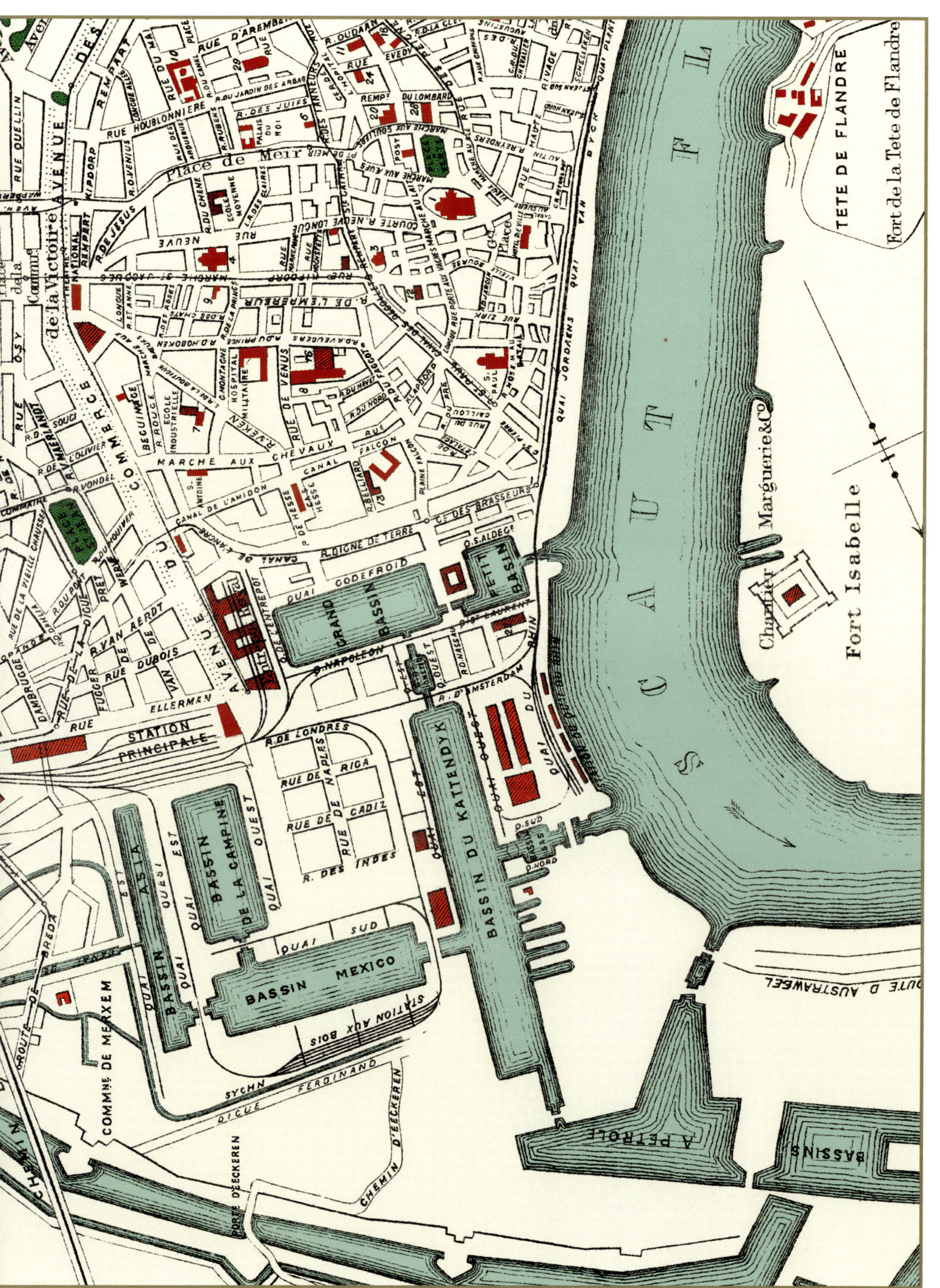

TETE DE FLANDRE
Fort de la Tete de Flandre
ESCAUT
F L
Chantier Marguerie & Co
Fort Isabelle
AVENUE de la Victoire
AVENUE DES
RUE QUELLIN
RUE HOUBLONNIERE
Place de Meir
RUE D'AREMBERG
RUE DU MA
REMPART
RUE NEUVE
RUE ST JACQUES
RUE DE L'EMPEREUR
MARCHE AUX CHEVAUX
RUE DE VENUS
RUE DES CHEVAUX
RUE FALCON
MARCHE AUX OEUFS
Gde Place
RUE DE L'HOPITAL MILITAIRE
HOSPITAL MILITAIRE
CANAL DE L'AMIDON
C.r DES BRASSEURS
R. DIGNE DE TERRE
O.S. ALDEG.
CODEFROID
QUAI
GRAND BASSIN
PETIT BASSIN
O. NAPOLEON
QUAI DU RHIN
R. D'AMSTERDAM
QUAI JORDANS
AVENUE DU COMMERCE
STATION PRINCIPALE
R. DE LONDRES
RUE DE NAPLES
RUE DE RIGA
RUE DE CADIZ
R. DES INDES
BASSIN ASIA
BASSIN DE LA CAMPINE
QUAI OUEST EST
QUAI OUEST
BASSIN DU KATTENDYK
QUAI OUEST
QUAI SUD
BASSIN MEXICO
STATION AUX BOIS
COMMUNE DE MERXEM
QUAI NORD
O. SUD
O. NORD
A PETROL
ROUTE D'AUSTRAWEEL
BASSINS
CHEMIN D'EECKEREN
DIGUE FERDINAND
PORTE D'EECKEREN
ELLERMAN
RUE DUBOIS
R. VAN AERDT
FUGGER
RUE
ROUTE DE BREDA
CHEMIN
ELLERMAN

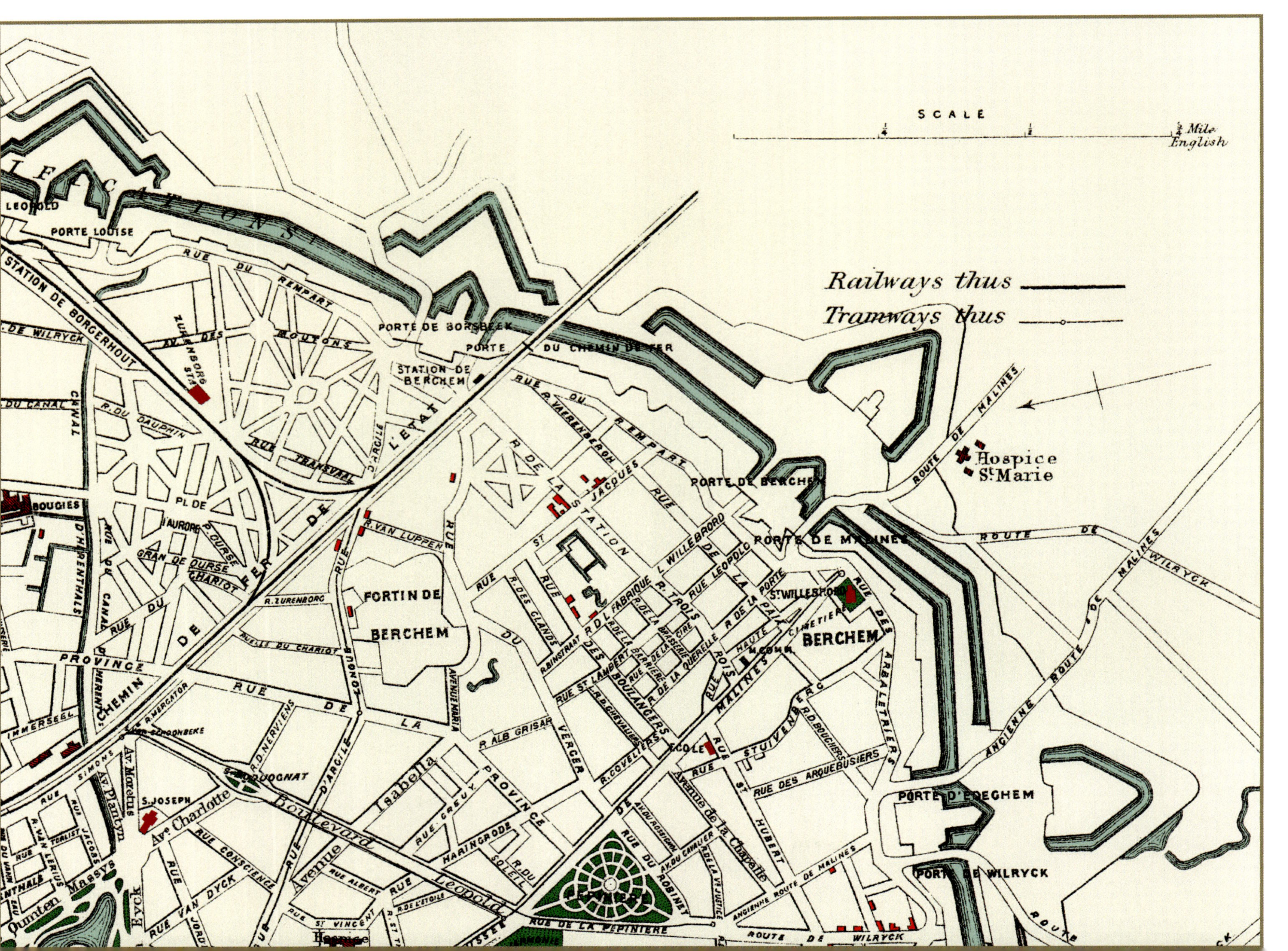
SCALE
1/4   1/2   3/4 Mile English
Railways thus
Tramways thus
LEOPOLD
PORTE LOUISE
STATION DE BORGERHOUT
R. DE WILRYCK
DU CANAL
CANAL
R. DU DAUPHIN
AV. DES MOUTONS
ZURENBORG STA.
RUE DU REMPART
PORTE DE BORSBEEK
PORTE DU CHEMIN DE FER
STATION DE BERCHEM
RUE DU R. VAERENBERGH
REMPART
R DE LA STATION
PORTE DE BERCHEM
ROUTE DE MALINES
Hospice St Marie
PORTE DE MALINES
ROUTE DE
WILRYCK
RUE DE MALINES
RUE TRANSVAL
D'ARGILE
L'ETAT
RUE DE FER
BOUGIES
D'HERENTHALS
PL DE L'AURORE
GRAN DE OURSE
CHARIOT
RUE DU CANAL
RUE DU
PROVINCE
CHEMIN DE
IMMERSEEL
R. ZURENBORG
FORTIN DE BERCHEM
RUELLE DU CHARIOT
RUE
DU
R. VAN LUPPEN
RUE ST JACQUES
ST WILLEBRORD
RUE DES GLANDS
RUE
R. DL FABRIQUE
R. DE LA BRASSERIE
RUE L WILLEBRORD
RUE LEOPOLD
R. DE LA PORTE
RUE DE LA PAIX
R. TROIS
PORTE
 St WILLEBRORD
BERCHEM
RUE DES ARBALETRIERS
PORTE D'EDEGHEM
PORTE DE WILRYCK
AVENUE MARIA
R. ALB GRISAR
VERGER
RUE ST LAMBERT
R. BINSTRAAT
R. DE LA QUERELLE
BARRIERE DE LA
RUE DES BOUZANGERS
R. B. CHEVALIERS
R. COVELIERS
ECOLE
CIMETIER
M. COMM.
RUE HAUTE
RUE DES ROIS
RUE STUIVENBERG
R. D. BOUCHERS
RUE DES ARQUEBUSIERS
ANGIENNE ROUTE
R. MERCATOR
R. D. NERVIENS
AV. Moretus
AV. Plantyn
SIMONS
AV. SCHOONBEKE
DRUOGNAT
S. JOSEPH
AV. Charlotte
Isabella
Boulevard
Avenue Leopold
D'ARGILE
PROVINCE
DE
LA
Quinten Massys
Eyck
RUE VAN DYCK
RUE JORD
R. VAN TERLIST
R. JACOBS
RUE DU HARM
R. ST VINCENT
R. D. L'ETOILE
RUE CONSCIENCE
RUE ALBERT
RUE GREUX
HARINGRODE
RUE DU SOLEIL
R. DU
RUE DU ROBINET
RUE DE LA PEPINIERE
AV. DU ROSSIGNOL
AV. DU CHEVALIER
R. DE LA V. JUSTICE
ANGIENNE ROUTE DE MALINES
ROUTE DE WILRYCK
ST HUBERT
RUE

CHAMP DES MANŒUVRES
RUE DES CENDRES
RUE DE WILRYCK
REMPART DE WILRYCK
LONGUE RUE DES AULNES
COURTE RUE DES AULNES
R. COIN DE FER
RUE DU BOOM
CIMETIÈRE DU KIEL
PLACE ST. CATHARINE
ST. BERNARD
R. DE LA BARRIÈRE
RUE DU POLDER
CHAUSSÉE D'HOBOKEN
CHEMIN DE FER DE POLDER D'ANVERS A BOOM
D'HOBOKEN
RUE DU PAIN
PORTE DU KIEL
PORTE LAURENT
REMPART DU KIEL
AVENUE DE LA BARRIÈRE
ÉCOLE NORMALE
RUE DE L'ANCIENNE ÉGLISE
ST. LAURENT
SCHOONBEKE
R. DES PETITS COPS
RUE BILLIAR
RUE DU CHEVREUIL
RUE DES BATTERIES
R. DE SAXE
RUE RUYWAARD
PLACE DU TRÔNE
STATION POUR VOYAGEURS
STATION DU SUD
PLACE DU SUD
PTE. ST. MICHEL
PARC D'ARTILLERIE
ARSENAL DE GUERRE
FABRIQUE DE MOITS
RUE DE BATAVIA
PALAIS DE JUSTICE
RUE DE LA JUSTICE
AVENUE DE L'INDUSTRIE
PLACE DE L'INDUSTRIE
RUE DES PEINTRES
RUE DES SCULPTEURS
RUE DE HORNES
R. DU RETRANCHEMENT
RUE D'EGMONT
P. COCKERILL
Q. DE LA STATION
ESCAUT
AVENUE DES ARTS
RUE RUBENS
RUE VAN BREE
REMPART DES BÉGUINES
R. DES CAPUCINES
PLACE GEORGES
RUE LÉOPOLD
RUE ST. ROCH
RUE DU LIVRE
PLACE DE LA NACELLE
RUE ST. JEAN
QUAI ST. MICHEL
STATION DU MIDI
RAILWAY

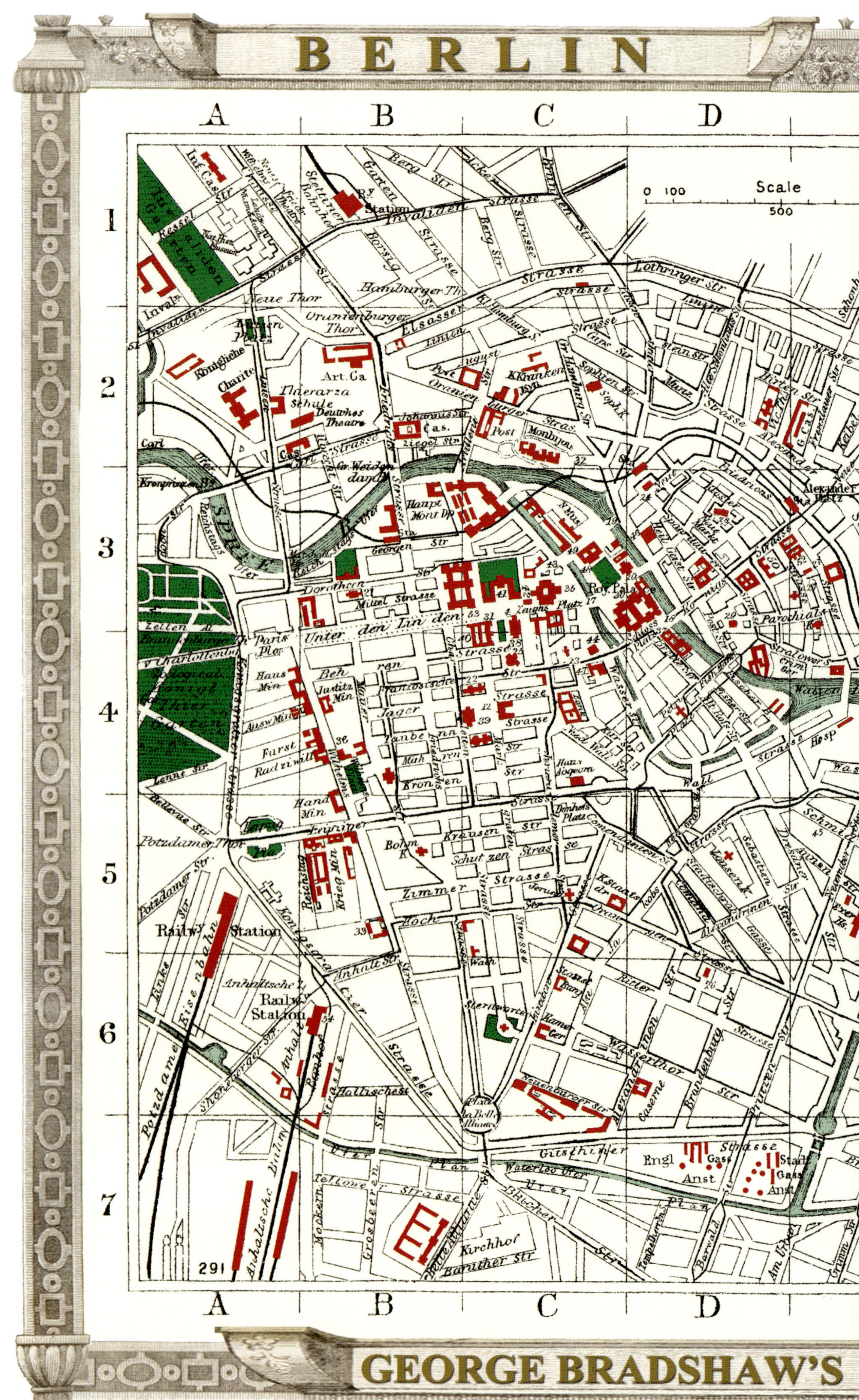
BERLIN
A B C D
Scale
0 100
500
Stettiner
Rathhaus
Ry Station
Berg Str
Invaliden Strasse
Berg Str
Lothringer Str
Borsig Str
Strasse
Strasse
Inf Cas
Ressel allée
Invaliden Gar
Nat Hist Museum
Invaliden Str
Neue Thor
Oranienburger Thor
Hamburger Th
Elsasser
Unter den
Strasse
Königliche
Charité
Thierarza Schule
Art Ga
Deutsches Theater
Augusta
Oranien
Pro August
K Kranken
Sophien Sr
Sopk
Maria
Linien Str
Johannis
Cas
Ziegel Str
Post
Monbijou
Strasse
Friedrichs
Alexander Platz
Carl
Kronprinzen Br
Reichstags
Haupt
Mont Dp
Georgen
Str
Roy Palace
Parochial
Dorothen
Mittel Strasse
Zeughs Platz
Unter den Linden
Strasse
Brandenburger Thor
v Charlottenb
Zoological
Königl
Thier garten
Paris Pla
Haus Min
Beh
Justiz Min
Franzosische
Str
Jager
Strasse
Mah
Auss W Min
Farst Radziwill
Jerusalem
Hausvogtei
Bellevue Str
Lenne Str
Hand Min
Leipziger
Thor
Bethm
Bolm K
Krausen
Str
Schutzen Stras se
Dönhofs Platz
Potzdamer Thor
Zimmer
Strasse
Jerusalem
Staats
dr
Potzdamer Str
Königgrätzer Str
Leipziger Str
Koch
Strasse
Wall
Railway Station
Anhalt St
Anhaltische
Railway Station
Wasser
Potzdamer Bahn
Stromberger Str
Anhalt
Bahnhof
Halleschest
Sheriworte
Kamel Ger
Wasserthor
Neuenburger Str
Caserne
Brandenburg Str
Plan
Waterloo Ufer
Ufer
Bleicher
Gitschiner
Engl Anst
Strasse Gass
Stadt Gass Anst
Mockern Str
Grossbeeren Strasse
Tempelhofer Ufer
Plan
Kirchhof
Baruther str
291

E F G H I

1000
Meters

Oeffentliche Plätze:

1 Der Schlossplatz D3
2 Der Lustgarten C3
3 Der Zeughausplatz C3
4 D Platz am Opernhaus C3
5 Der Platz an der Königswache, sche 42.
6 Der Platz vor den Linden,
   siehe 13.
7 Der Pariser Platz A4
8 Der Wilhelms Platz B4
9 Der Leipziger Pl A5

10 D Belle Alliance Pl C6
11 Der Dönhofs Platz C5
12 D Gensdarm Markt C4
13 Unter den Linden B3
14 Friedrichsstrasse B4
15 Leipzigerstrasse B5
16 Königsstrasse D3

Brücken:

17 Schlossbrücke C2
18 Die lange Brücke D3
19 Neu Friedrichs Br. C3

Kirchen und andere öffentliche Gebäude:

20 Die Domkirche D3
21 Dorotheenkirche B3
22 Französische Kirche C4
23 Friedrichswerdersche K. C4
24 Garnisonkirche D3
25 Hedwigskirche C4
26 Die neue Jacobskirche D6
27 Klosterkirche E3
28 Marienkirche D3
29 Nicolaikirche D3
30 Das königl Schloss C3
31 Königliches Palais C3
32 Monbijou C2
33 Palais d Prinzen Albert B5
34 Pal. d. Prinz. v. Preussen C3
35 Zeughaus C3
36 Palais des Prinzen Carl B4
37 Marstall D3
38 Opernhaus C3
39 D neue Schauspielhaus C4
40 Die Bibliothek C4
41 D. Universitätsgebäude C3
42 Neue Königswache C3
43 Singakademie C3
44 Die Bauakademie C4
45 Georgen Kirch E2
46 Börse C3
47 Die neue Münze C4
48 Das Museum C3
49 Das neue Museum C3
50 Ger Gewb. Inst. D3
51 Das Zellengefängniss A2
52 Das Lagerhaus E3
53 Die Akadem d Kunste B3

Eisenbahnhöfe:

54 Bahnhof d Anhalt schen Bahn B6
55 d Potsdamer Bahn A5
56 d Frankfurter Bahn G5
57 d Berl Stettin Bahn B1

E F G H I

REFERENCE.

1	Hotel de Ville.	18	Beguinage.	33	Thea. Alcazar Royal.
2	Minimes.	19	Banque Nationale.	34	Notre Dame des Victories.
3	Old Palace de Justice.	20	Palais du Roi.	35	Palais des Academies.
4	Musée Historie Naturelle	21	Ch. of Deputies & Senate.	36	Prison Civil.
5	da Peinture et Sculpture.	22	Hospital des Orphelines.		
6	Prison Civil et Militaire.	23	S. Jacques sur Caudenberg		
7	Hotel du Gouvernment.	24	G. Hospice P. des Villards.		
8	Hospital Militaire.	25	Pal. of the duc. d. Aramberg.		
9	Theatre Royal du Parc.	26	Monnaie.		
10	N.D. de la Capelle.	27	Cathedral of S. Gudule.		
11	Bourse.	28	Theatre Royal.		
12	Post Office.	29	Manège.		
13	Ecole Publique.	30	Maison de Bain.		
14	Hospice Pacheco.	31	Pal. of the Count of Flandres.		
15	Riches Claires	32	Manége Royal Aufsism		
16	Mannekin Pis.				
17	S. Catherine.				

BOULEV. LEOPOLD II.
Rue de l'Intendant
Rue du Coton
ABATTOIR
BOULEV. BARTELEMY
BOULEV. DE L'ENTREPOT
Caserne du
Petit Château
Entrepot
Quai au bois de Construction
Bassin
Gd Bassin
Quai des Houilles
BOULEVARD ANSPACH
Bassin
17
13
24
Canal de Willebroeck
ALLEE VERTE
STATION
DES MARCANDISES
Bruxelles au Port de Laeken
Route de
Rue du Frontispice
Rue Herry
Chaussee d'Anvers
Rue des Roses
Augustins BOULD DE LA SENNE
12
RIVIERE
26
Rue Jolly
BOULEVARD DU NORD
Rue du Marche
Rue Gaucheret
Grande Place
Place de la Reine
Rue du Progres
35
Place des Martyrs
Station
Chemin de Fer du Nord
Rue de Cologne
RAIL TO OSTEND ANTWERP COLOGNE
Rue de
BOULEVARD DU JARDIN BOTANIQUE
Jardin
Botanique
Rue de Pavimentan
Verte
Rue de Brabant
Hopital St Jean
Rue de Secours
Rue des Palais
Rue de la Poste
Place du Congres
RUE ROYALE
Rue Royale
Rue Royale
R. Royale
Ste Marie
PARC
9
Place de la Liberté
BOULEVARD DE L'OBSERVATOIRE
Hoecht
RER DUCALE
BOULEVARD DU REGENT
Josaphat
Jonghat
Abattoir
Rue Merinos
Maelbeek
QUARTIER
LEOPOLD
Pl. de la
Société Civile
Verboeckhoven
Rue Van Baden
Venck

REFERENCE.
1 Hotel de Ville.
2 Minimes.
3 Old Palace de Justice.
4 Musée Historie Naturelle.
5 do Peinture et Sculpture.
6 Prison Civil et Militaire.
7 Hotel du Gouvernment.
8 Hospital Militaire.
9 Theatre Royal du Parc.
10 N.D. de la Capelle.
11 Bourse.
12 Post Office.
13 Ecole Publique.
14 Hospice Pacheco.
15 Riches Claires.
16 Mannekin Pis.
17 S.t Catherine.
18 Beguinage.
19 Banque Nationale.
20 Palais du Roi.
21 Ch.r of Deputies & Senate.
22 Hospital des Orphelines.
23 S. Jacques sur Caudenberg.
24 G.t Hospice P.t des Villards.
25 Pal. of the duc d'Aramberg.
26 Monnaie.
27 Cathedral of S.t Gudule.
28 Theatre Royal.
29 Manége.
30 Maison de Bain.
31 Pal. of the Count of Flandres.
32 Manége Royal Aufsisn
33 Thea Alcazar Royal.
34 Notre Dame des Victories.
35 Palais des Academies.
36 Prison Civil.
STATION DU MIDI
B. JAMAR
Place de la Constitution
Rue Fiennes
MIDI
DU HAINAUT
BOULEVARD
MUSEE
Place du Jeu de Balle
Place Rouppe
Vieux Marché

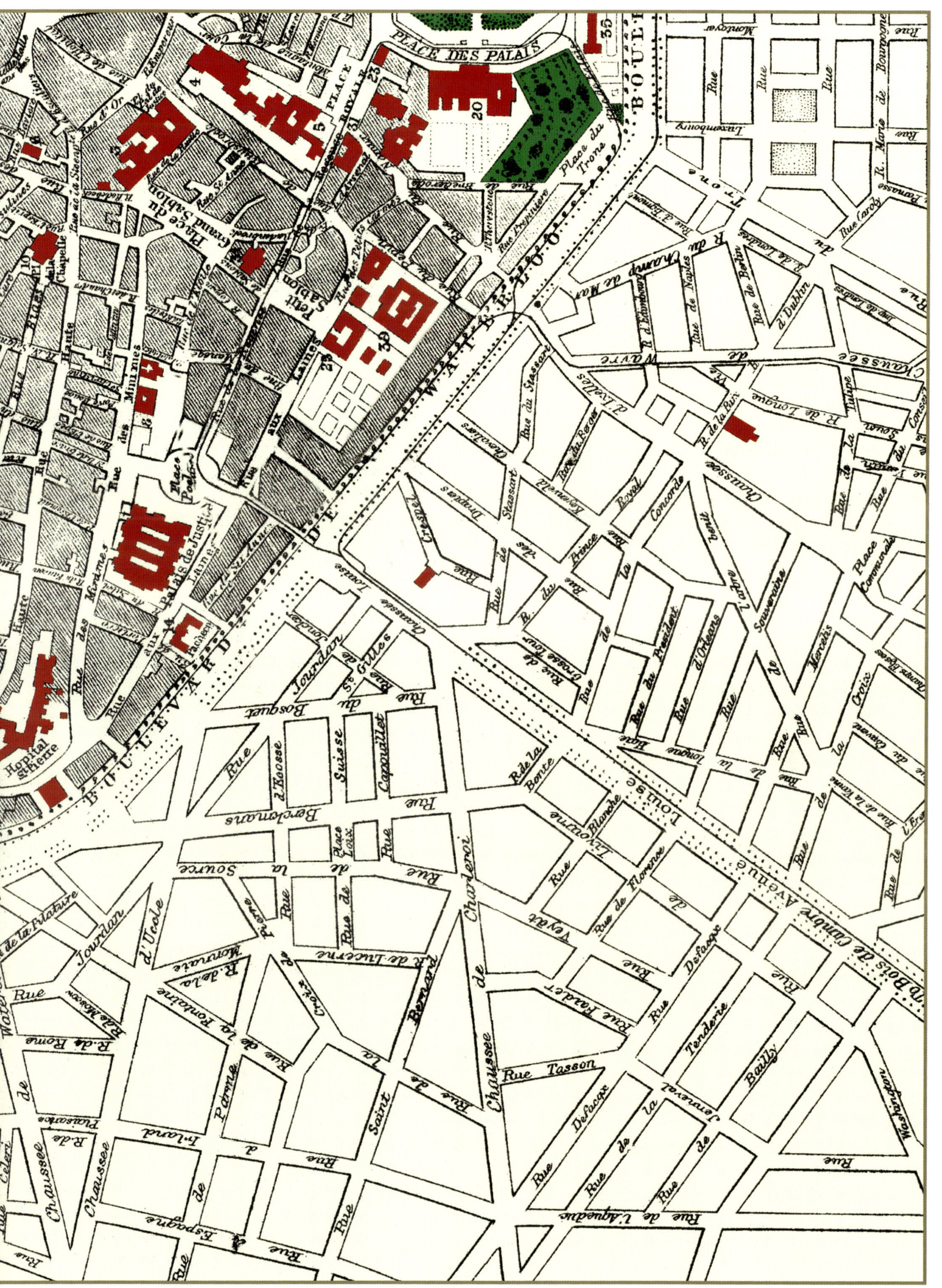

PLACE DES PALAIS
Place du Trône
BOULEVARD
Place du Luxembourg
Rue Montoyer
Rue de Luxembourg
Rue du Luxembourg
Rue Montoyer
Rue Marie de Bourgogne
Rue du Parnasse
Rue Lardy
Rue du Longue
Rue du Congrès
Rue de Naples
Rue de Berlin
Rue d'Dublin
Rue d'Edimbourg
Rue du Champ de Mars
CHAUSSÉE DE WAVRE
Rue de Stassart
Rue du Stassart
Rue Keyenveld
Rue de la Paix
Rue de Vallée
Rue de Londres
Rue Jacobs
Rue du Prince Royal
Rue de la Concorde
Rue du Trône
Chaussée d'Ixelles
Chaussée de Wavre
Rue Crespel
Rue de Stassart
Rue Capouillet
Rue de la Bonté
Rue Livourne
Rue de Florence
Rue Souveraine
Place Communale
Rue Mercelis
Rue de la Croix
Rue de la Tulipe
Rue du Président
Rue de l'Orléans
Rue de la Longue Haie
BOULEVARD DE WATERLOO
Rue Jourdan
Rue du Bosquet
Rue des Gilles
Rue de Tombeur
Chaussée de Louise
Rue de Rooze
Rue Suisse
Rue Berckmans
Place du Jeu de Balle
Rue de la Source
Place Loix
Rue de la Victoire
Rue de Lucerne
Rue Morinale
R. de la Fontaine
Rue de Parme
Rue Saint Bernard
Chaussée de Charleroi
Rue Tasson
Rue Vydt
Rue Blanche
Rue de Florence
Rue Hôtel des Monnaies
Rue Defacqz
Rue Faider
Rue Tenderie
Rue Bailly
Rue Defacqz
Rue de la Réforme
Rue de l'Aqueduc
Avenue du Bois de la Cambre
AVENUE LOUISE
Chaussée de Waterloo
Rue Jourdan
Rue d'Uccle
Rue Africaine
Rue de Rome
Chaussée de Forest
Chaussée de Waterloo
Rue Berckmans
Rue de la Pelature
Rue Célèbre
R. de Rome
Rue Plasschaerts
Rue d'Espagne
Hôpital St Pierre
BOULEVARD DE WATERLOO
Rue des Minimes
Rue Haute
Rue des Minimes
Place de la Chapelle
Rue aux Laines
Rue des Alexiens
Rue de Rollebeek
Place du Petit Sablon
Place du Grand Sablon
Palais de Justice
Rue de la Régence
Rue Ernest Allard
Rue Watteau
Rue des Sablons
Place Poelaert
Rue de la Paille
20
23
31
4
5
39
10
55

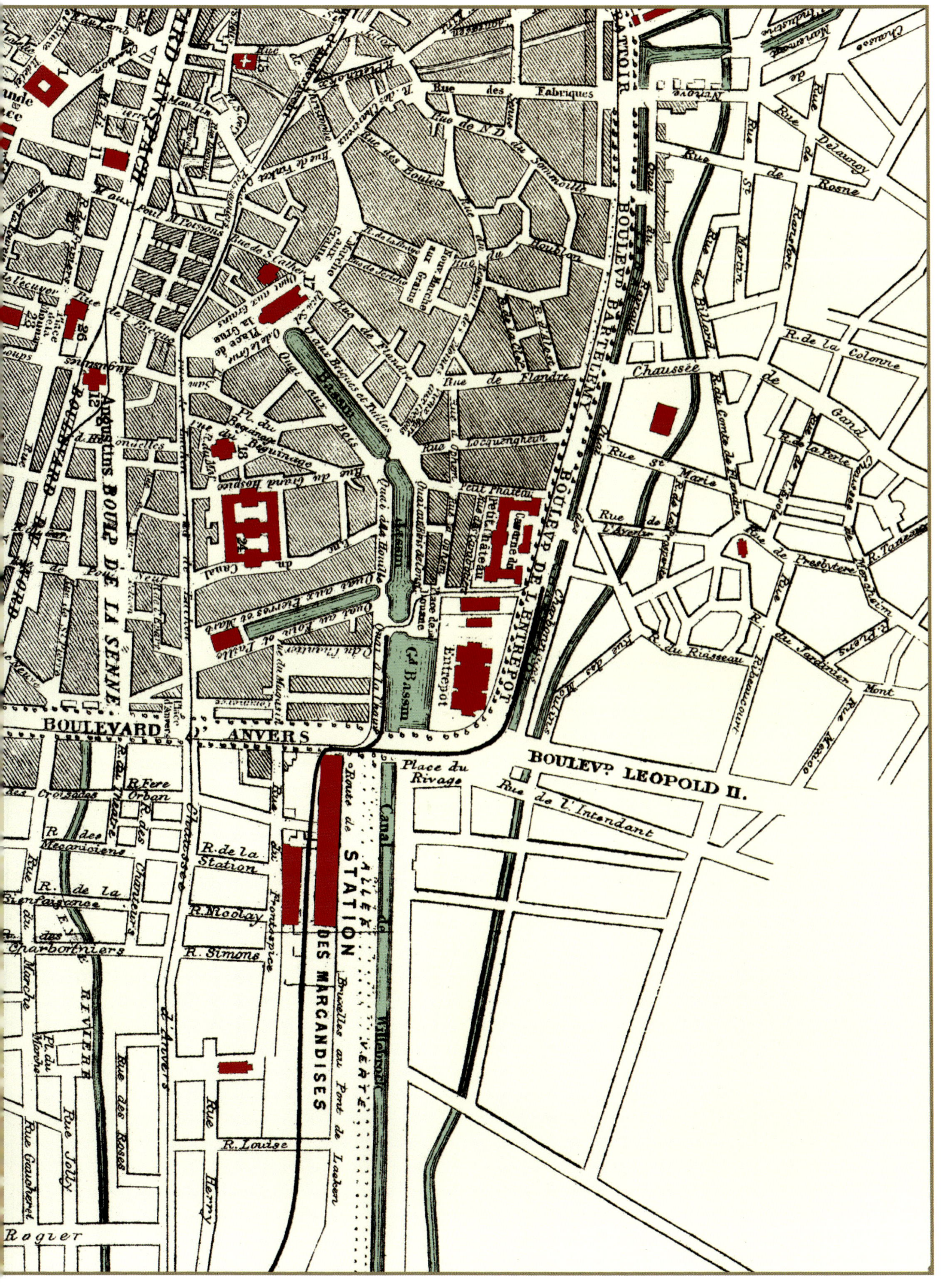
BOULEVARD ANSPACH
ABATTOIR
Rue des Fabriques
Rue des Boulets
Rue de N. D.
Nouv. Marché aux Grains
R. de la Vierge
Rue de St Alain
Rue de Flandre
Place de la Grue
O. de la Grue
Quai aux Bois
Rue Bogard et Tilleu
Quai au Foin et Paille
Quai aux Pierres et Marb
Gd Bassin
Entrepot
Caserne du Petit Château
BOULEVᴰ DE L'ENTREPOT
BOULEVᴰ BARTHÉLÉMY
Rue Locquenghein
Rue St Marie
Rue de l'Anvers
Chaussée
Rue du Comte de Flandre
Rue St Martin
Rue de Renkort
Rue de Rosne
R. de la Colonne
de Gand
Rue de la Porte
R. de Presbytère
R. Tasse
Ninove
Rue Delaunoy
Industrie
Chaussée
Mont
Rue Mexico
Augustins BOULᴱ DE LA SENNE
BOULEVARD DU NORD
Augustinelles
BOULEVARD ANVERS
Rue du Grand Hospice
Pl. du Béguinage
Rue du Béguinage
Canal
Rue Neuve
Quai aux Pierres et Marb
Quai au Foin et Paille
Place du Rivage
BOULEVᴰ LEOPOLD II.
Rue de l'Intendant
Canal de Willebroek
ALLÉE VERTE
STATION DES MARCANDISES
Route de Bruxelles au Pont de Laeken
R. de la Station
R. Moolay
R. Simons
Frontispice
R. Fère Orban
R. des Croisades
R. des Mécandiens
R. de la Bienfaisance
R. des Chanteurs
d'Anvers
des Charbonniers
RIVIÈRE
Pl. du Marché
Rue des Roses
Rue Jolly
Rue Gauchepet
R. Louise
Herry
Roger

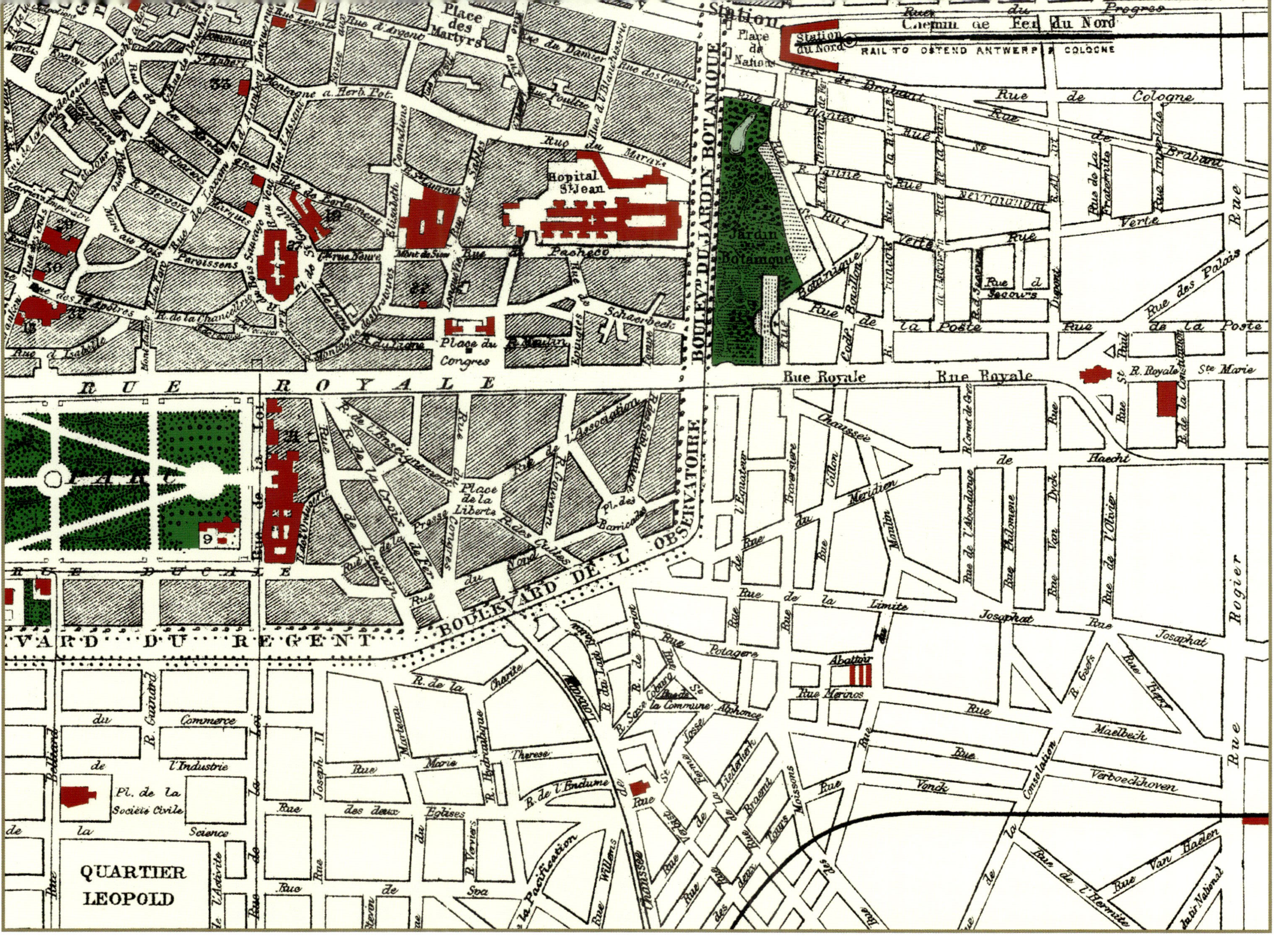

Station
Chemin de Fer du Nord
RAIL TO OSTEND ANTWERP & COLOGNE
Rue du Progrès
Station du Nord
Place de Nations
Place des Martyrs
Rue d'Argent
Rue de Damier
Rue des Comtes
Rue de Cologne
Rue de la Fraternité
Rue Verte
Rue Verte
Rue Impériale
Rue de Brabant
Chemin de Fer de Brabant
Rue des Plantes
Rue de la Rivière
Rue Dupont
Rue d. Secours
Rue des Palais
Rue de la Poste
Rue de la Poste
Rue St Paul
R. Royale Ste Marie
Rd de la Constitution
Rue du Marais
Hopital St Jean
Jardin du Botanique
BOULEVᴰ DU JARDIN BOTANIQUE
Rue Botanique
Place du Congrès
R. Moulan
Pacheco
Schaerbeek
RUE ROYALE
Rue Royale
Rue Royale
Rue Royale
Haecht
Chaussée
Cullen
Meridien
L'Equateur
Traversière
Rue du Dyck
Rue Van Dyck
Rue de l'Abondance
Rue Philomene
Rue de l'Olivier
PARC
RUE DUCALE
Place de la Liberté
R. de l'Enseignement
R. de la Croix de Fer
R. des Cultes
Rue du Congrès
Pl. des Barricades
BOULEVARD DE L'OBSERVATOIRE
Rue de la Limite
Josaphat
Josaphat
Rogier
Rogier
Rue Martin
Abattoir
Rue Merinos
BOULEVARD DU REGENT
R. Guinard
Commerce
du
de
l'Industrie
Pl. de la Société Civile
Science
Rue de la Loi
Joseph II
Rue Marie
Rue Thérèse
R. Hydraulique
R. de l'Endume
R. de la Charité
R. de Boite
la Commune
St Alphonce
Rue Potager
Rue des deux Eglises
Rue de Spa
la Pacification
Rue Willems
R. Verviers
QUARTIER LEOPOLD
Vonck
Maelbeek
Verboeckhoven
Rue Van Haelen
Rue de l'Hermite
R. Gaels
Rue Figuy
Consolation
Rue des Deux Tours
Rue des deux Moissons
33

RAILWAY TO BONN &c
LUXENBURGER STRASSE
TÜLPICHER STRA
HOHENSTAUFFEN RING
HOHENSTAUFFEN RING
MAURITIUS WALL
HANNEN WALL
BALDUIN STR
BENES
SALTER RING
EIFEL STRASSE
MAURITIUS
HUMBOLD STR
BOB STRASSE
ST MAURITIUS
ALTE MAUER
AM LAACH
NEU MARKT
PANTALEON RLY STA
PANTALEON K.
FESTGE BAUND
THIEBOLDS
BURG HOSP
STPETER
TELEGRAPHEN AMT
ST CACILIEN
CACILIEN KL
WAISENHAUS
SACHSEN
CARTHAUSE
PROVIANT MAG
RUBENS MARIA DE MEDICI
GARNISON BACKEREI
FRIED WILH GYMNASIUM
ST GEORG
REICHS BANK
GEORG P
BÖRSE
NEUE EVANGL KIRCHE
IM ELEND
POWDER MAG
ZWIRNER STRASSE
BAUMWOLL SPINNEREI
KÖNIGSHALLE
HOLZMARKT
ZUCKER FABRIK
RHEIN BERG
THURNMARKT
BAYENTHURM
BAYEN THOR
BADESCHIFFE
Rheinau Hafen
KÖLN AU
DÜSSELDORFER DAMPFBOOTE
DAMPFBOOTE
R I V E R
Hafen
SIEGBURGER
DÜSSELDFR DAMPFBOOT
D E U T
GLACIS WEG
CASEMATTEN
KIRCHE
MATHILDEN STRASSE
DÜSSEL
CASEMATTEN
SCALES
0 10 20 30 40 50 100 200
Metres
1 2 3 4 5
ENVIRONS of COLOGNE
Longerich
Rhine R.
Dünwald
Merheim
R? to Neuss &c
Bickendorf
R? to Aix la Chapelle
Nipps Zoolog. Gard.
Mulheim
Gladbach & Bensb? R?
Central Station
Lind
Buchheim
COLOGNE
(CÖLN)
Deutz
Brack
Komar
Venast
Der Königs
Forst
Poll
Rodenkirchen
Ensen
Kalschuiren
Weiss
Porz
R? to Bonn
Rhine Riv?
R? to Giessen
Brühl
Railways thus

STADT GARTEN
Railways shown thus ———
GOODS STATION
RHINE
Footroad to Mulheim
GOODS STATION
CONTINENTAL CITY PLANS 1896

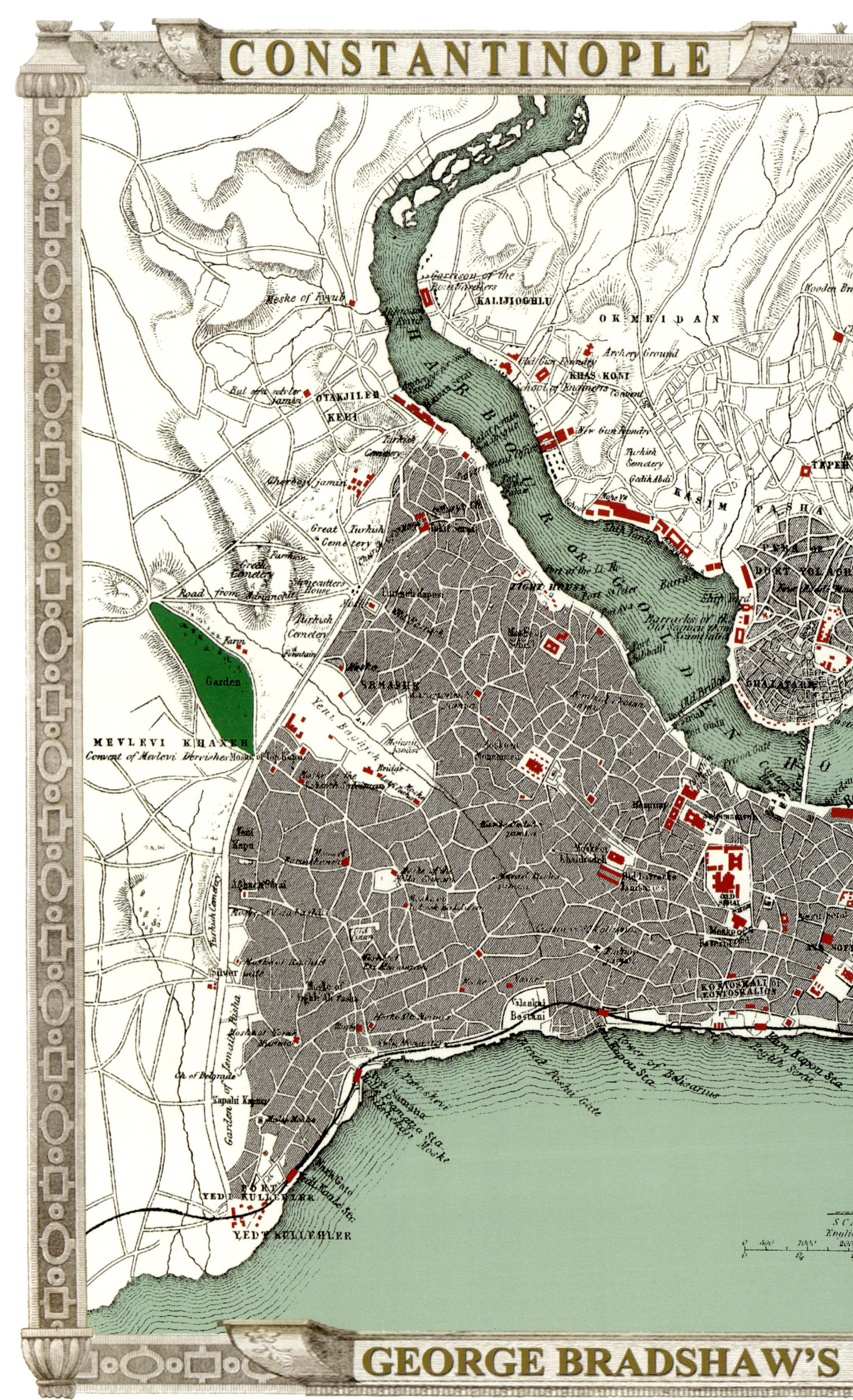

Garrison of the Bombardiers
KALIJIOGHLU
OKMEIDAN
Mosque of Eyoub
Archery Ground
KHAS KOI
New Gun Foundry
Turkish Cemetery
OTAKJILER KEHI
Greek Cemetery
Turkish Cemetery
Great Turkish Cemetery
LIGHT HOUSE
KASIM PASHA
Barracks of the Old Seraglio
GHALATA
Road from Adrianople
Garden
MEVLEVI KHANEH
Convent of Mevlevi Dervishes
Yeni Baghtch
Mosque of Khaireddin
Old Barracks
OLD SERAI
KOMIOSKALI or KOMIOSKALION
Bostani
Silver Gate
Mosque of Sheikh Ali Pasha
Garden of Ismaili Pasha
FORT YEDI KULLEH
YEDI KULLEHLER
SCALE English

BESHIKTASH
Ruins of an Aqueduct
Turkish Cemetery
of St Demtrius
DEMTRIUS
an Dimitri
Fountain
Volunteers Farm
Armenian Cemetery
Palace of the Sultau Begum
Moske of Suian Pasha
Beshiktash Landing Place
Roman Catholic Cemetery
Tchifilik
DOLMA-BAGHCHEH
Fountain Hotel
Garden
Fountain
Moske of Mustaki Efendi
Palace of Beshiktash
BOSPORUS
wir of Pera
ASHI
New Artillery Barracks
Landing Place
Fatal
Findiklu Moske
Begte Buynk
Port of Scu
Moske of Sali-bazari
Moske of Shamsi Pasha
Artillery Barracks
Landing Place of Top Khaneh
Kiosk of the Sultan
Palace of Top Khaneh
Port Egri Crooked Gate
Moske of Mohammed Pasha
Salayah Ishelebi
Fort Kirey Lime Gate
Fort Munkhauch Wax Gate
Kiz Kullehsi
Tower of Leander
SKUTARI OR SKUDAR
Kiosk
Grand Pavilion
Graphic Point Serai Burnu
Odajah Ishelebi
Port Serai
Kiosk of Marble Great Port Battery
Esqmi Ishelehsi Sacred Stairs
New Kiosk
B O S
Infirmary
Mosk
SERAI
Harem
Record Office
Jewel
Darseuse Landing
Hospital
Balik-Khaneh Fish-House
Barracks
Fountain Abdoullah Efendi
Marble Gate
Military Hospital
Convent
Haider Pascha
Haider Pascha Sta
Haider Pascha Ishelesi
Fountains
KADIKUI
F.
Feet
5000   5000 5000 5200
Mile

DRESDEN
Dresdener Heide
ELBE
OSTRAWIESE ODER DAS GROSSE GEHEGE
KLEINE GEHEGE
NEUSTADT
ALTSTADT
BERLINER STRASSE
TAUENTZIEN STR.
KLEIN HAMBURG
FREIBERGER VORSTADT
WILSDRUFFER VORSTADT
STERN PL.
Railway shown thus
Stations
Scale
0   100   200   300   600   900   1200
Dresd. Ellen.

Alaun Platz
Neust Kirchhof
Scheunen
Neue Welt Hof
Kammerdieners od. Schonbrunn
Gasthof Grünen Tanne
Jordan u Timaus Chocoladin Fabrik
Gas Anst
Pichhaus
LÖSSNITZ
Railway from Berlin
Leipzig Dresden Bahnhof
HELLER STR
Schlesischer Bahnhof
Railway Sta
Artesb
ALBERT
ALBERT THEATER
Theater Lincke's Bad
UFER ST
Leipziger Thor
KAISER WILHELMS PLATZ
Böhm. Stift Armen Schule Garnison Schule
Japan. Gas
Militär Straf Anst
Hospital Pl.
Ober Elb Thor
Artillerie Caserne
Militär Hosp
Bader Thor
Elb Wiesen-Thor
Militär Requisite Schuppen
Thurm u. d. Ritter akad.
Sachsen Platz
Jäger Cas
AUGUSTUS BRÜCKE
Baths
Bade u. Schwim Anstalten
DIE ELBE
ALBERT BRÜCKE
Theater
Theater Platz
Kath Hof K.
Landhausplatz
Brühlsche Terrassen Ufer
Brühl'sche Gart
Konigl Schl
HOLBEINPLATZ
DÜRER STRASSE
STRASSE
BLUMEN STR
NEU MARKT
ALT MARKT
Synagoge
Thierarzneischule
STRIESSENER PLATZ
STRIESSENER STRASSE
Johannis
JOHANNE K. P. Kirchhof
Pirnaischer Schlag
Restauran
KONIGL.
Kaitz Bach

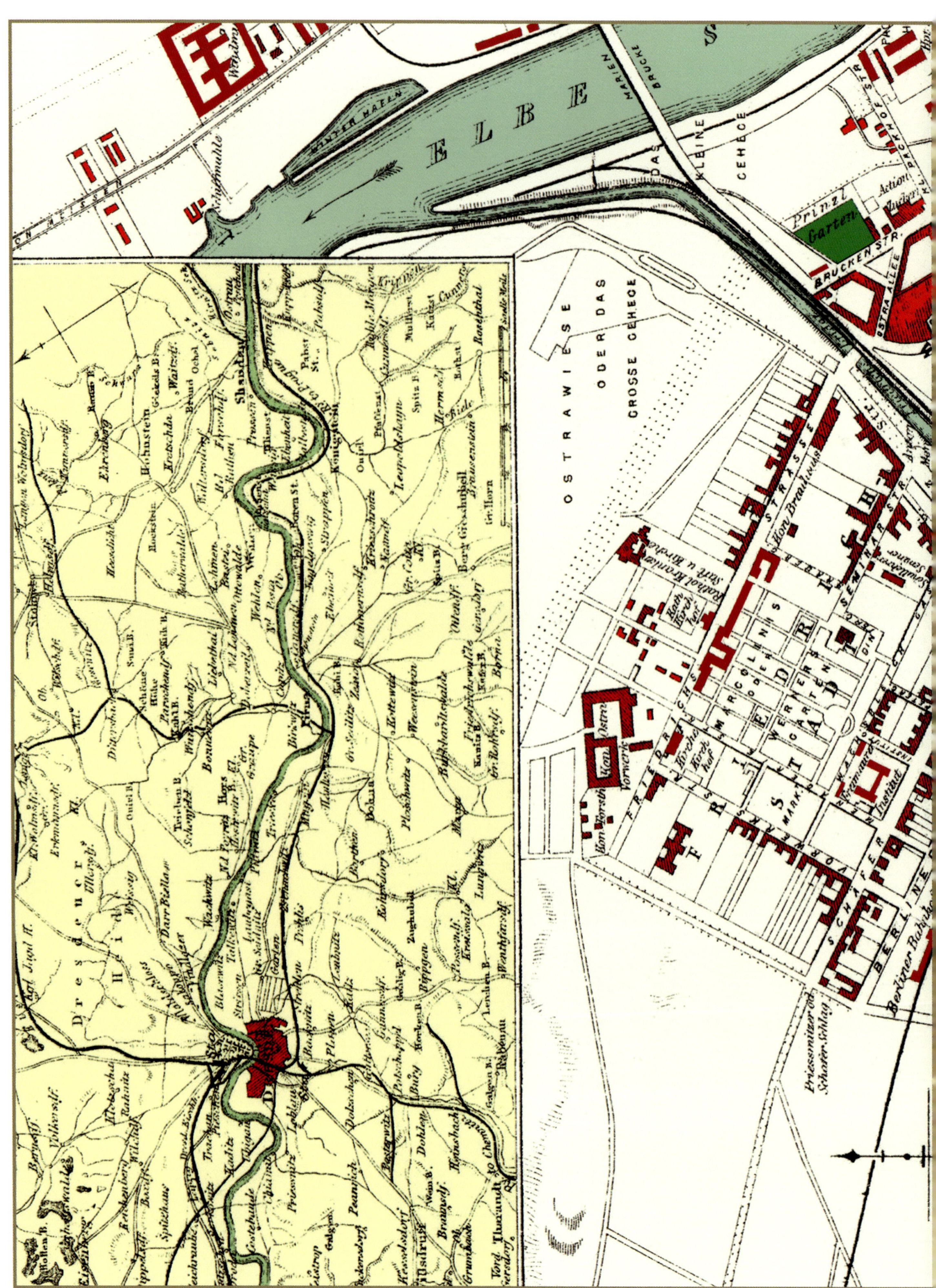

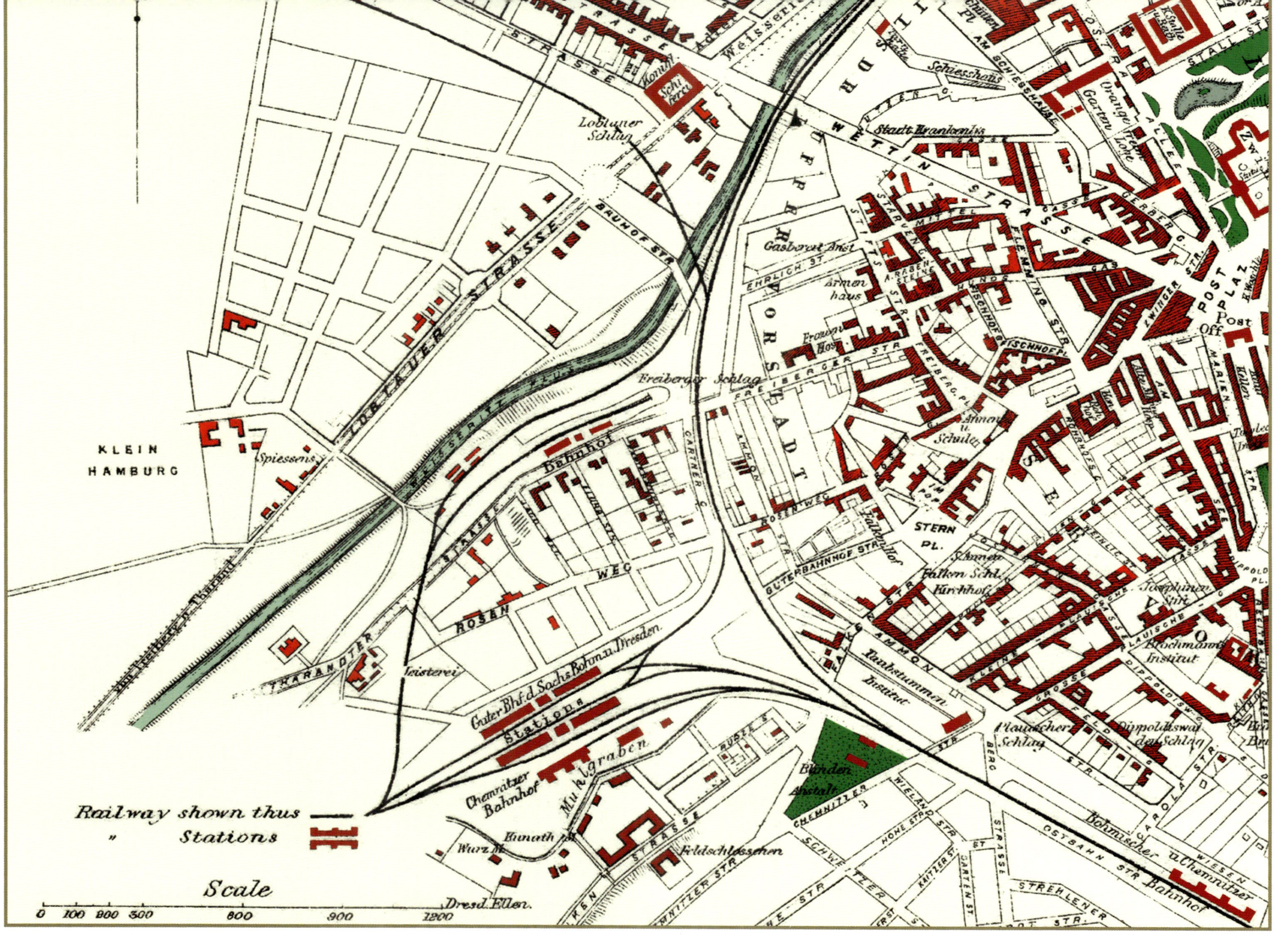

KLEIN HAMBURG
LÖBTAUER STRASSE
BAHNHOF STR.
WEISSERITZ FLUSS
Löbtauer Schlag
Schützen
Spiessens
THARANDTER
Meisterei
ROSEN
WEG
Bahnhof
Freiberger Schlag
Güter Bhf. d. Sachs. Bahn u. Dresden
Stations
Chemnitzer Bahnhof
Muldgraben
Hunath
Wurz.
Feldschlösschen
CHEMNITZER
SCHW. STR.
HOHE STRASSE
WIELAND STR.
GARTEN ST.
KAPTER STR.
STRELENER STR.
Railway shown thus
" Stations
Scale
0 100 200 300   800   900   1200
Dresd. Ellen.
Stadt Krankenhaus
Gasberst Anst.
EHRLICH ST.
Armen haus
STIFTS STR.
A. RABEN-STEINE
STARVENG.
MITTEL
WETTIN STRASSE
FLEMMING STR.
Frauen Hof.
GERBER G.
FREIBERG PL.
FREIBERGER STR.
FISCHHOF
FISCHHOFL.
Ahnen u. Schulen
AM POP
ROSEN WEG
GÜTERBAHNHOF STR.
STERN PL.
Falkenhof
Falken Schl. Kirchhof
AMMON
Taubstummen Institut
Blinden Anstalt
Plauenscher Schlag
BERG
Schiesshaus
PL. AM SCHIESSHAUSE
Orange Freih. Garten Lone
ALLEE
OSTRA
ZWINGER
POST PLATZ
Post Off.
K.Wort-bl.
MARIEN STR.
Keller
AM
Kn. Rohr.hof.
Josephinen Stift
LAUISCHE
Brochmann Institut
DIPPOLDIS.
Dippoldiswalder Schlag
STALL STR.
Böhmischer u. Chemnitzer Bahnhof
OSTBAHN STR.
STREHLENER STR.
WIESEN STR.
STRASSE
VORSTADT

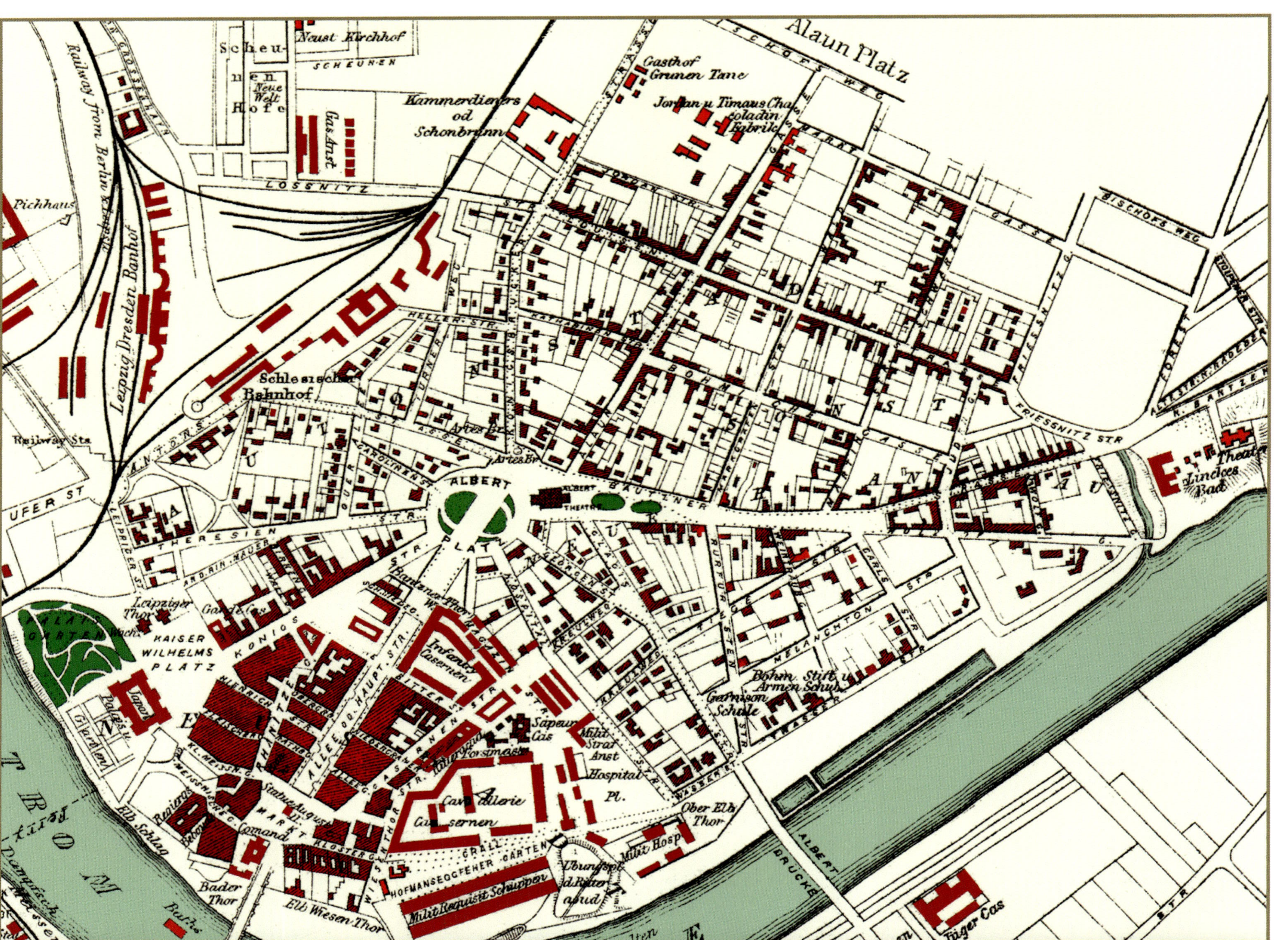

Alaun Platz
Neust Kirchhof
Scheunen
SCHEUNEN
Neue Welt Hofe
Gasthof zum Grünen Tanne
Jordan u Timaus Chocoladin Fabrik
Kammerdieners od Schonbrunn
Railway from Berlin & Leipzig
Pichhaus
Gas Anst
LOSSNITZ
Leipzig Dresden Banhof
BISCHOFS WEG
TOLPENER STR
FRIESSNITZ STR
R BARTLER
HELLER STR
BOHM STR
Schlesischen Bahnhof
Railway Sta
ANTONS STR
UFER ST
CAROLINEN STR
Aртes Br
ALBERT
Albert Theater
BAUTZNER STR
Theater Lindes Bad
THERESIEN STR
PLATZ
RURFURSTEN STR
CARLS STR
MELANCHTHON STR
Bohm Stift u Armen Schul
Garnison Schule
Leipziger Thor
Garten Cas
KAISER WILHELMS PLATZ
KONIGS STR
HEINRICH STR
ALLEE OD HAUPT STR
Infanterie Caserne
Sapeur Cas
Milit Straf Anst
Hospital Pl.
Japan Palais u Garten
Gärtel Garten
KL NEY STR
WEISSENBURGER STR
MARKT
Statue August II
Cavallerie Casernen
Unter Forstmach
Ober Elb Thor
Milit Hosp
Regiers Command
Elb Schlag
Bader Thor
Rathé
Elb Wiesen Thor
Milit Requisit Schuppen
Hofmanseogfeher Garten
GRÄL
Übungspl d Ritter apud
ALBERT BRUCKE
Tiger Cas
TROM
Danzisch Meissen

STRAESSE
Striessener Platz
STRIESSENER STRASSE
HOLBEIN STRASSE
DÜRER STR.
HOLBEINPLATZ
ZIEGET STR.
BLUMEN
Sachenplatz
ELIAS STR.
BLOCHMANNSTR.
BAULBACH STRASSE
MATHILDEN STR.
SEIDN. STR.
GRUNAER STR.
PIRNAISCHER PLATZ
Pirnaischer Schlag
KÖNIGL.
GARTEN
GROSSE
STEINS
LÜBEN STR.
MAIEN ALLEE
Restauration
ALBRECHTS
PRINZEN
DIE
ELBE
Bade u. Schwimm Anst.
Bruehlsche Terrassen
JOHANNIS
GASSE
UNTERE
CASSE
MORITZ ALLEE
PIRNAISCHER PLATZ
DOHNAISCHE
GASSE
PARK
BRÜCKE
AUGUSTUS
Theater Pl.
Theater
Platz
Brühl'sche
Zwinger
Zeughof
Prinz
NEU IN LAMPIENE G.
MORITZ STR.
FRAUENSTR.
GEORGE
PLATZ
JÜDENTEGH
FERDINANDS STR.
VICTORIA
AUGUSTUS
Schloss
FISCHER G. STR.
BADER G.
GR. FROHNG.
SCHULE
WAISEN HAUS STR.
JOHANNES
FRIEDRICHS ALLEE
WILSDRUFER G.
SCHEFFEL G.
WEBER G.
ZAHNS G.
BREITE
SEE STR.
Alt
MARKT
AND MAUER
SCHLEHR STR.

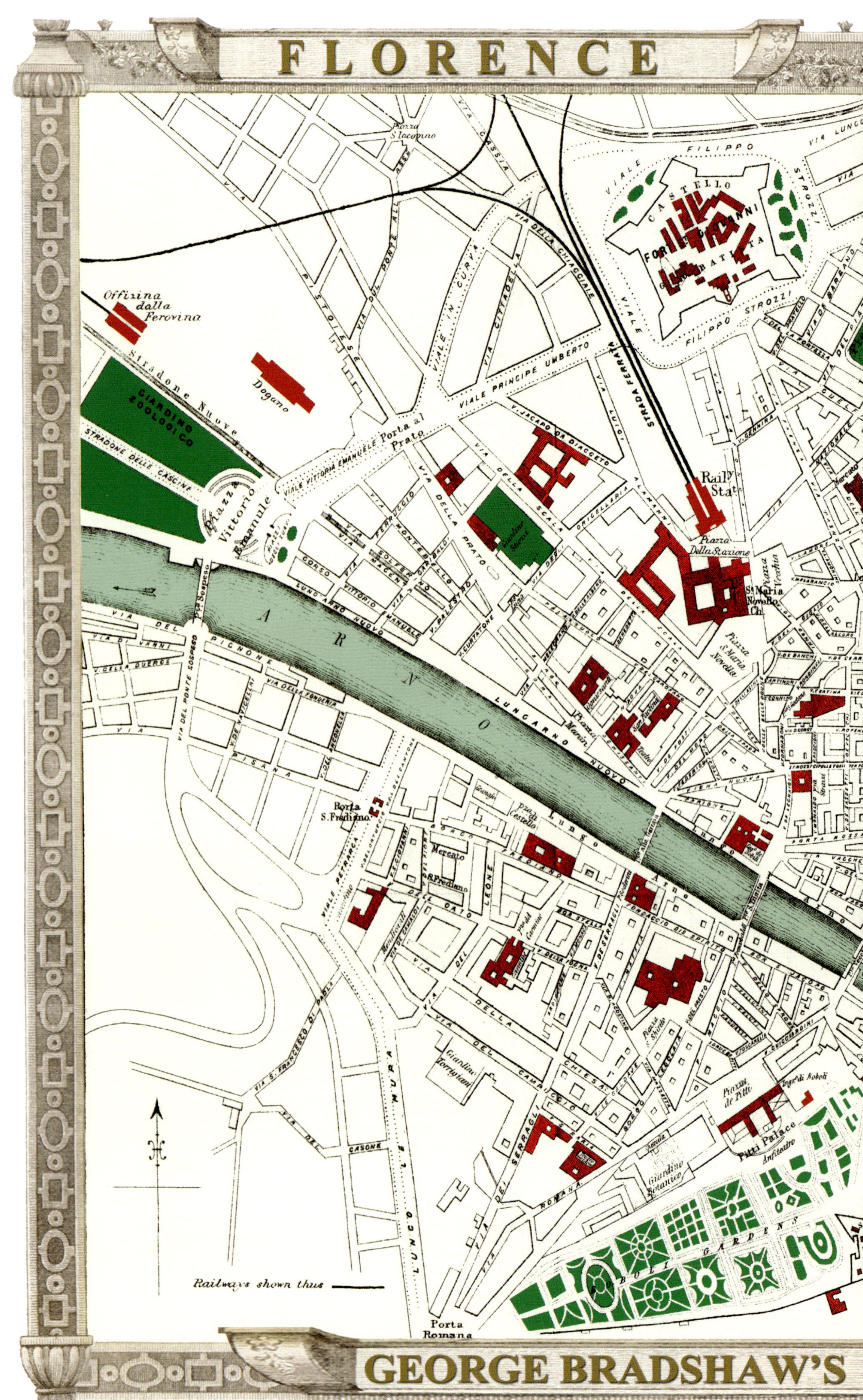

Offizina dalla Ferovina
Stradone Nuove
Dogana
GIARDINO ZOOLOGICO
STRADONE DELLE CASCINE
Piazza S.Iacopino
VIA CASSIA
VIA N. CURVA
VIA CITTADELLA
VIA DELLA CHIACCAIE
VIALE FILIPPO STROZZI
CASTELLO
FORTE BASSO DA BATESO
VIALE FILIPPO STROZZI
STRADA FERRATA
Piazza Vittorio Emanuele
Viale Vittoria Emanuele Porta al Prato
VIALE PRINCIPE UMBERTO
V. JACAPO DA DIACCETO
ALAMANNI
VIA DELLA SCALA
VIA DELLA PRATO
Giardino Sforza
Rail Stat
Piazza Della Stazione
S.Maria Novella Ch.
Piazza S.Maria Novella
ARNO
LUNGARNO NUOVO
VIA DEL VANNI
VIA DELLA DUERCE
Ponte Sospeso
VIA DEL PONTE SOSPESO
PIGNONE
VIA DELLA FONDERIA
VIA PISANA
Porta S.Frediano
VIALE PETRARCA
Prato d'Ognissanti
Mercato S.Frediano
LUNGARNO
VIA DEL LEONE
VIA DEL CAMPUCCIO
VIA DELLA CHIESA
Giardino Torrigiani
VIA S. FRANCESCO DI PAOLA
VIA DEL CASONE
VIA ROMANA
VIA DEL SERRAGLIO
LUNGARNO
Piazza Pitti
de' Pitti
Pitti Palace
Ing: di Boboli
Anfiteatro
Giardino Botanico
BOBOLI GARDENS
Porta Romana
Railways shown thus ——

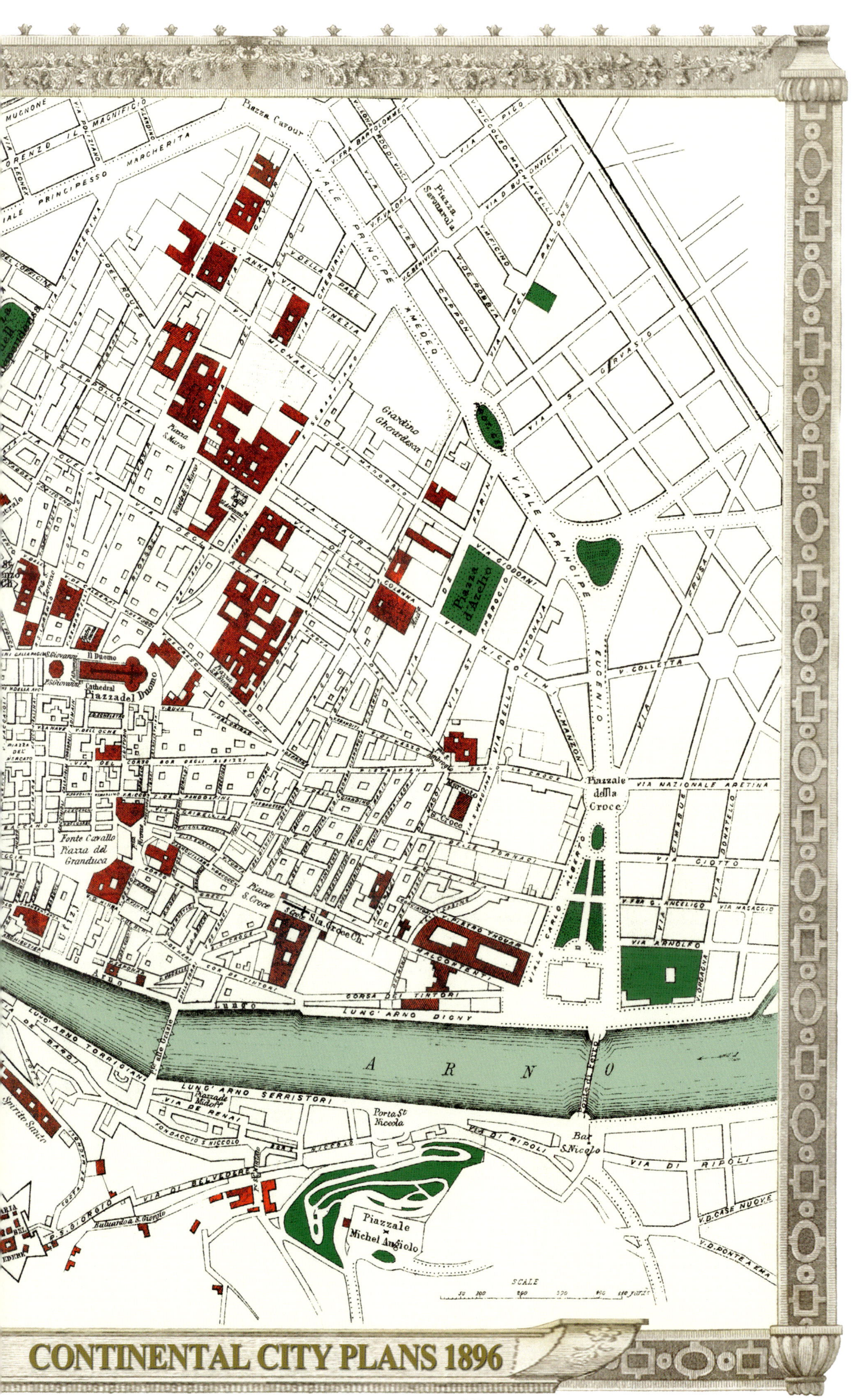

MUGNONE
Piazza Cavour
LORENZO IL MAGNIFICO
PRINCIPESSA MARCHERITA
VIALE PRINCIPE AMEDEO
Piazza Savonarola
Giardino Gherardesca
Piazza S. Marco
Piazza d'Azeglio
VIA GIORDANI
VIALE PRINCIPE EUGENIO
VIA NAZIONALE ARETINA
Il Duomo
Cathedral
Piazza del Duomo
VIA COLLETTA
Fonte Cavallo
Piazza del Granduca
Piazza S. Croce
Piazzale della Croce
Sta. Croce Ch.
VIA CIMABUE
VIA GIOTTO
VIA MASACCIO
VIA ARNOLFO
CORSO DEI TINTORI
LUNG' ARNO DIGNY
A R N O
LUNG' ARNO SERRISTORI
Piazza de' Mozzi
VIA DE' RENAI
Porta St. Niccola
VIA DI RIPOLI
Bar S. Nicolo
VIA DI RIPOLI
FONDACCIO S. NICCOLO
S. Spirito Sanio
VIA DI BELVEDERE
Baluardo S. Giorgio
Piazzale Michel Angiolo
V. D. CASE NUOVE
V. D. PONTE A EMA
SCALE

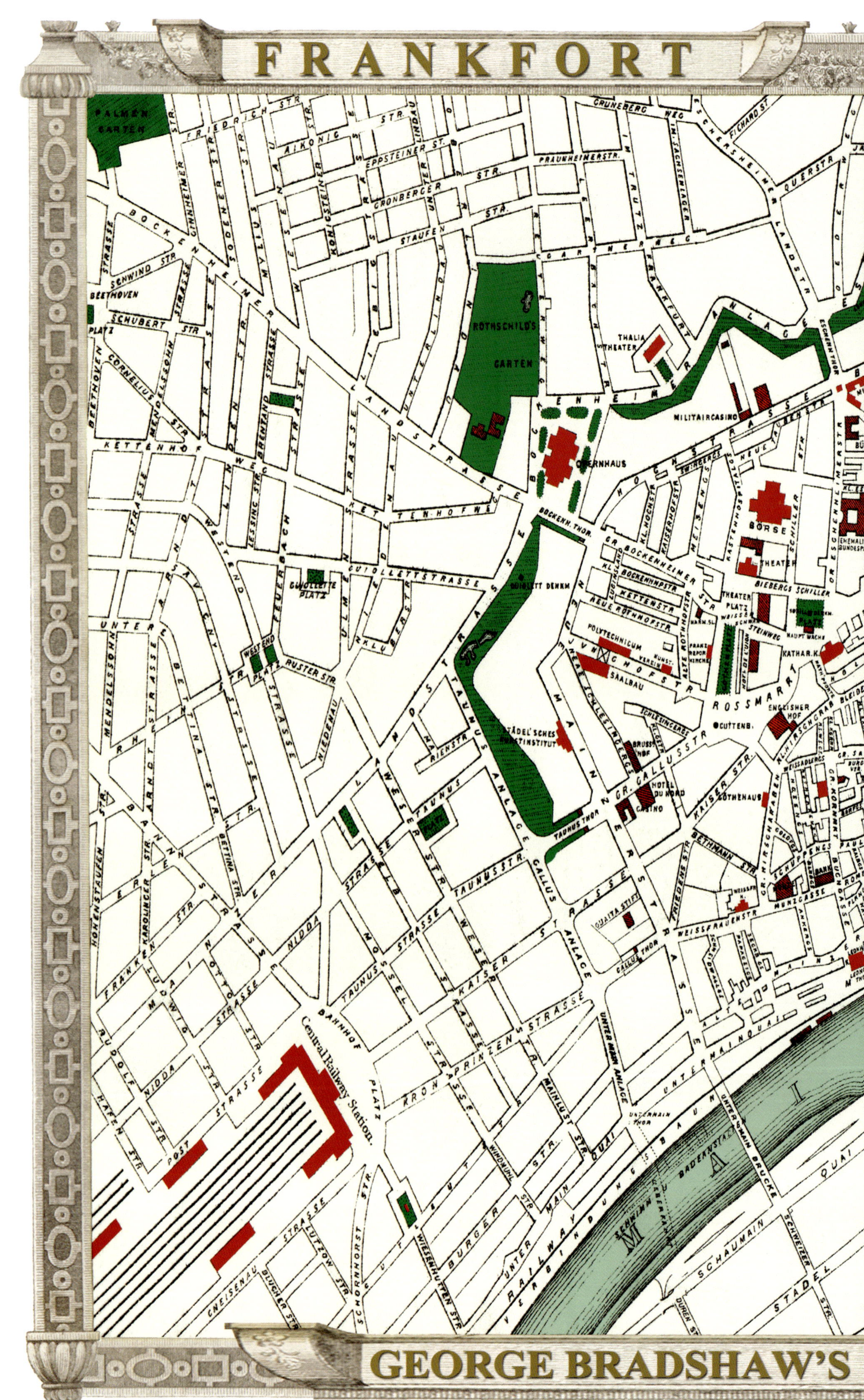
PALMEN GARTEN
GRUNEBERG WEG
FRIEDRICH STR
AIKONIG
EPPSTEINER ST.
GRONBERGER STR
STAUFEN STR
PRAUNHEIMERSTR.
ROTHSCHILD'S GARTEN
THALIA THEATER
MILITAIRCASINO
BOCKENHEIMER STRASSE
SCHWIND STR
BEETHOVEN
SCHUBERT PLATZ
BEETHOVEN
CORNELIUS STR
MENDELSSOHN STR
KETTENHOF
OPERNHAUS
BOCKENH. THOR.
KLKNESTR
KLKBOCKENHEIMER
KETTENSTR
BORSE
THEATER
BIEBERGS SCHILLER
THEATER PLATZ
SCHILLER DENKM.
GUIOLLETT DENKM
NEUE ROTHHOFSTR
POLYTECHNICUM
STEINWEG
HAUPT WACHE
KATHAR. K.
GUIOLLETTSTRASSE
GUIOLLETTE PLATZ
WESTEND
WESTEND PLATZ
RUSTER STR
SAALBAU
ROSSMARKT
ENGLISHER HOF
GUTTENB.
UNTER
MENDELSSOHN STR
NIEDENAU
STADEL'SCHES KUNSTINSTITUT
SCHLESINGERS HOF
BRUSS. HOF
GR. GALLUSSTR
HOTEL DU NORD
CASINO
KAISER STR
ROTHENAU
HOHENSTAUFEN STR
FRANKEN
KAROLINGER STR
ARNDT STR
BETTINA STR
OTTO STR
NIDDA STRASSE
TAUNUS THOR
TAUNUSSTR
BETHMANN STR
KRONPRINZEN STRASSE
MAINZST STR
GALLUS ANLAGE
GALLUS THOR
WEISSFRAUENSTR
MUNZGASSE
LUDWIG STR
NIDDA STR
POST STRASSE
BAHNHOF PLATZ
Central Railway Station.
SCHORNHORST STR
GNEISENAU STRASSE
WIESENHUTTEN STR
WINDMUHL STR
UNTER MAIN ANLAGE
UNTERMAIN THOR
UNTERMAINQUAI
UNTERMAIN BRUCKE
RAILWAY
SCHAUMAIN QUAI
SCHWEIZER
STADEL
BAUM
M A I N

Railways shown thus ____
GAUSS STRASSE
FRIEDBURGER THOR
HESSENWEG
ANLAGE
BETHMANN'S MUSEUM
ARIADNE
Der Hessen
BETHMANNS DENKMAL
MITTLERE BURGERSCHULE
KURSAAL MILANI
KONIGSWARTER STR.
AM THIERGARTEN
ZOOLOGISCHER GARTEN
VERSORGUNGSHS
WAISENHS
HOHERE BURGERSCHULE
BLINDENANST
STAATS GYMNASIUM
KATH. SCHULE
EHEMAL ST STEPH
PETERS
STIFT
BURGERHOSP
KL. FRIEDBSTR
KREUZGASSE
CIRGUS
NEUE ZEIL
GR. BLEICHGARTEN
KINDER HOSPITAL
ROMISCHER KAISER
POST OFF
CONST WACHE
BAUGRABEN
NEUER MARKTPLUTZ
ALBUS STRASSE
VICT HO
Hanau Bebra Ry Station
ALLERHEILIGEN THOR
ALLERHEILIGENSTRASSE
JUDENB
CASSE
EHEMALIGER ISR. BEGRABNISS PLATZ
LBFR.K.
UEBFRAUEN BURG
ISR REALSCHULE
Rechneigraben
SCHNUR GASSE
BARRACKS
DOMINIKANERGS
JUDEN MARKT
ISR. KRANKENKASSE
RECHNEIGRABENSTR
RECHNEISTR
SYNAGOGE
SCHWANENSTR
ANDWIRTHS VEREIN
TO ZOOLOGICAL GARDEN
OSTENDSTRASSE
DOMPLATZ
GYMNASIUM
DOM
FISCHER FELDSTR
FREMDEN HOSPITAL
ROMER BERG
WECKMARKT
HINTER DER SCHON AUSSICHT
STADT-BIBLIOTH
ENGLISCH. GASFABRIK
METZGERTHOR
BRUCKENQUAI
SCHONE AUSSICHT
MAIN THOR
OBERMAINSTRASSE
OBERMAINQUAI
RAILWAY
F   L   U   S   S
MAIN BRUCK
OBER MAIN BRUCKE
OBER FAHRT
DEUTSCHHERRN QUAI
DEUTSCH ORDENS HAUS U KIRCHE
VIEHHOF
ELISABETHENSTR
KL. KLAPPERG
NEUER WALL
OPPENHEIM PLATZ
OFFENBACHER MAINWASENWEG
FUSSWEG
Station
OFFENBACH RAILWAY
ROCHUS HOSPITAL

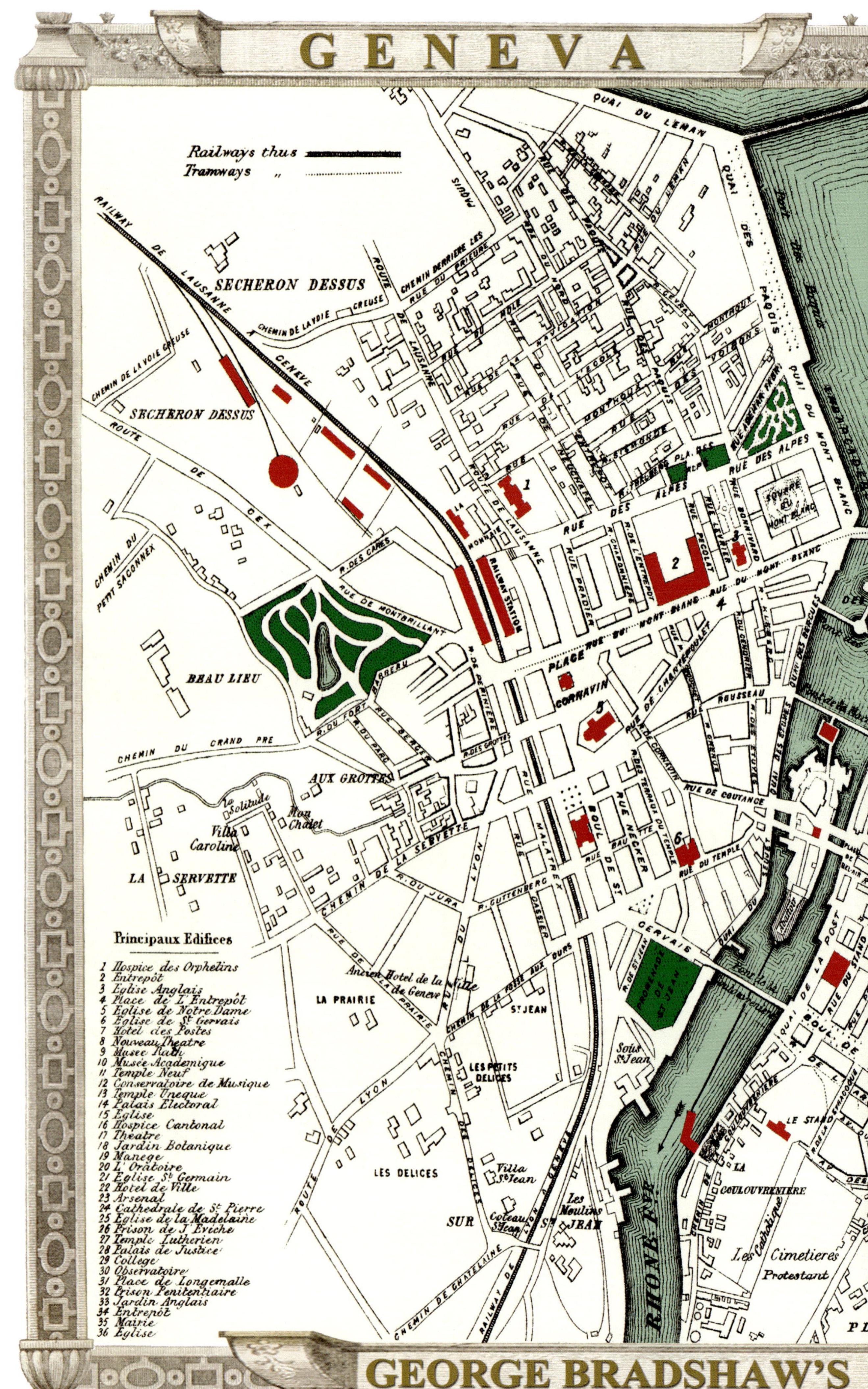
Railways thus
Tramways „
SECHERON DESSUS
SECHERON DESSUS
CHEMIN DE LA VOIE CREUSE
CHEMIN DE LA VOIE CREUSE
ROUTE DE LAUSANNE
CHEMIN DERRIERE LES
RUE DU PRIEURE
QUAI DU LEMAN
QUAI DES PAQUIS
Port des Barques
EMBARCADERE
RAILWAY DE LAUSANNE
CHEMIN DE GENEVE
ROUTE DE GEX
ROUTE DE LAUSANNE
RUE DE LAUSANNE
CHEMIN DU PETIT SACONNEX
BEAU LIEU
R. DES CAPES
RUE DE MONTBRILLANT
RUE BERGERE
R. DU PARC
R. DU FORT BARBERIN
RAILWAY STATION
RUE DES ALPES
RUE PECOLAT
RUE BONIVARD
RUE DU MONT-BLANC
QUAI DU MONT BLANC
SQUARE DU MONT BLANC
RUE PRADIER
RUE DE L'ENTREPOT
RUE CHAPONIERE
PLACE CORNAVIN
RUE DU MONT-BLANC
RUE DE CHANTEPOULET
ROUSSEAU
RUE ROUSSEAU
CHEMIN DU GRAND PRE
AUX GROTTES
R. DES GROTTES
RUE DE CORNAVIN
RUE DE COUTANCE
Le Solitude
Mon Chalet
Villa Caroline
LA SERVETTE
CHEMIN DE LA SERVETTE
R. DU JURA
R. GUTTENBERG
BOUL. DE ST. GERVAIS
RUE NECKER
BOUL. DU TEMPLE
RUE DU TEMPLE
RUE DE SVIZAN
PROMENADE DE ST JEAN
ROUTE DE LYON
RUE DE LYON
Ancien Hotel de la Ville de Geneve
LA PRAIRIE
CHEMIN DE LA FOSSE AUX OURS
St JEAN
Sous St Jean
CHEMIN DE LYON
LES PETITS DELICES
LES DELICES
Villa St Jean
Coteaux St Jean
Les Moulins St JEAN
LA COULOUVRENIERE
LE STAND
RHONE RIVER
QUAI DE LA POST
RUE DU STAND
Les Cimetieres Protestant
SUR
RAILWAY DE LYON
CHEMIN DE CHATELAINE
Principaux Edifices
1 Hospice des Orphelins
2 Entrepôt
3 Eglise Anglais
4 Place de L'Entrepôt
5 Eglise de Notre Dame
6 Eglise de St Gervais
7 Hotel des Postes
8 Nouveau Theatre
9 Musee Rath
10 Musee Academique
11 Temple Neuf
12 Conservatoire de Musique
13 Temple Uneque
14 Palais Electoral
15 Eglise
16 Hospice Cantonal
17 Theatre
18 Jardin Botanique
19 Manege
20 L'Oratoire
21 Eglise St Germain
22 Hotel de Ville
23 Arsenal
24 Cathedrale de St Pierre
25 Eglise de la Madelaine
26 Prison de J'Eveche
27 Temple Lutherien
28 Palais de Justice
29 College
30 Observatoire
31 Place de Longemalle
32 Prison Penitentiaire
33 Jardin Anglais
34 Entrepôt
35 Mairie
36 Eglise

LAKE OF GENEVA
EAUX-VIVES
BEL-AIR
JARGONNANT
36
LA TERRASSIERE
MALAGNOU
PRE L'EVEQUE
CHEMIN DU PRE L'EVEQUE
VILLE REUSE
Bryn Bella
32
RUE DE VERSONNEX
RUE DU RHONE
15
A. DU RHONE
34
CHEMIN DES TRANCHEES
JARDIN ANGLAISE
33
QUAI DU RHONE
RUE PIERRE
D'ITALIE
RUE DE LA CROIX D'OR
COURS DE RIVE
RUE DE RIVE
LES TRANCHEES DE RIVE
GRANDE QUAI
HELVETIQUE
RUE DE MALAGNOU
CONTAMINES
MONT BLANC
RUE DU RHONE
31
PL. DU COLLEGE
RUE STURM
RUE TOPEFER
CHEMIN DU SQUARE
RUE DES BERGUES
PROMENADE DE ST ANTOIN
30
R. DE L'OBSERVATOIRE
RUE DE MONNETIER
BOULD DES TRANCHEES
CHAMPEL
RUE DU MARCHE
29
28
RUE DES CASEMATES
RUE ST VICTOR
RUE C. BONNET
11
RUE DE LA CORRATERIE
23
26
24
BOURG DE FOUR
HELVETIQUE
DE L'ATHENEE
20
19
RUE DES BASTIONS
COURS DES CASEMATES
PL. DE CHAMPEL
10
RUE
22
PROMENADE DE LA TREILLE
NOUVELLE RUE
RUE DES BASTIONS
LES PHILOSOPHES
9
17
PROMENADE DES BASTIONS
8
PLACE NEUVE
UNIVERSITE
RUE DE CAN
CHEMIN DES GRANDS
16
HOSPICE CANTONAL
BOUL DU THEATRE
12
RUE GENERAL
14
RUE DU CONSEIL GENERAL
RUE DE
BOULEVARD
LES TRANCHEES
13
DE PLAINPALAIS
LA CLUSE
BOULEVARD DE PLAINPALAIS
CHEMIN DES TERRASSIERS
PLAINE DE PLAINPALAIS
PLAINPALAIS
LES PHILOSOPHES
LE JEU DE MAIL
CHEMIN DU MAIL
15
CONTINENTAL CITY PLANS 1896

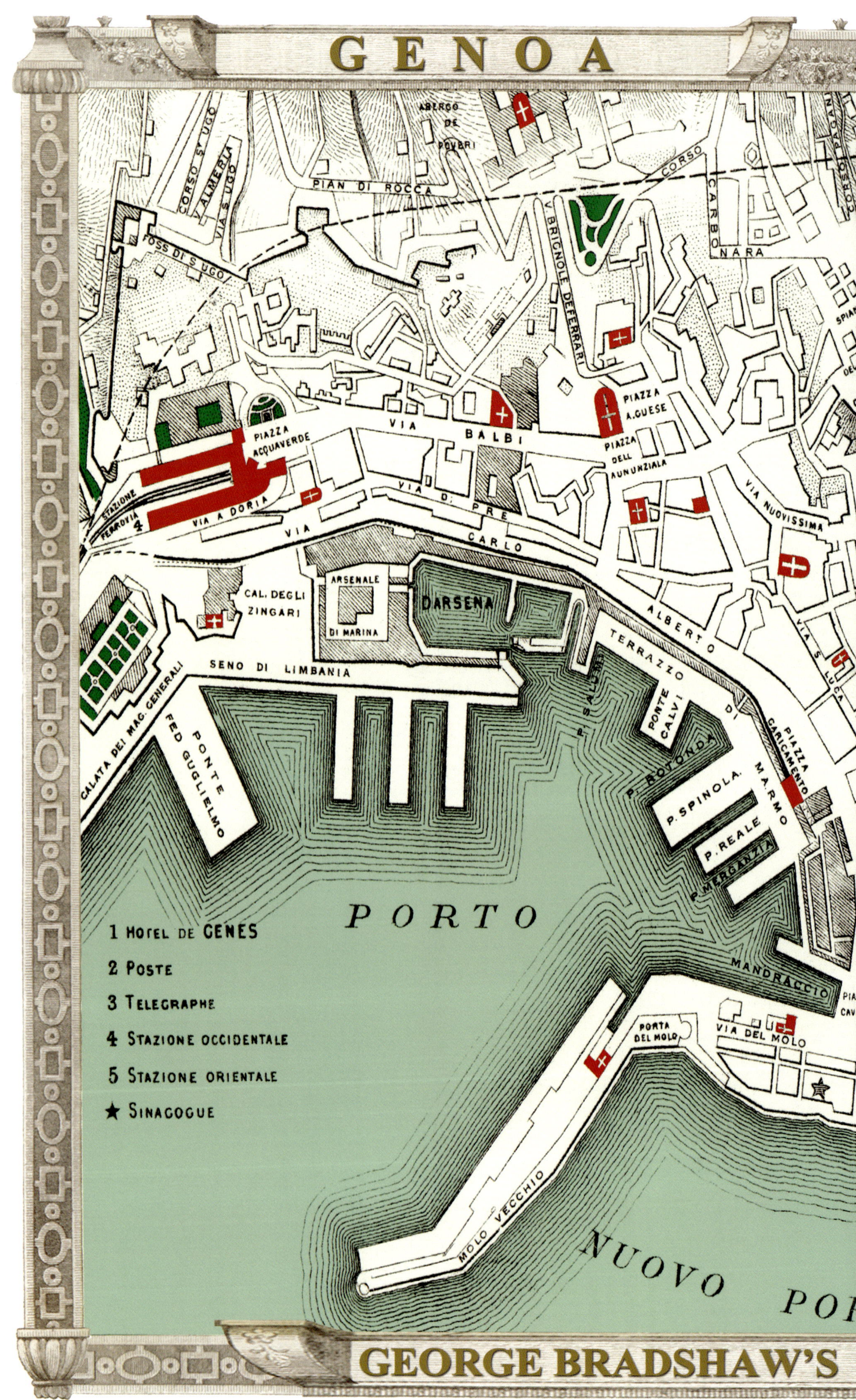

GENOA
ALBERGO DE POVERI
PIAN DI ROCCA
CORSO S.T UGO
VIA S.T UGO
V. ALMERIA
FOSS DI S. UGO
CORSO CARBONARA
V. BRIGNOLE DEFERRARI
VIA BALBI
PIAZZA ACQUAVERDE
PIAZZA A. GUESE
PIAZZA DELL' ANUNZIALA
VIA NUOVISSIMA
STAZIONE FERROVIA 4
VIA A. DORIA
VIA D. PRE
VIA CARLO ALBERTO
VIA S. LUCA
CAL. DEGLI ZINGARI
ARSENALE DI MARINA
DARSENA
TERRAZZO DI
PIAZZA CARICAMENTO
SENO DI LIMBANIA
CALATA DEI MAG. GENERALI
PONTE FED GUGLIELMO
B. SAULI
P. ROTONDA
PONTE CALVI
P. SPINOLA
MARMO
P. REALE
P. MERGANZIA
PORTO
MANDRACCIO
PIAZ CAVO
1 HOTEL DE GENES
2 POSTE
3 TELEGRAPHE
4 STAZIONE OCCIDENTALE
5 STAZIONE ORIENTALE
★ SINAGOGUE
PORTA DEL MOLO
VIA DEL MOLO
MOLO VECCHIO
NUOVO PORTO
GEORGE BRADSHAW'S

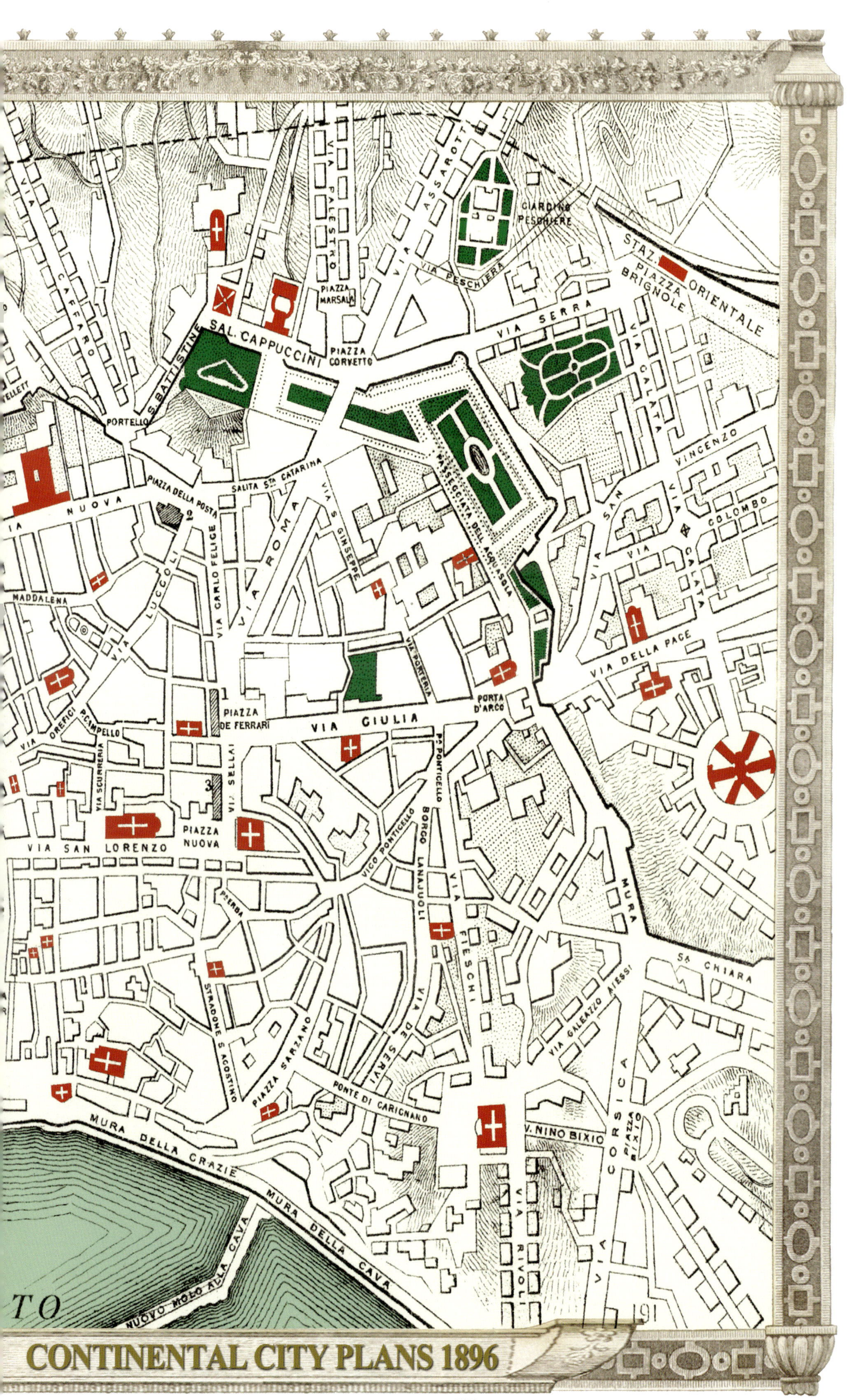

VIA PALESTRO
VIA ASSAROTT
GIARDINO PESCHIERE
VIA PESCHIERA
STAZ. ORIENTALE
PIAZZA BRIGNOLE
PIAZZA MARSALA
VIA SERRA
VIA CALATA
SAL. CAPPUCCINI
SAL. BATTISTINE
PIAZZA CORVETTO
VIA SAN VINCENZO
PORTELLO
PIAZZA DELLA POSTA
SALITA STA CATARINA
VIA ROMA
VIA GINSEPPE
PASSEGGIATA DELL'ACQUASOLA
VIA SAN
VIA COLOMBO
VIA CALATA
NUOVA
LUCCOLI
VIA CARLO FELICE
VIA PORTERIA
VIA DELLA PACE
MADDALENA
PORTA D'ARCO
PIAZZA DE FERRARI
VIA GIULIA
VIA OREFICI
P. CAMPELLO
VIA SELLAI
VIA SCURRERIA
PIAZZA NUOVA
P. PONTICELLO
VICO PONTICELLO
BORGO LANAJUOLI
VIA FIESCHI
MURA
VIA SAN LORENZO
P. ERBA
SA CHIARA
PIAZZA SARZANO
STRADONE S. AGOSTINO
VIA DE SERVI
VIA GALEAZZO ALESSI
PONTE DI CARIGNANO
V. NINO BIXIO
CORSICA
PIAZZA SARZANO
VIA RIVO
MURA DELLA GRAZIE
MURA DELLA CAVA
NUOVO MOLO ALLA CAVA
T O
191

EXPLANATION
1 Eglise Cathed de St Bavon
2 do St Jacques
3 St Nicolas
4 St Michel
5 St Martin
6 St Sauveur
7 N.D. St Pierre
8 Ste Anne
9 Ste Anne (New)
10 des Augustins
11 Dominicains
12 Recollets
13 P. Jesuites
14 Couvent de Doorseele
15 du Nouveau-Bois
16 des Carmes Chausses
17 Theresiennes
18 Grand Séminaire
19 Collège Ste Barbe
20 Hospice de Schreyboom
21 des Incurables
22 Sourds et Muets
23 Enfants trouves
24 Orphelins (Garcons)
25 Filles Corps Bleu
26 Rouge
27 Maison d'insenses pour hommes
28 femmes
29 Grand Beguinage
30 Petite Beguinage
31 Jardin Botanique
32 Palais de Justice
33 l'Université
34 Entrepôt de Commerce
35 Tribunal Civil
36 Grand Theatre
37 Maison de Detension
38 Manege et ecole Industrielle
39 Maison de Ville
40 Hopital Militaire
41 do Civil
42 Hospice de Vielles Femmes
43 des Vieillards
44 Mont de Piete
45 Tour du Beffroi
46 Casino
47 Athenee
48 Eveche
49 Ecole d'Armes et Gymnace
50 Caserne des Sapeurs Pompier
51 Marechausses
52 de Cavalerie
53 d'Infanterie No 1
54 No 2
55 d'Artillerie
56 Academie de Dessin et Museum
57 Atelier de Bienfaisance
58 Bureau de Bienfaisance
59 Douane
60 l'Octroi
61 Bibliotheque Pubque
62 Grande Boucherie
63 Petite
64 Ancien Chateau des Comtes
65 Establissement du Gaz No 1
66 No 2
67 Poste aux Chevaux
68 Lettres
69 Theatre de la Rethorique
70 Moulin a Vapeur
71 Magasin d'habillement Militaire No 1
72 No 2
73 Marché aux qu. 2
74 Bains Publique
75 Grande Garde Militaire
76 Halle aux Toiles
77 Atelier du Phenix
78 Maternite
PLAINE St PIERRE
ZOOLOGICAL GARDENS
Terrain de Golf
NEW HOSPITAL
RAILWAY STATION
PLACE DE LA STATION
BOULD DES HOSPICES
BOULEVARD DE LA CITADELLA
CHEMIN DE FER DE L'ETAT A OSTEND
BOULEVARD DU JARDIN ZOOLOGIQUE
BOULEVARD FRERE ORBAN
RAMPART DE LA PORTE DE BRUXELLES
PORTE ST LIEVIN
PORTE DE BRUXELLE
PECHERIE
HOSPICE LOUSBERGS
NORTH
WEST
EAST
SOUTH

Tir
à la cible
BOULEVARD DES HOSPICES
Railways thus
St Jean
77
COUPURE
LA COUPURE
Station
PROMENADE
Ancien
Cloitre des
Chartrex
MARCHE DU VENDREDI
MARCHE AU GRAINS
PECHERIE

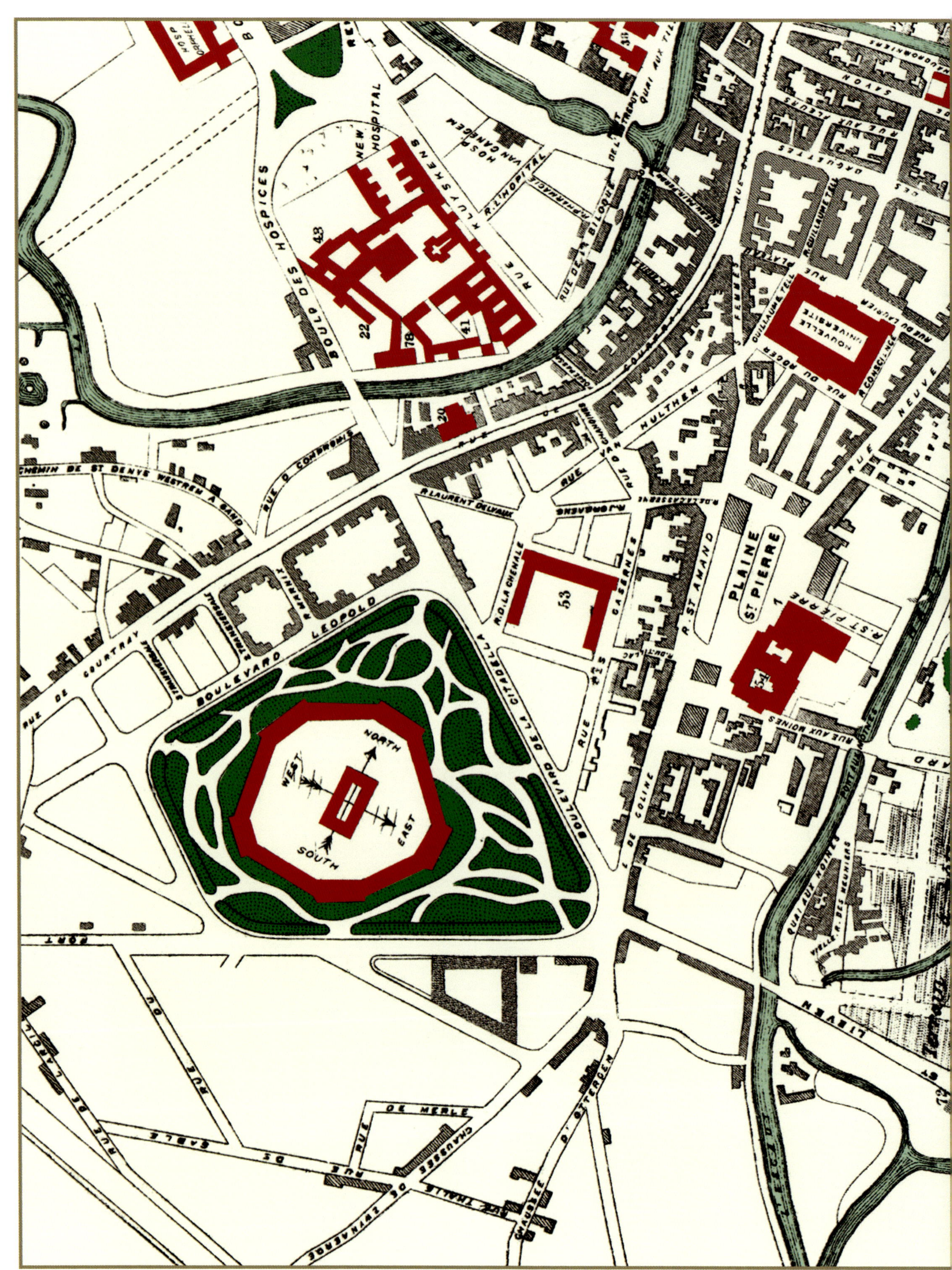

HOSP. ORPHELINS
BOULD
NEW HOSPITAL
HOSP. KLUYSKENS
HOSP. VAN CANEGEM
R. L'HOPITAL
R. PHARMACIE
RUE DES HOSPICES
RUE DE LA BILOQUE
BOULD DES HOSPICES
48
22
78
41
20
RUE DE
RUE D. CONDUMIS
CHEMIN DE ST DENYS WESTREM A GAND
RUE DE COURTRAY
R. LAURENT DELVAUX
RUE VAN HULTHEM
R. ORGAGNE
R. DELACASSERNE
CASERNE
RUE DES
RUE DE COLINE
R.D. LA CHENALE
53
PLAINE ST. PIERRE
R. ST. PIERRE
1
54
R. ST. ANAND
RUE AUX MOINES
R. MARNIX
BOULEVARD LEOPOLD
BOULEVARD DE LA CITADELLE
NORTH
WEST
EAST
SOUTH
QUAI AUX TIL
RUE DU STREPOT
DEL STREPOT
SAVON
RUE AUX VACHES
RUE DES DAGUETTES
NOAS
RUE DU ROGER
NOUVELLE UNIVERSITE
A CONSCIENCE
RUE DU LAURIER
RUE GUILLAUMTEL
NEUVE
LIEVEN
PONT
RUE DES GABLE
RUE DES CARELI
CHAUSSEE D'ZWYNAERDE
RUE DE MERLE
D. OTTERGEM
QUAI AUX MOINES
QUAI DES REUNIES
TERNEUS

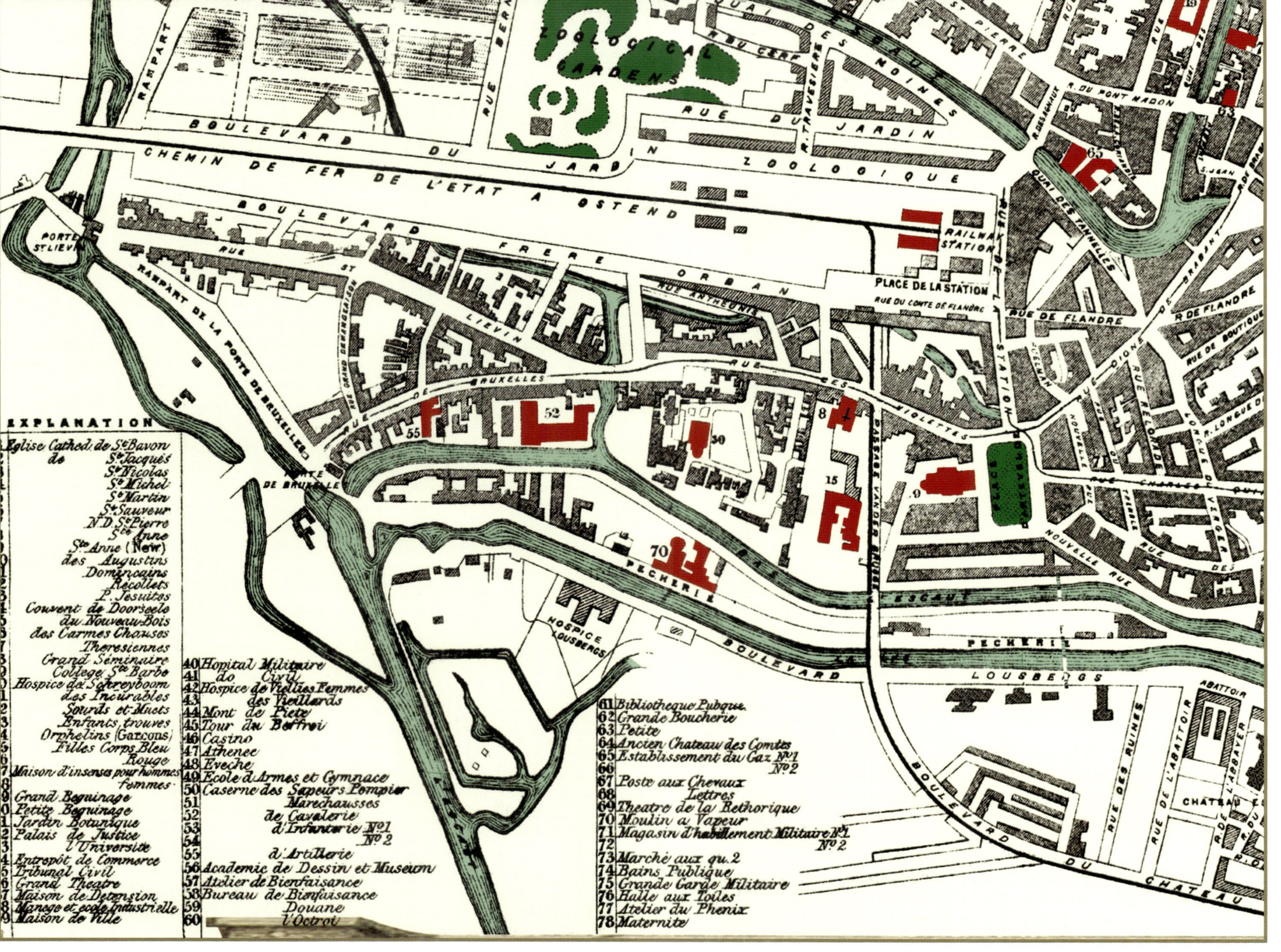

ZOOLOGICAL GARDENS
RAMPART
RUE BERN
RUE DU CERF
R. TRAVESIERE
RUE DU JARDIN
QUAI DES ESCLIS
RUE DES NOINES
ST PIERRE
R. DU PONT NADON
QUAI DES TANNELLIES
BOULEVARD DU JARDIN ZOOLOGIQUE
CHEMIN DE FER DE L'ETAT A OSTEND
BOULEVARD FRERE ORBAN
PORTE ST LIEVIN
RAMPART DE LA PORTE DE BRUXELLES
RUE DE GRAND DERANGATION
RUE DE BRUXELLES
LIEVIN
RUE ANTHEUNIS
RUE DES VIOLETTES
RAILWAY STATION
PLACE DE LA STATION
RUE DU CONTE DE FLANDRE
RUE DE FLANDRE
R DE FLANDRE
R DE BOUTIQUE
R. LONGUE DE
PORTE DE BRUXELLE
PECHERIE
HOSPICE LOUSBERGS
BOULEVARD
ESCAUT
PLACE D'ARTEVELD
NOUVELLE RUE
PECHERIE
LOUSBERGS
BOULEVARD DU CHATEAU
RUE DES RUINES
RUE DE L'ABATTOIR
ABATTOIR
CHATEAU

EXPLANATION
1 Eglise Cathed. de St Bavon
2 do St Jacques
3 St Nicolas
4 St Michel
5 St Martin
6 St Sauveur
7 N.D. St Pierre
8 Ste Anne
9 Ste Anne (New)
10 des Augustins
11 Dominicains
12 Recollets
13 P. Jesuites
14 Couvent de Doorzeele
15 du Nouveau-Bois
16 des Carmes Chausses
17 Theresiennes
18 Grand Séminaire
19 Collège St Barbe
20 Hospice de Schreyboom
21 des Incurables
22 Sourds et Muets
23 Enfants trouves
24 Orphelins (Garçons)
25 Filles Corps Bleu
26 Rouge
27 Maison d'insensés pour hommes
28 Femmes
29 Grand Béguinage
30 Petite Béguinage
31 Jardin Botanique
32 Palais de Justice
33 l'Université
34 Entrepôt de Commerce
35 Tribunal Civil
36 Grand Theatre
37 Maison de Détention
38 Manège et école Industrielle
39 Maison de Ville
40 Hopital Militaire
41 do Civil
42 Hospice de Vieilles Femmes
43 des Vieillards
44 Mont de Pieté
45 Tour du Beffroi
46 Casino
47 Athenee
48 Eveche
49 Ecole d'Armes et Gymnace
50 Caserne des Sapeurs Pompier
51 Marechausses
52 de Cavalerie
53 d'Infanterie No.1
54 No.2
55 d'Artillerie
56 Academie de Dessin et Museum
57 Atelier de Bienfaisance
58 Bureau de Bienfaisance
59 Douane
60 l'Octroi
61 Bibliotheque Pubque.
62 Grande Boucherie
63 Petite
64 Ancien Chateau des Comtes
65 Establissement du Gaz No.1
66 No.2
67 Poste aux Chevaux
68 Lettres
69 Theatre de la Rethorique
70 Moulin a Vapeur
71 Magasin d'habillement Militaire No.1
72 No.2
73 Marché aux qu.2
74 Bains Publique
75 Grande Garde Militaire
76 Halle aux Toiles
77 Atelier du Phenix
78 Maternité

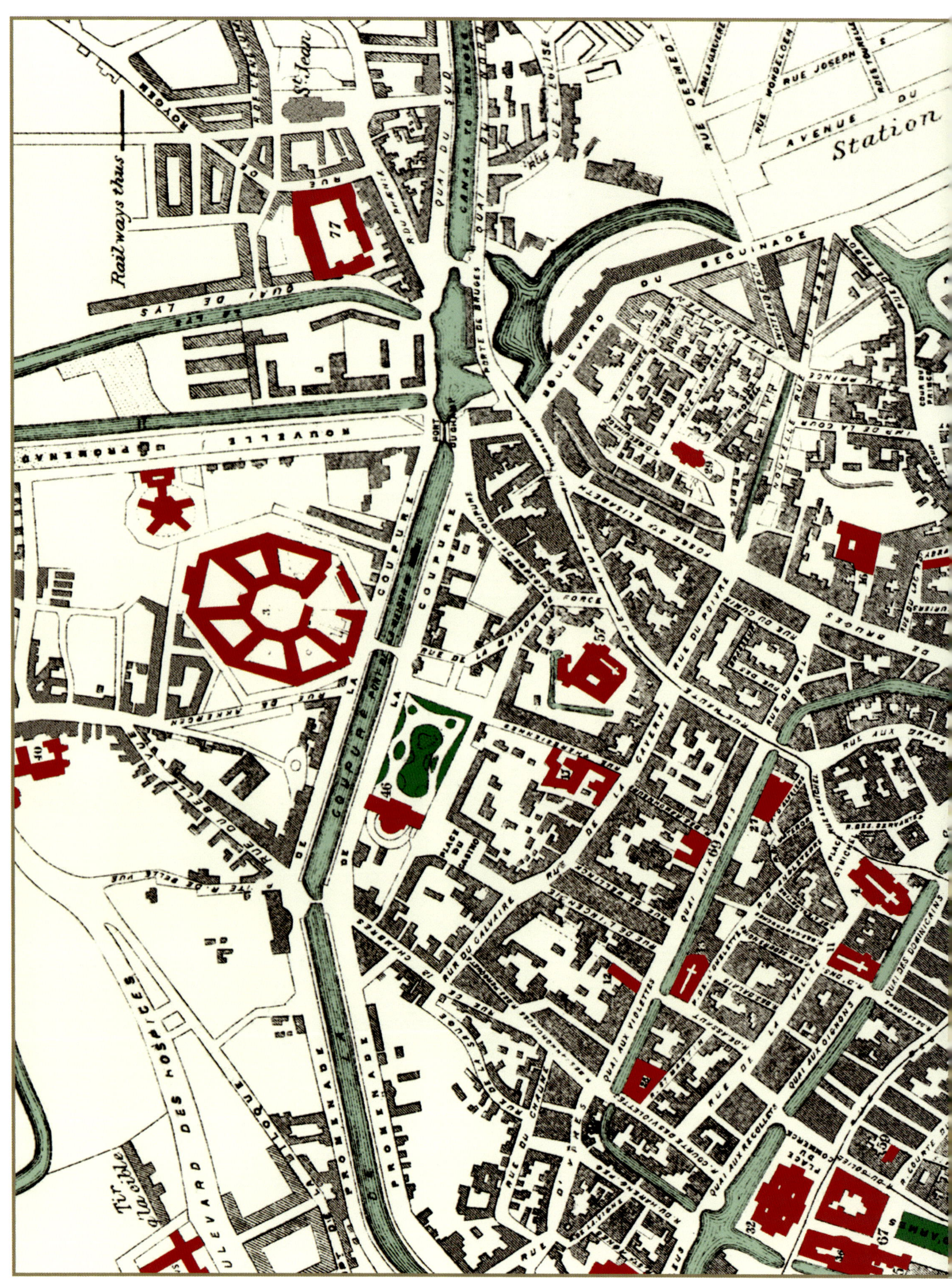

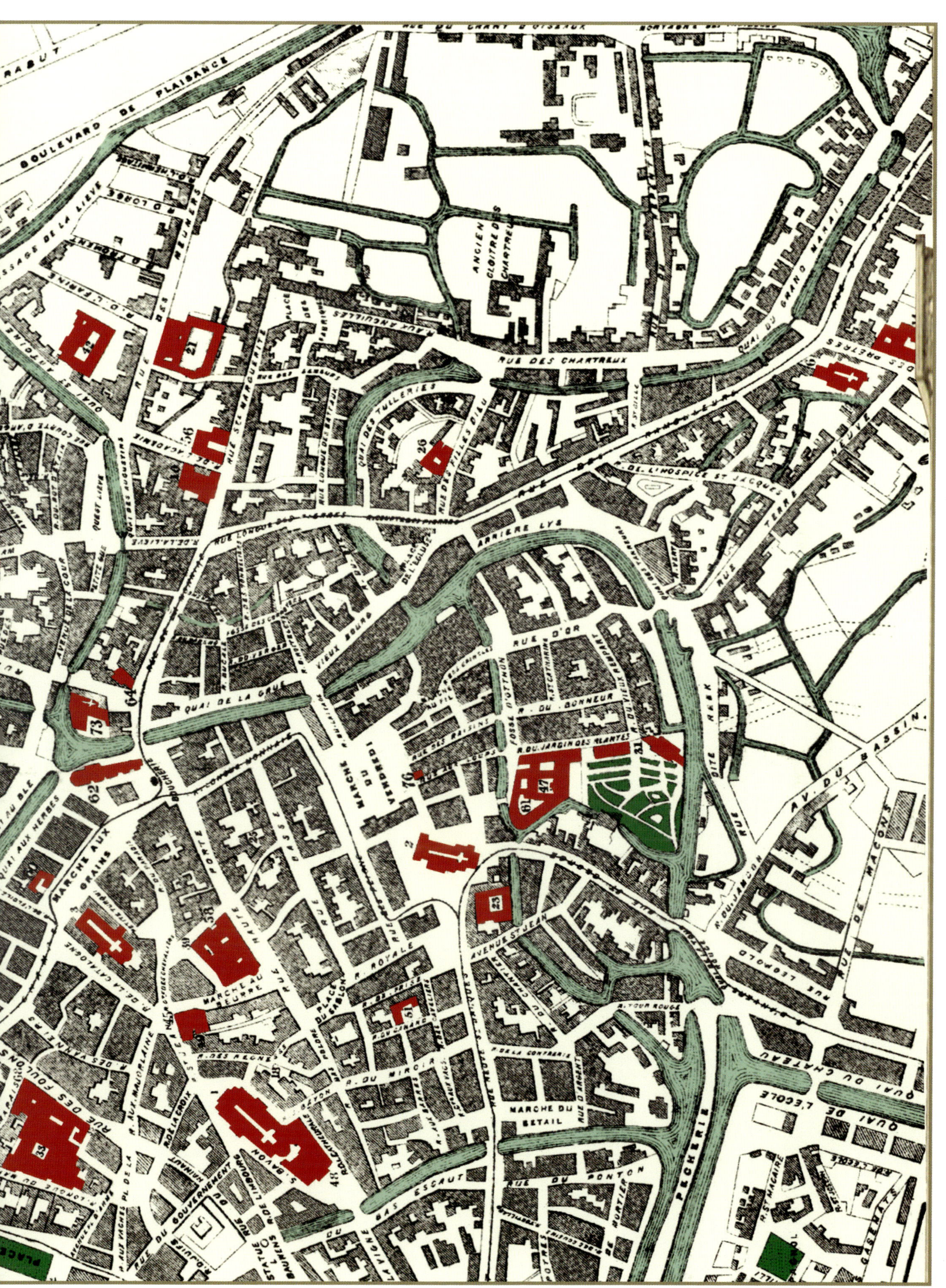

RABUT
BOULEVARD DE PLAISANCE
PASSAGE DE LA LIEVE
QUAI DES PIERRES
QUAI D'ARS
RUE DES CHARTREUX
ANCIEN CLOITRE DES CHARTREUX
RUE DES TULLERIES
DE L'HOSPICE ST JACQUES
ARRIERE LYS
QUAI DU GRAND MARAIS
DES PRETRES
RUE D'OR
R. DU BONHEUR
R. DU JARDIN DES PLANTES
QUAI DE LA GRUE
MARCHE DU VENDREDI
AV. DU BASSIN
QUAI AUX HERBES
MARCHE AUX GRAINS
MARCHE AU BEURRE
RUE LEOPOLD
QUAI DU CHATEAU
AVENUE ST JEAN
R. TOUR ROUGE
R. ROYALE
R. DU MIROIR
MARCHE DU BETAIL
QUAI DE L'ECOLE
RUE DES FOULONS
RUE DU GOUVERNEMENT
STATUE DE JACQUES VAN ARTEVELDE
R. BAS ESCAUT
RUE DU PONTON
PECHERIE
PLACE

Explanation of the numbers:

1. Royal Palace .... Paleis v. z. M. d. Koning
2. King's Mews .... 's Konings Stallen
3. Prince of Orange's Palace
        Paleis v. z. K. H. de Prins van Orange
4. Minister of Finance's office .. Ministerie van Finantien
5. .... Salon d'Exposition
6. Cloister Church .... Klooster Kerk
7. Royal Riding school .... 's Konings Manège
8. Barracks .... Oranje Kazerne
9. Library .... Bibliotheek
10. Portuguse Synagogue .. Portugeesche Synagoge
11. Estab. for boring Canon .. Boorhuis
12. Canon foundery .... Kanongietery
13. Post horses office .... Paordenpostery
14. Prince Frederic's Palace .. Paleis v. z. K. H. Prins Frederik
15. Government offices for South Holland
        Gouvernement van Zuid Holland
16. French Roman cath. Ch. .. Fransche Roomsche Kerk
17. Theatre .... Schouwburg, Théâtre
18. King's Palace .... Paleis v. z. M. den Koning (Plein)
19. Poor house .... Arme inrigting
20. Museum .... Museum
21. Government offices .... Ministerium
22. States General 1. Chamb. .. Staaten Generaal 1. Kammer
23.   „   2.   2.   „
24. Roman Cath. Chapel .... Roomsche Kapel
25. Lottery office and Criminal Court of Justice
    Binnenhof, Loteryzaal en Hoog Geregtshof
26. Principal Guard house .. Hoofdwacht
27. Government offices of National and Colonies,
    and Minister of Justice's offices
    Ministerie v. d. nationale Nyverheid en Kolonien
        & Ministerie v. Justice
28. French Church .... Fransche Waalsche Kerk
29. .... Pastors Kerk
30. Old Men's Hospital .. Oude Mannenhuis
31. English Chapel .... Engelsche Kerk
32. Jansenist Chapel .... Janseniste Kerk
33. Exhibition of Works of Art
    Tentoonstelling van Kunstwerken
34. Town Hall .... Stadhuis
35. Post office .... Postkantoor
36. Principal Church .. Groote Kerk
37. .... Fundatiehuis
38. Rom. Catho. Church .. Roomsche Kerken
39. Lutheran Church .... Luthersche Kerk
40. New Church .... Nieuwe Kerk
41. Old Women and Children's Hospital
    Oude Vrouwen en Kinderhuis

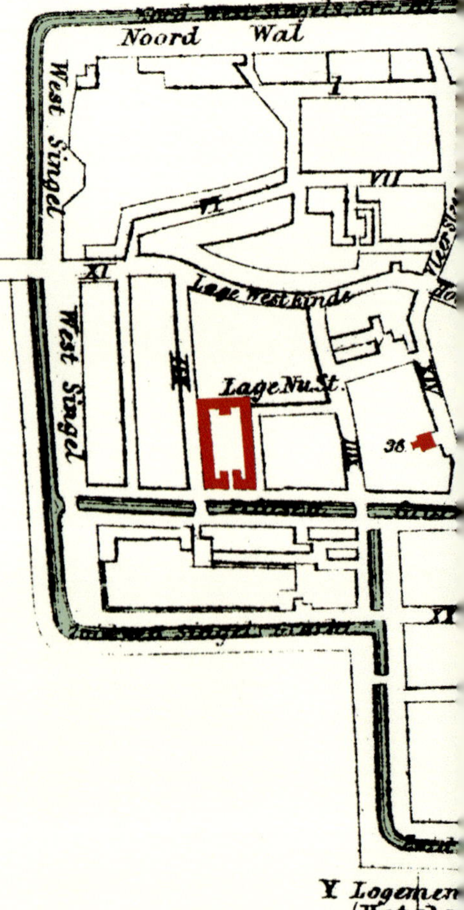

I. Ledig Erf   II. Breed Straat   XIII. Groote Lombard Str.   XXI. Vlaming Str.
III. Snoek Straat   XIV. Lorren of Assendelft   XXII. Lange Poten
IV. Korte Molen Straat   XV. Jan Hendrik Str.   XXIII. Korte Poten
V. Molen Straat   XVI. School Str.   XXIV. Groote Markt
VI. Het Korte Bosch   XVII. Nieuwe Str.   XXV. Het Hooge Zand
VII. Slik Einde VIII. De Geest XVIII. Veene Str.   XXVI. Lange Beesten Markt
IX. Nobel Str. X. Groen Markt. XIX. Goort Str.   XXVII. Bockhorst Straat
XI. Loosduiner Brug   XX. De Loan   XXVIII. Ged. Burgwal
XII. Slop de drie Boeren   XXIX. Gedempte Gracht
                              XXX. Kalveren Markt
                              XXXI. Paddenmoes
                              XXXII. Fluweelen Burgwal

Java Straat
WIL HEMS
Wilhelms Park
Sophia Laan
Willems
Alexander Straat
Noord Straat
Bazaar
P A RK
Noord Singels Gracht
Hooge Wal
BENOORDEN
HOUTSCHE
Frederik St.
Fredericks
Zoological & Botanic Gardens
Wal
Prin cessen Tuin
Princessen
Nord Einde
Park St.
Willems St.
Denne Weg
Kazerne Weg
Kazerne Weg
Malie Baan
Achter de Stallen
8
Lang Vourhout
Wyde Voorhout
Paaden Mt.
10
2
1
3
4
7
6
9
28
32
29
30 31
Kloeater Dyk
Korte
Tournooi Veld
YY
12
13
11
15
14
16
35
37
Chu.
34
De Plaats
Lang Vyver Berg
Y
VIJ VER
Buiton Hof
Groen M.
33
Hoog St.
West Einde
36
Visch M.
25
26
23
24
27
18
19
5
38
Het Plein
Koe Kamp
Heeren Gr.
Beruiden houtsche Weg
Kazern. v. d. Artillerie
Spui Str.
Groote Mkt.
39
40
Willems Hospital
Amunitieh
Zwarte Str.
Zuid Wal
Het Bade
Kl. Grosne Weg
Grosne Weg
41
Vanden Duin St.
Huigens Begr. Gardens
Oranje Plein
Van Hogendorp St.
Van Limburg St.
Noord Polder
Rotterdam Str.
Railway Station
ROTTERDAM RAILWAY

HAMBURG
ZOOLOGISCHE GARDEN
GRAND CUBE
Reform
Begr Pl S. Johannis
Katholischer Begr Pl
Begr Pl St Petri
Begr Pl St Michaelis
St Pauli Bg Pl
St Catharinen
RUDOLPHUS
RINGSTRASSE
KIRCHHOFEN
HEILIGENGEIST
FELD
VALENTINS STR
KONIGS
PANORAMA
STEINWEG
MARKT
MUHLEN STR
GRAVENKAMP
MICHAELIS
NICOLAI
HOLZ SCHAAR
SCHAARSTEINWEG
Elbhöhe
Hafenthor Thc.
Hopfen Markt
BINNEN HAFEN
SANDTHOR
NORDER
ST PAULI
LANGEREIHE
SPIELBUDEN PL
REEPERBAHN
MARIEN STR
KIELER STR
HEILIGENGEIST FELD
THE ENVIRONS
-OF-
HAMBURG & ALTONA
Railways thus
Barmbeck
Uhlenhorst
WANDSBECK
Poseldorf
Eimsbüttel
Hamm
Hammerbrook
ST GEORG
Hammerdeich
Ottensen
Kl. Grasbrook
Gr. Feddel
NORDER ELBE
Billwarder Elbe
Dille R.
Berlin Raily
GRASBR

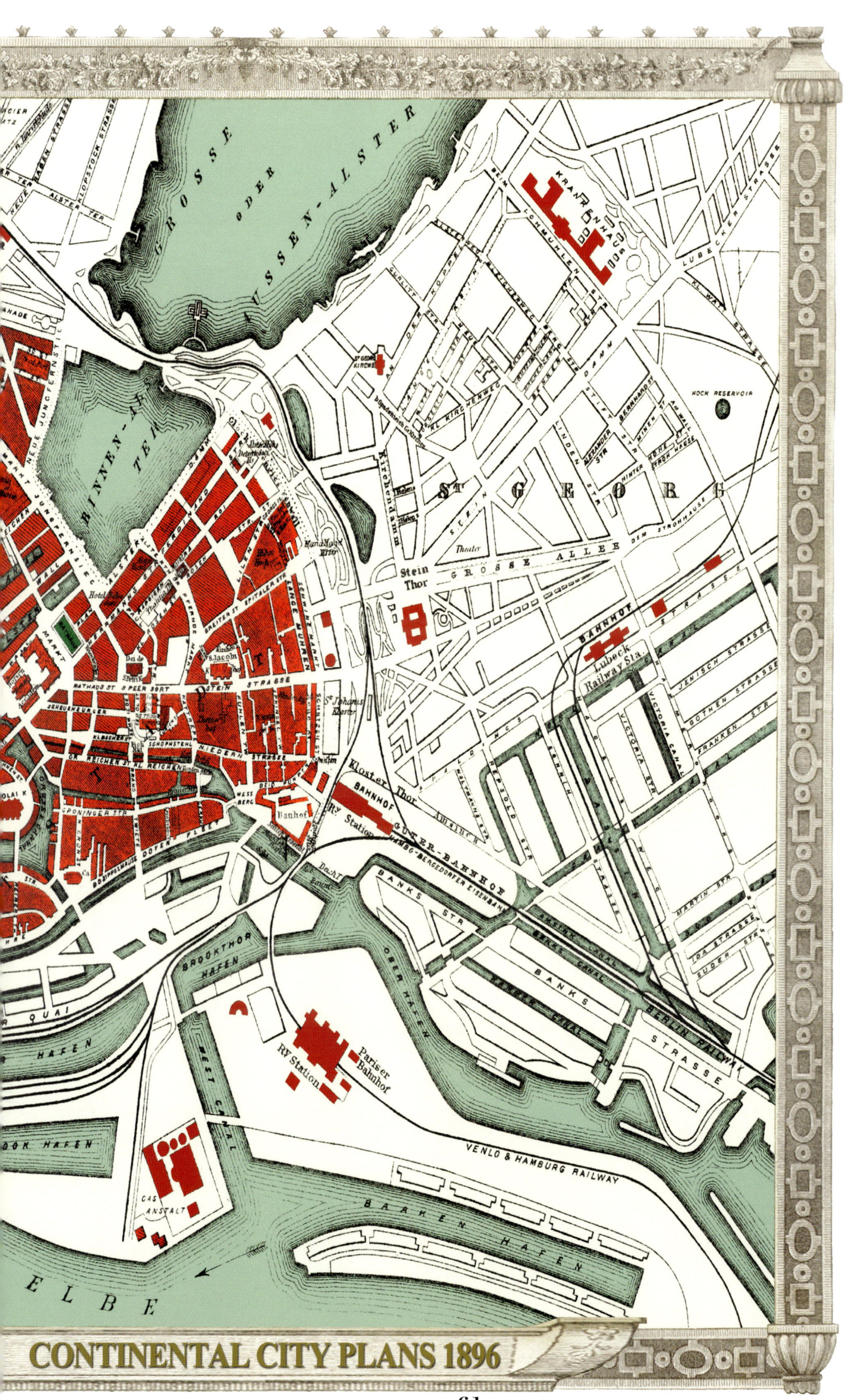

GROSSE ODER AUSSEN-ALSTER
BINNEN-ALSTER
St GEORG
HOCH RESERVOIR
KRANKENHAUS
St GEORG KIRCHE
Stein Thor
GROSSE ALLEE
Theater
Bahnhof
Lübeck Railway Sta.
JENISCH STRASSE
GÖTHEN STRASSE
VICTORIA CANAL
FRANKEN STR.
Kloster Thor
BAHNHOF
GÜTER-BAHNHOF
HAMBG-BERGEDORFER EISENBAHN
Ry Station
BANKS STR.
OBER HAFEN
BANKS
BROOKTHOR HAFEN
WEST CANAL
RY Station
Pariser Bahnhof
BERLIN RAILWAY
STRASSE
VENLO & HAMBURG RAILWAY
GAS ANSTALT
BAAKEN HAFEN
DOCK HAFEN
HAFEN
QUAI
ELBE

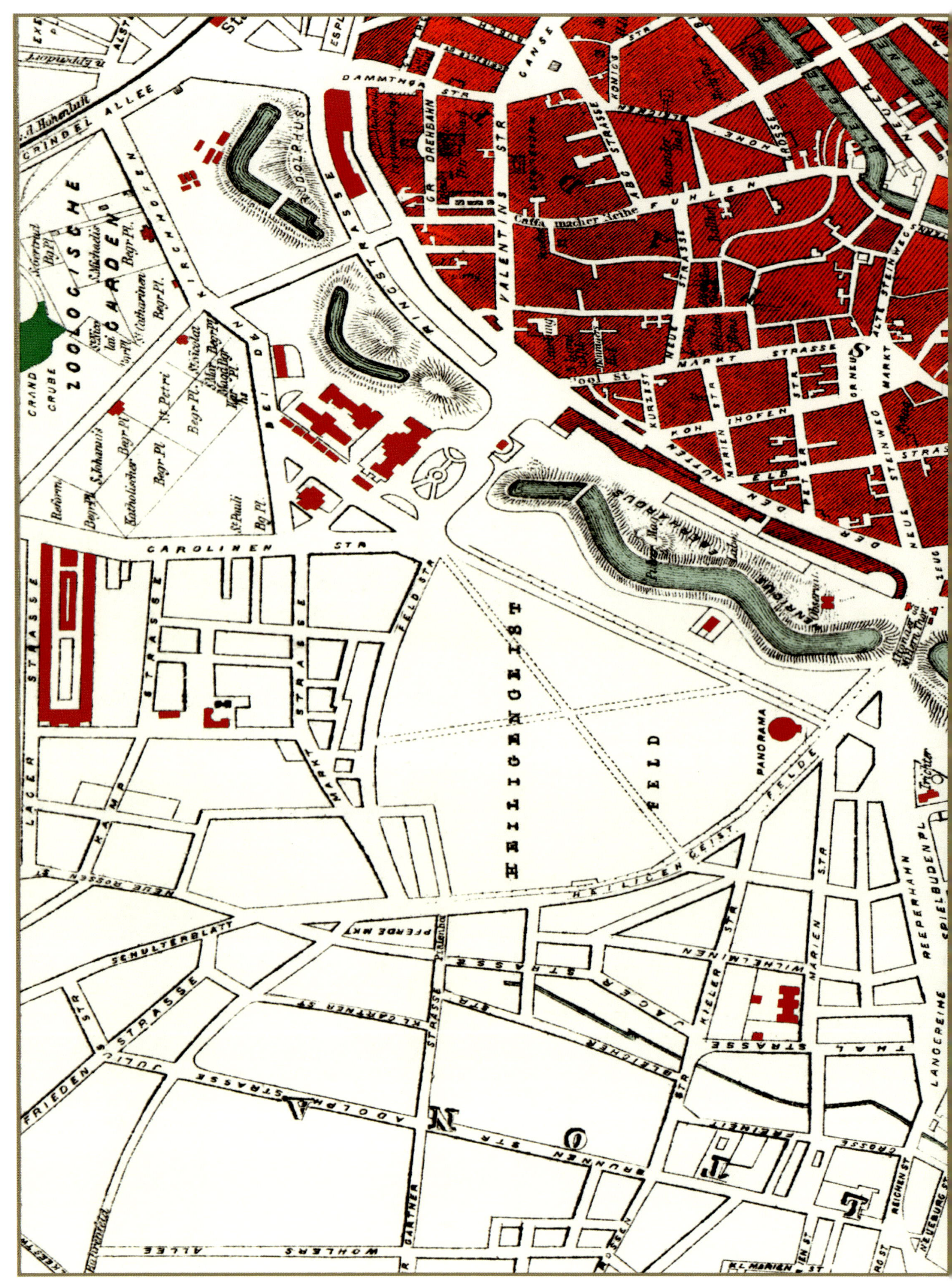

GRINDEL ALLEE
ZOOLOGISCHE GARTEN
RICHMODEN
KIRCHHOFEN
RINGSTRASSE
BEI DEN
DAMMTHOR STR
GR DREHBAHN
VALENTINS STR
GANSE
STRASSE KONIGS
FUHLEN
NEUE
MARKT
STRASSE
Caffamacher Reihe
Cool St
KURZ ST
KOH
MARIEN STR
IHOFEN
GR NEUE STR
STEINWEG
NEUE
STRAS
DEN MUTTEN
ELB
PETER
NEUE MARKT
ZEUG
CAROLINEN STR
FELD STR
STRASSE
MARKT
PANORAMA
HEILIGENGEIST FELD
LAGER STRASSE
KAMP
NEUE ROSEN
SCHULTERBLATT
FRIEDEN STRASSE
JULIUS
STRASSE
ADOLPH STR
PFERDE MKT
VALENTIN
KL GARTNER ST
STRASSE
JAGER STRASSE
BLEICHEN
HEILIGENGEIST FELDE
WILHELMINEN STR
MARIEN STR
KIELER STR
THAL
LANGEREIHE
REEPERBAHN
SPIELBUDEN PL
Trichter
WOHLERS ALLEE
R GARTNER STR
BRUNNEN STR
REICHEN ST
GROSSE FREIHEIT
KL MARIEN ST
NEUBURG

NORDER
Hopfen Markt
Eng Planke
JACOB
GRUNE
SOOD
THE ENVIRONS
-OF-
HAMBURG & ALTONA
Railways thus
Barmbeck
Uhlenhorst
WANDSBECK Rail.y
Lubeck Rail.y
Hamm
GEORG
Hammerbrook
Hammerdeich
Dille R.
Berlin Rail.y
Billwarder Elbe
NORDER ELBE
Gr. Feddel
Kl. Grasbrook
Poseldorf
Grosse Alster
Eimsbüttel
Ottensen
Kiel & Altona R.y

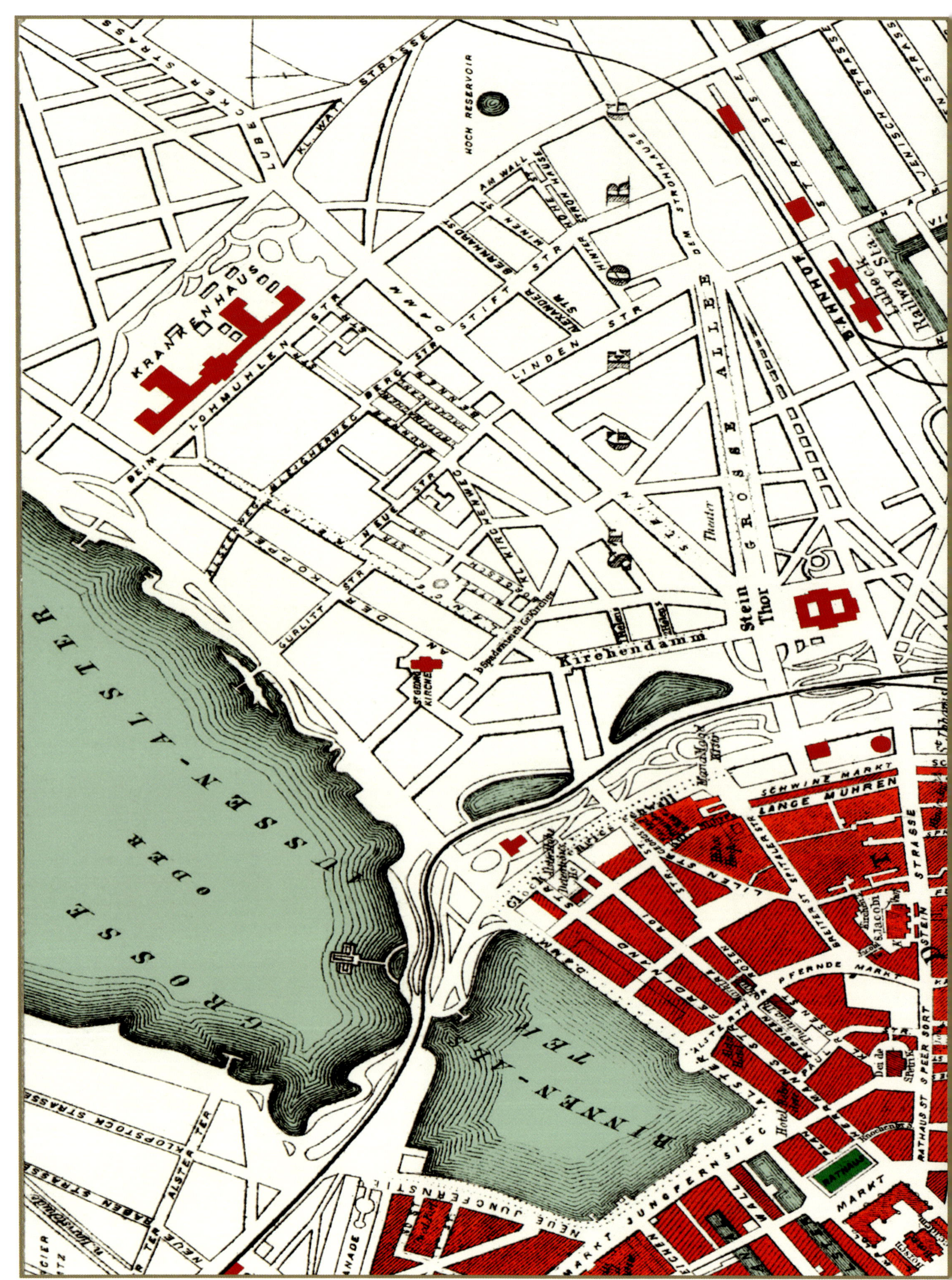

HOCH RESERVOIR
KRANKENHAUS
LÜBECKER STRASSE
KL WALL STRASSE
AM WALL
STIFT STR
ALEXANDER STR
LINDEN STR
LOHMÜHLEN STR
GURLITT STR
ST GEORG KIRCHE
LÜBECK
BAHNHOF
Railway
GROSSE ALLEE
Theater
Stein Thor
Kirchendamm
DER GROSSE ALSTER
ODER
DIE BINNEN-ALSTER
KLOPSTOCK STRASSE
RABEN STRASSE
LANGE MÜHREN
SCHWINE MARKT
PFERDE MARKT
RATHAUS
ST JACOBI
STEINSTRASSE
NEUE JUNGFERNSTIEG
MARKT
JUNGFERNSTIEG
ALSTER DAMM
JENISCH STRASSE

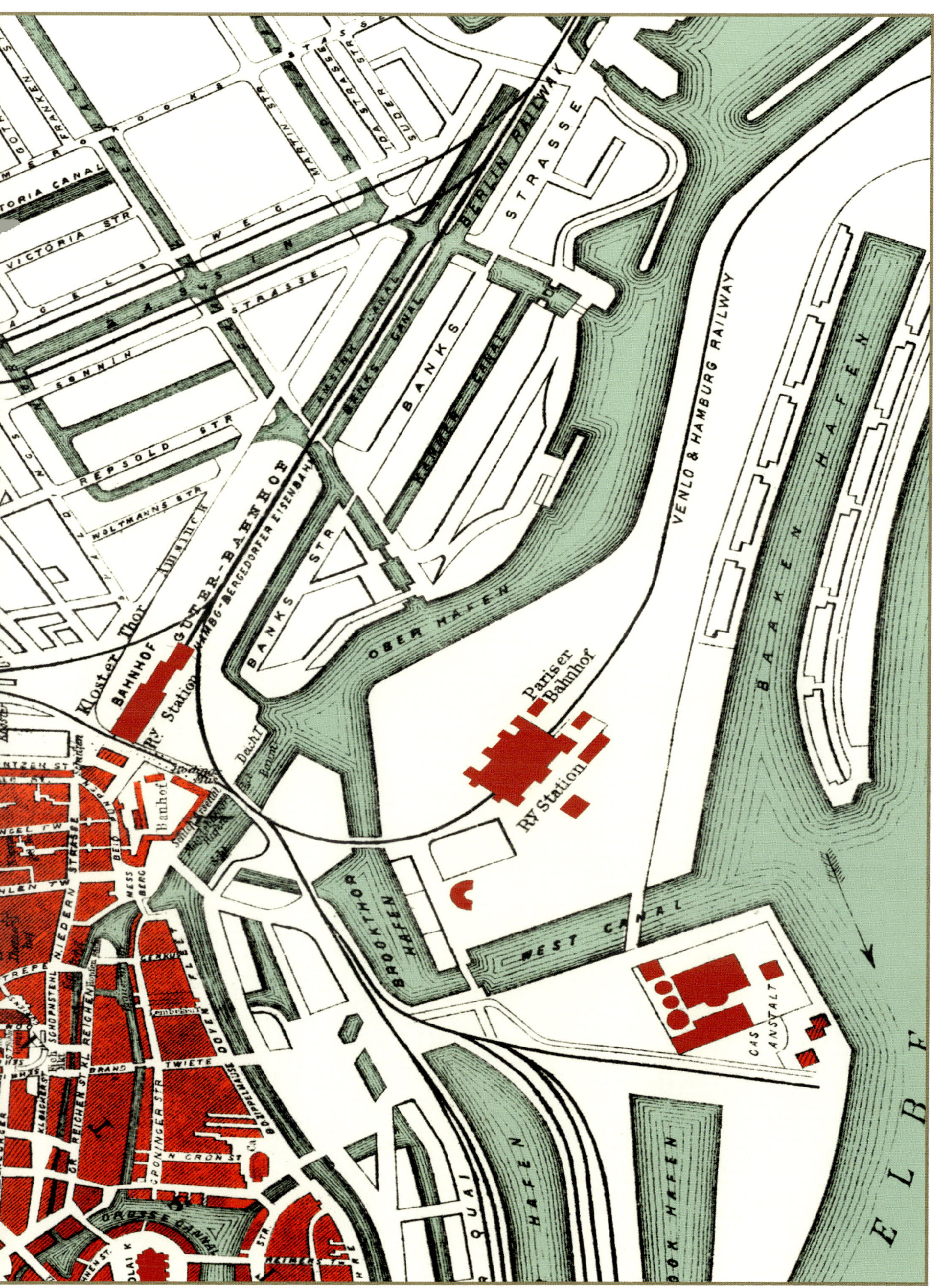
FRANKEN STR
GOTHA STR
VICTORIA CANAL
VICTORIA STR
BROOK
MARTIN STR
IDA STRASSE
SUDER STR
BASSIN
STRASSE
BERLIN RAILWAY
STRASSE
REPSOLD STR
SENNIN
AMSINK CANAL
BERGES CANAL
CENTRAL CANAL
BANKS
WOLTMANNS STR
KLOSTER THOR
BAHNHOF GUTER-BAHNHOF
HMBG-BERGEDORFER EISENBAHN
Ry Station
BANKS STR
BANKS STR
OBER HAFEN
VENLO & HAMBURG RAILWAY
BAAKEN HAFEN
Bahnhof
Pariser Bahnhof
Ry Station
BROOKTHOR HAFEN
WEST CANAL
GAS ANSTALT
BRAND
TWIETE
GROSSE CANAL
QUAI HAFEN
BROOK HAFEN
ELBE

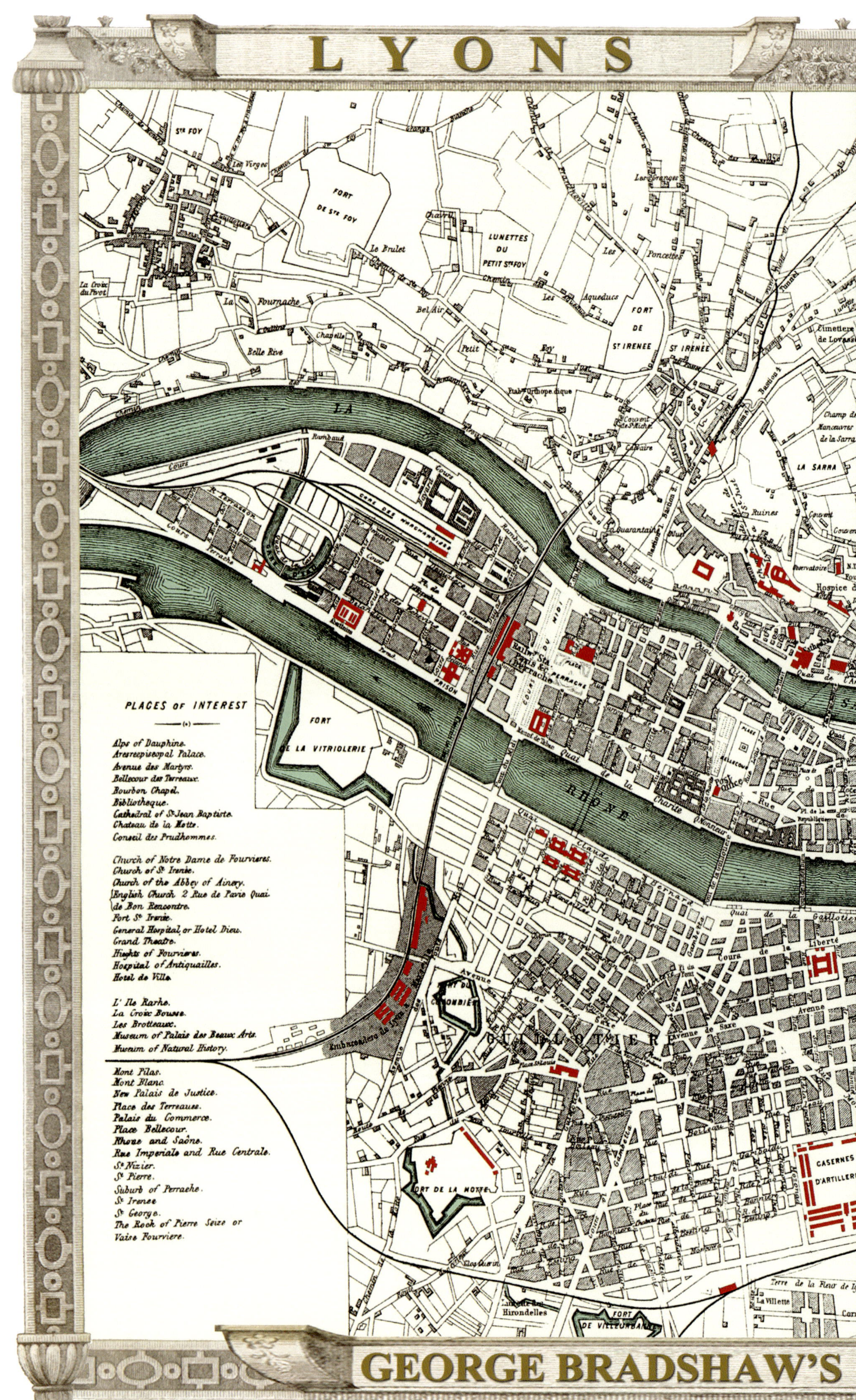

LYONS
PLACES of INTEREST
Alps of Dauphine.
Arcsreepiscopal Palace.
Avenue des Martyrs.
Bellecour des Terreaux.
Bourbon Chapel.
Bibliotheque.
Cathedral of St Jean Baptiste.
Chateau de la Motte.
Conseil des Prudhommes.

Church of Notre Dame de Fourvieres.
Church of St Irenie.
Church of the Abbey of Ainery.
English Church 2 Rue de Paris Quai
de Bon Rencontre.
Fort St Irene.
General Hospital or Hotel Dieu.
Grand Theatre.
Heights of Fourvieres.
Hospital of Antiquailles.
Hotel de Ville.

L' Ile Rarhe.
La Croix Bousse.
Les Brotteaux.
Museum of Palais des Beaux Arts.
Museum of Natural History.

Mont Pilas.
Mont Blanc.
New Palais de Justice.
Place des Terreaux.
Palais du Commerce.
Place Bellecour.
Rhone and Saône.
Rue Imperiale and Rue Centrale.
St Nizier.
St Pierre.
Suburb of Perrache.
St Irenee.
St Georgs.
The Rock of Pierre Seize or
Vaise Fourviere.

STE FOY
FORT DE STE FOY
LUNETTES DU PETIT STE FOY
Le Brulet
La Croix du Pevot
La Fournache
Bel Air
Chapelle
Belle Rive
FORT DE ST IRENEE
ST IRENEE
Cimetiere de Lovasse
Champ de Manoeuvres de la Sarra
LA SARRA
La Quarantaine
FORT DE LA VITRIOLERIE
RHONE
PRISON
FORT DE LA MOTTE
FORT DE VILLEURBANNE
GAILLOTIER
CASERNES D'ARTILLERIE
Quai de la Gaillotier
La Villette
Les Hirondelles

PLAN OF LYONS
Note — Railways & Stations thus
VAISE
FORT DE LOYASSE
FORT DE VAISE
Abattoir
Ecole Veterinaire
Antiquaille
de Mendicité
LA CROIX ROUSSE
CUIRE
Eglise de Cuire
Cimetiere
Couvent
FORT DE CALUIRE
RIVIERE
FLEUVE
FORT DE MONTESSUY
Quai de Brotteaux
Quai de l'Est
Quai de la Tête d'Or
Station
Caserne
Embarcadère de Brotteaux
FORT DES BROTTEAUX
PARC DE LA TÊTE D'OR
Jardin Botanique
Conservatoire
Grande Ile
Marquioles
Chemin de Fer de Lyon et Geneve
COMMUNE DE VILLEURBANNE

LA SARRA
Champ de Manœuvres de la Sarra
Cimetière de Loyasse
Chemin de Lumière
Ruines
St Just
Bastion 1
FORT DE ST IRENÉE
ST IRENÉE
Les Aqueducs
Les Roches
LUNETTES DU PETIT STE FOY
Le Brûlot
FORT DE STE FOY
STE FOY
Bel Air
Chapelle
Belle Rive
La Fourvache
Hospice de
Convent
Observatoire
N.D. de Fourvière
Quai de l'Archevêché
Prison
Rambaud
Cours des Archers
Cours
Perrache
Gare de Perrache
Quai de la
LA
PLACES DE INTÉRÊT

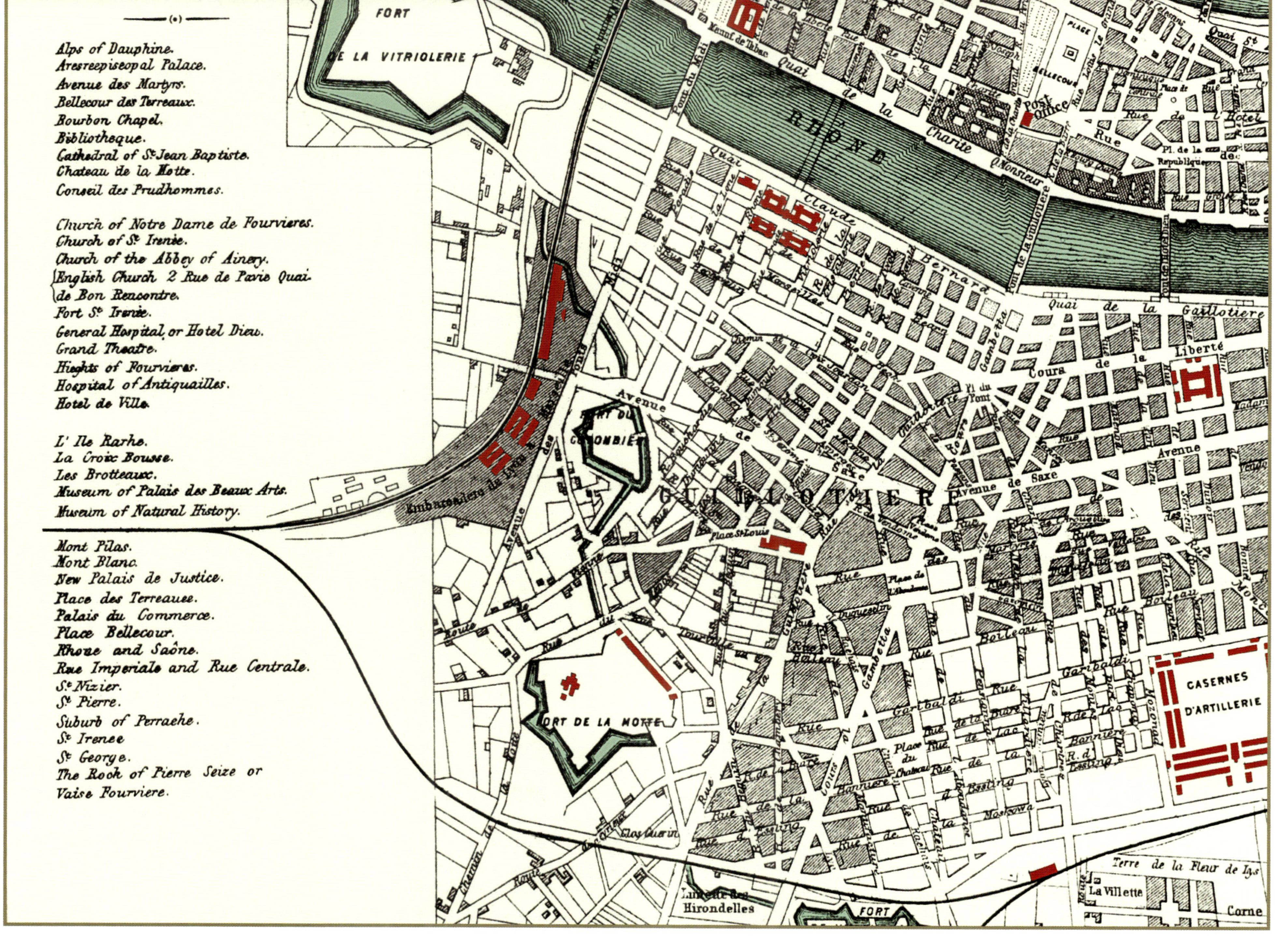

Alps of Dauphine.
Archiepiscopal Palace.
Avenue des Martyrs.
Bellecour des Terreaux.
Bourbon Chapel.
Bibliotheque.
Cathedral of St Jean Baptiste.
Chateau de la Motte.
Conseil des Prudhommes.

Church of Notre Dame de Fourvieres.
Church of St Irenée.
Church of the Abbey of Ainay.
English Church 2 Rue de Pavie Quai
de Bon Rencontre.
Fort St Irenée.
General Hospital or Hotel Dieu.
Grand Theatre.
Heights of Fourvieres.
Hospital of Antiquailles.
Hotel de Ville.

L' Ile Barbe.
La Croix Rousse.
Les Brotteaux.
Museum of Palais des Beaux Arts.
Museum of Natural History.

Mont Pilas.
Mont Blanc.
New Palais de Justice.
Place des Terreaux.
Palais du Commerce.
Place Bellecour.
Rhone and Saône.
Rue Imperiale and Rue Centrale.
St Nizier.
St Pierre.
Suburb of Perrache.
St Irenee
St George.
The Rock of Pierre Seize or
Vaise Fourviere.

PLAN OF LYONS
Note – Railways & Stations thus
RIVIERE
VAISE
LA CROIX ROUSSE
CUIRE
FORT DE LOYASSE
FORT DE VAISE
Abattoir
La Claire
Pépinière
Pépinère
Ecole Vétérinaire
Fort de St Jean
Champ de Manœuvres
Tour de la Belle Allemande
Antiquaille
et de Mendicité
les Lazaristes
Embarcadère du Chemin de fer de Lyon a Paris Vaise
Chemin de Fer de Paris a Lyon
Quai de Vaise
Couvent
Cimetière
Eglise de Cuire
Route Dep

FORT DE CALUIRE
FORT DE MONTESSUY
Chemin de Fer de Sathonay
Marginoles
Bresse
Route
Le Lambert
Quai de la Tete D'or
Grande Ile
FLEUVE
PARC DE LA TETE D'OR
Conservatoire
Jardin Botanique
Orangerie
Chemin de Fer de Lyon et Geneve
COMMUNE DE VILLEURBANNE
Quai de l'Est
Nord
de Bareme
Rue Duguarne
Montgolfier
Grillon
Tronchet
Boulevard Du
Caserne
Station
Debarcadere debarcadere
FORT DES BROTTEAUX
Quai de Brotteaux
Cours Morand
Cours
Rue Bugeaud
Vauban
Lafayette
Rabelais
de Cerf

MER MEDITERRANÉE
BASSIN DE LA GARE MARITIME
BASSIN D'ARENC
BASSIN DU LAZARET
BASSIN DE LA JOLIETTE
Place du Lazaret
Marché du Temple
Cimetière St Charle
Place de la Joliette
AVANT PORT
Cathedrale
Fort St Jean
OLD PORT
Batterie du Phare
Champ de Manœuvres du Pharo
Château du Pharo
Fort St Nicolas
Boulev. du Pharo
Citadelle
Ave de la Pesene
JARDIN PUGET
Boulevard de la Corderie
Boulevard
Cours du Quatre Septembre
Fort N.D. de la Garde
Note—Railways & Stations shown thus

CONTINENTAL CITY PLANS 1896

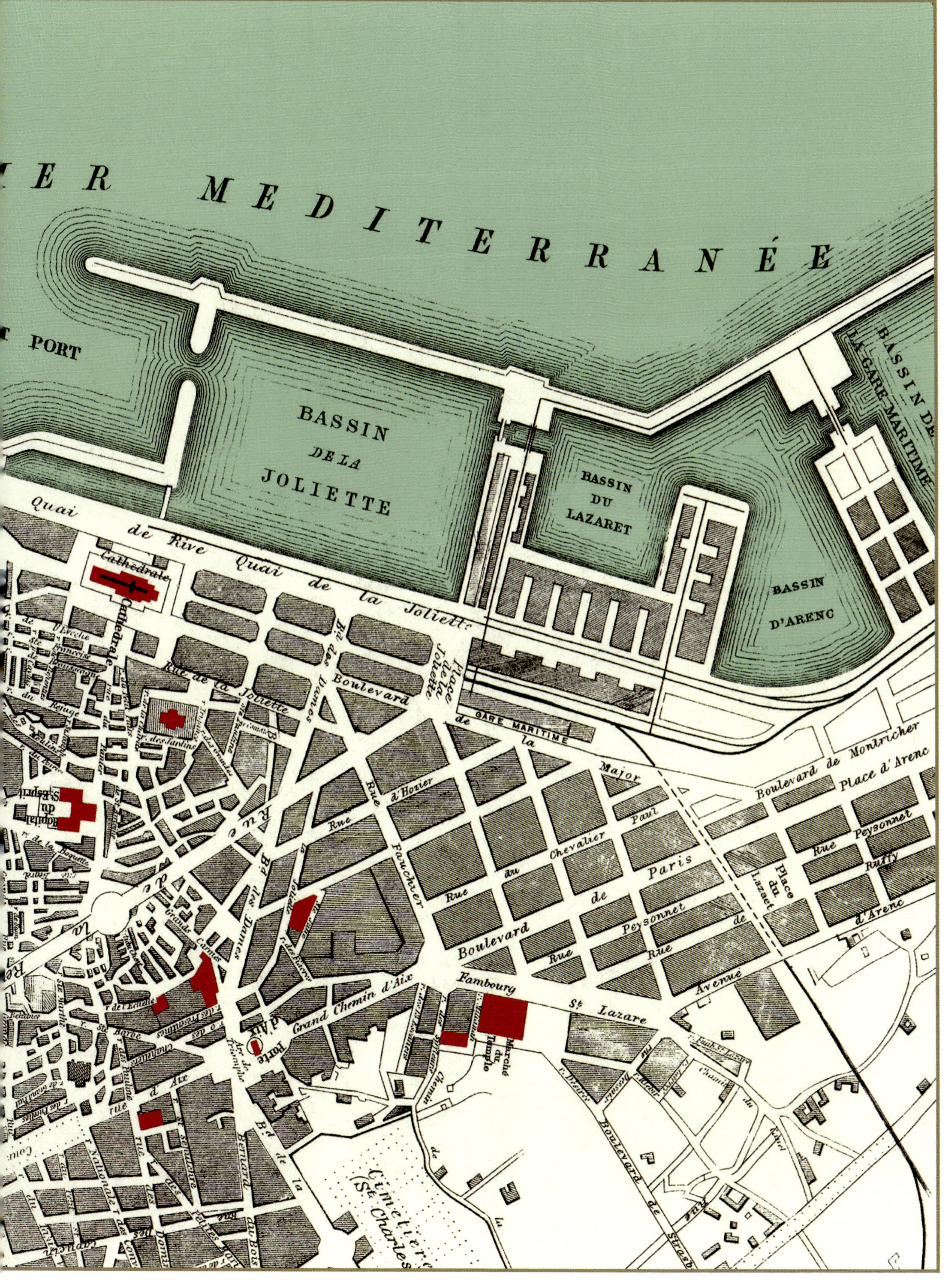

MER MÉDITERRANÉE
PORT
BASSIN DE LA JOLIETTE
BASSIN DU LAZARET
BASSIN D'ARENC
BASSIN DE LA GARE MARITIME
Quai de Rive
Cathédrale
Quai de la Joliette
Bd des Dames
Boulevard
Rue de la Joliette
Place de la Joliette
GARE MARITIME de la
Hôpital du S.Esprit
Rue
Rue d'Hozier
Rue Foucher
Major
Paul
du Chevalier
Boulevard de Paris
Rue
Rue Peysonnet
Rue
Boulevard de Montricher
Place d'Arenc
Rue Peysonnet
Ruffy
Place du Lazaret
d'Arenc
de
Avenue
Famboury
St Lazare
Grand Chemin d'Aix
Marché du Temple
Porte d'Aix
Bd de la
Boulevard de
Cimetière (St Charles)

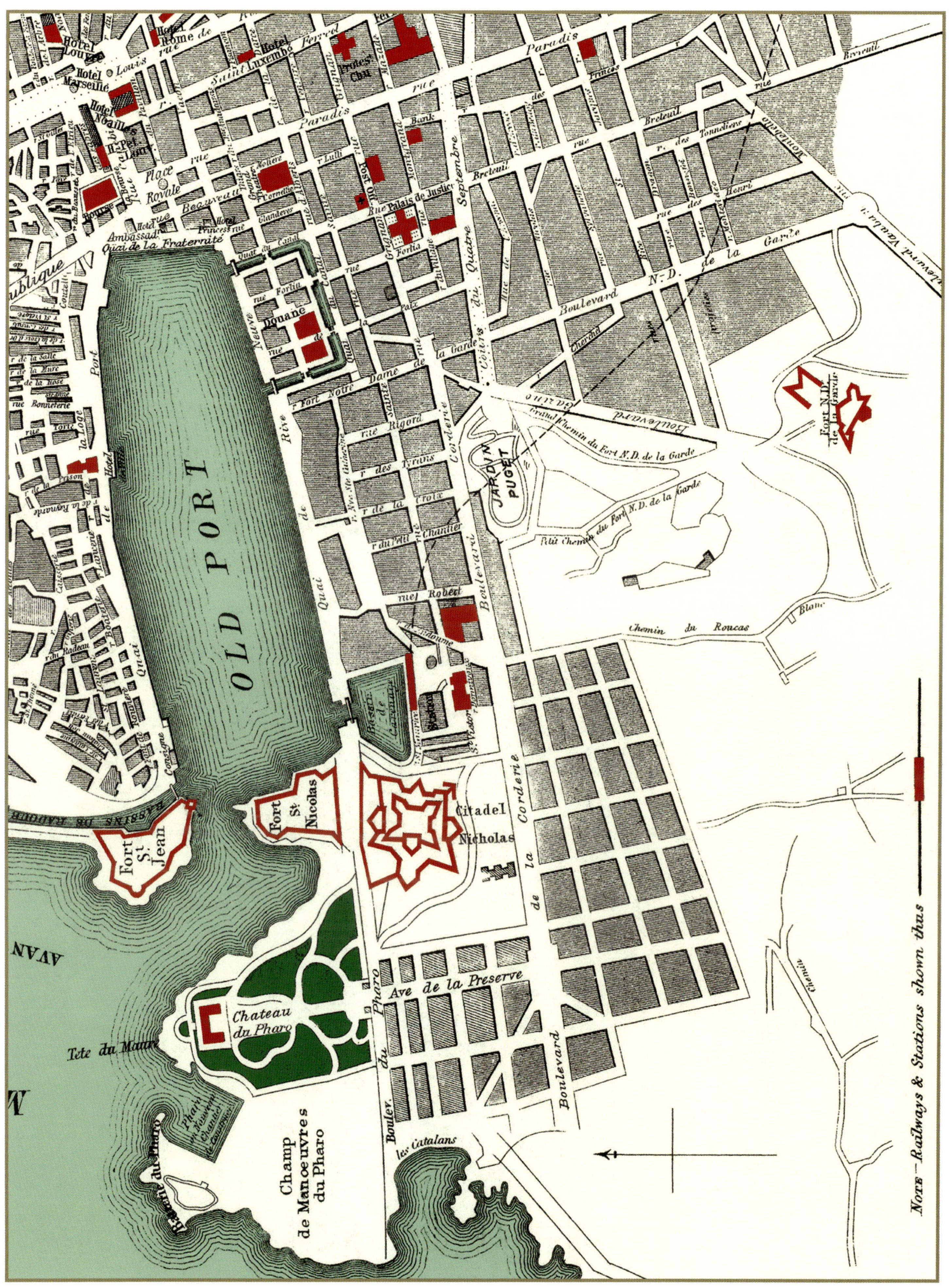

OLD PORT
Hotel Louvre
Hotel Marseille
Hotel Noailles
Hotel Rome de
Place Royale
Douane
Fort St. Jean
Fort St. Nicolas
Citadel Nicholas
Chateau du Pharo
Champ de Manoeuvres du Pharo
Tete du Maure
les Catalans
Ave de la Preserve
JARDIN PUGET
Fort N.D. de la Garde
N.-D. de la Garde
Boulevard
Chemin du Roucas
Paradis
rue
Rue Palais de Justice
Quai de la Fraternité
Ambassad.
Protest. Cht
Quatre Septembre
Boulevard du Pharo
BASSINS DE RADOUB
AVAN
Note—Railways & Stations shown thus

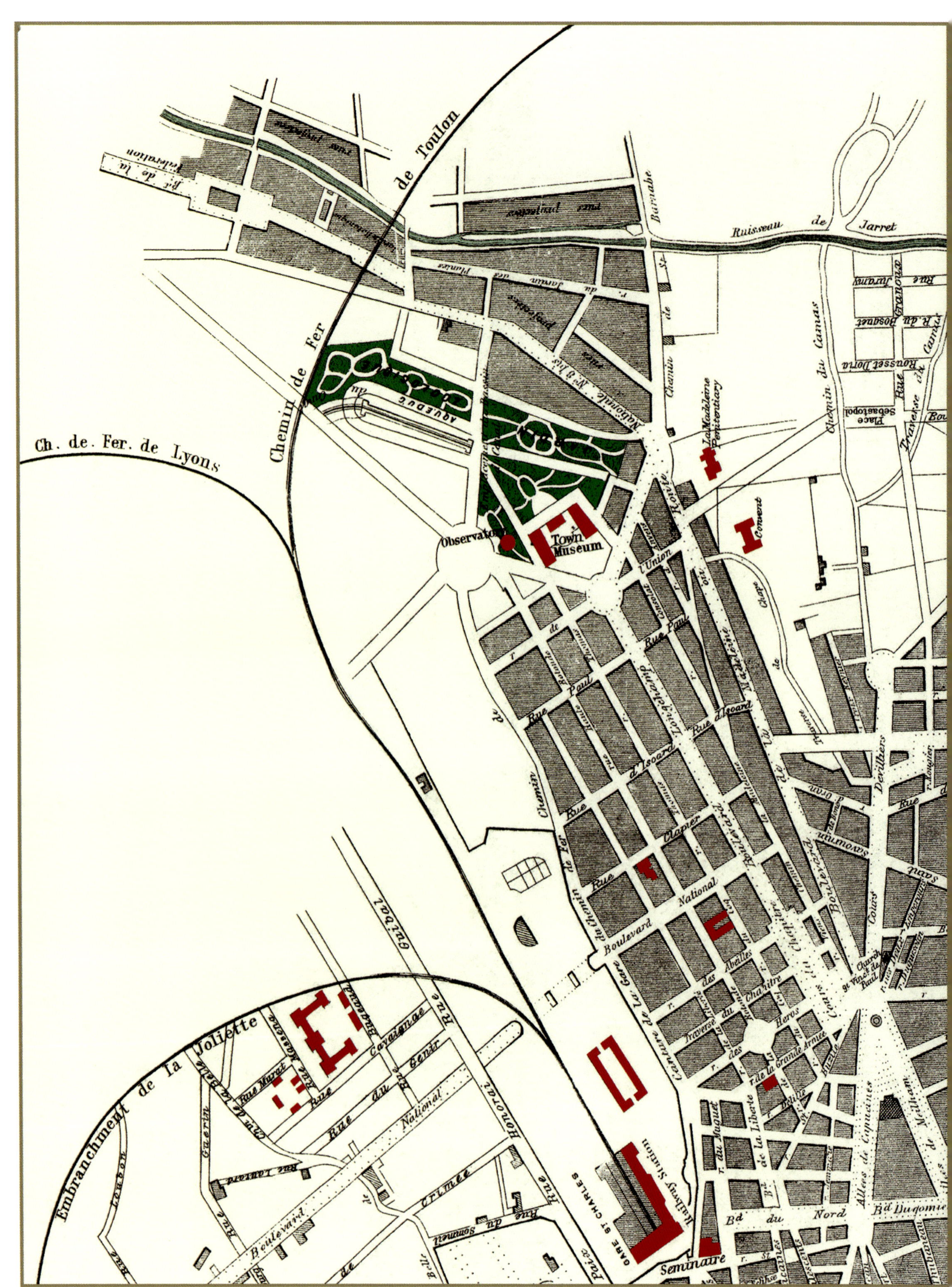

de Toullon
Ruisseau de Jarret
Ch. de. Fer. de Lyons
Chemin de Fer
Observatory
Town Museum
La Madeleine Penitentiary
Convent
Place Sébastopol
Rousset Doria
R. du Bosquet
Embranchment de la Joliette
Rue Guiban
Boulevard National
Rue Honorat
Rue du Genir
Rue Cavaignac
Rue Murat
Rue Guerin
GARE ST CHARLES
Seminaire
Bd du Nord
Bd Dugomi
Allées de Capucines
Cours
Boulevard National
Rue Clapier
Rue Paul
Rue d'Isoard
Rue d'Isoard
Rue Devilliers
l'Union
Chemin du Camas

Asile des Alienés
Lunatic Asylum
Ruisseau de Jarret
Chave
Jarret
Boulevard
de l'Epée
Prison Departementale
Sebastopol
de l'Abbé
Chemin Terruse
R. Bergere
Cté.
de
Pierre
St.
Chemin
Jarret
Hospital de la Conception
Prison
Convent du Refuge
Traverse des Quatre Portails
Menpenti
Rome
Chemin du Rond
Chemin de l'Âme
construction
Vincent
de
Vincent
Usine
Redway
GARE DU
Ferrandi
du Progres
du Progres
Boulevard
Merentie
Boulevard
Rivoli
du Brays
du Brays
Terruse
Renard
du
Chateau
Pavan
des
Bons
Infants
Loch
Boulevard
Grand
Titsit
Titsit
Place St. Michel
Nev de l'Amandier
des Cypres
Chemin
Berrin
Sollier
rue Morengo
Grande
Cours
Liautaud
Rome
de
Rome
Chemin de St. Tinie
Le Prado
Barthelemy
Petits Peres
Curiol
Senac
Musée
Cours Julien
Rome
Cours
Liautaud
d'Aubagne
Rue de l'onsale
Place Castellane
St.
Philomen
Biblioth.
des
Porte de Rome
Grand
de
Rome
Chemin de Rome
Prefecture
Paradis
Place St.
Montaux
rue

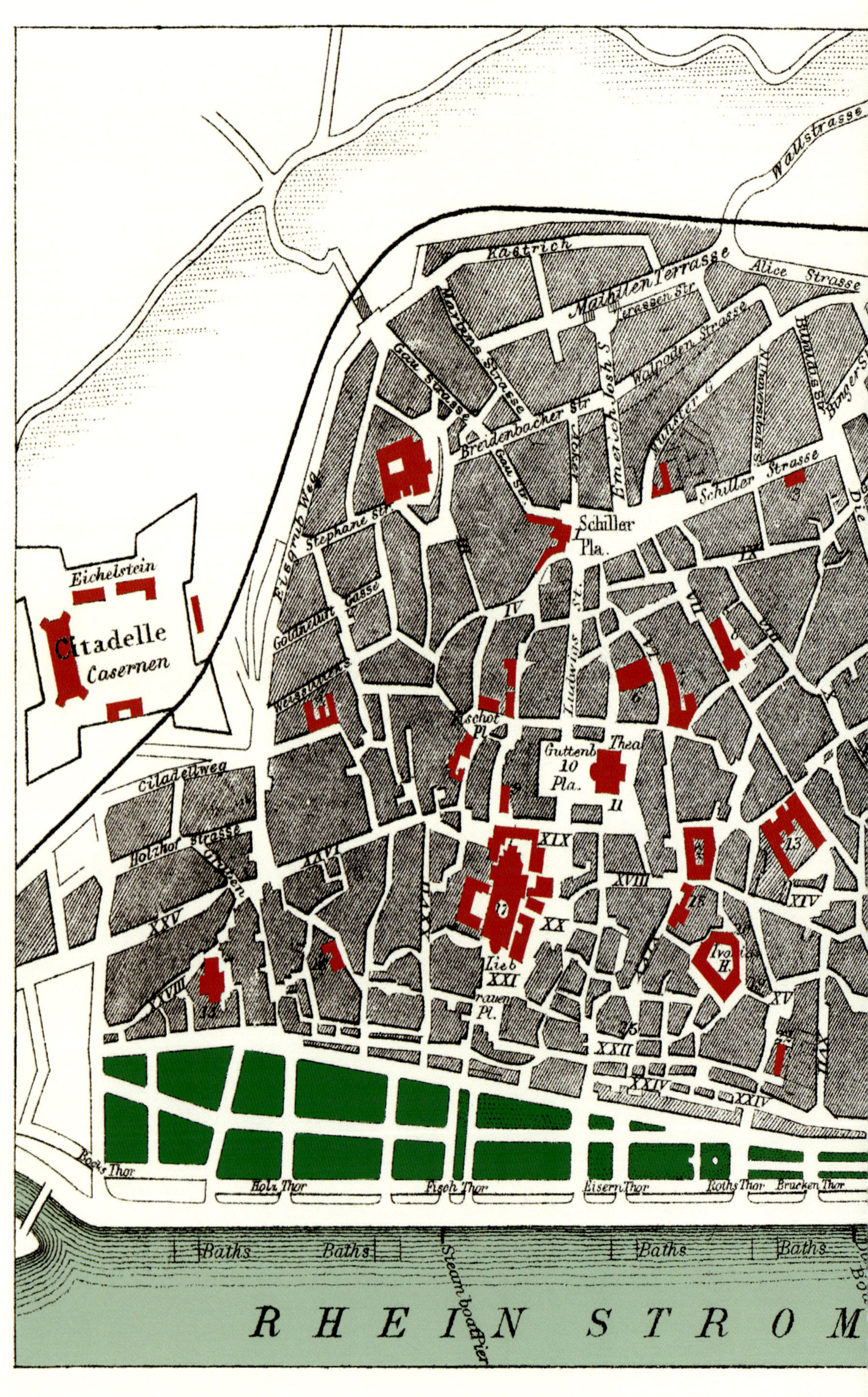

Wallstrasse
Kastrich
Maihilen Terrasse
Alice Strasse
Grasse Str
Walpoden Strasse
Breidenbacher Str
Gau Strasse
Gau Str
Schiller Strasse
Schiller Pla.
Eichelstein
Citadelle
Casernen
Stephanie Str
Eisgrub Weg
Goldenbrunnen Gasse
Schot Pl.
Guttenb 10 Pla.
Thea
11
Citadellweg
Holzhof Strasse
Ludwigs Str
XIX
XVIII
Ivo H.
XXV
Lieb XXI
XX
XIV
XV
Frauen Pl.
XXII
XXIV
Bocks Thor
Holz. Thor
Fisch Thor
Eisern Thor
Roths Thor
Brücken Thor
Baths
Baths
Baths
Baths
Steamboat Pier
R H E I N S T R O M

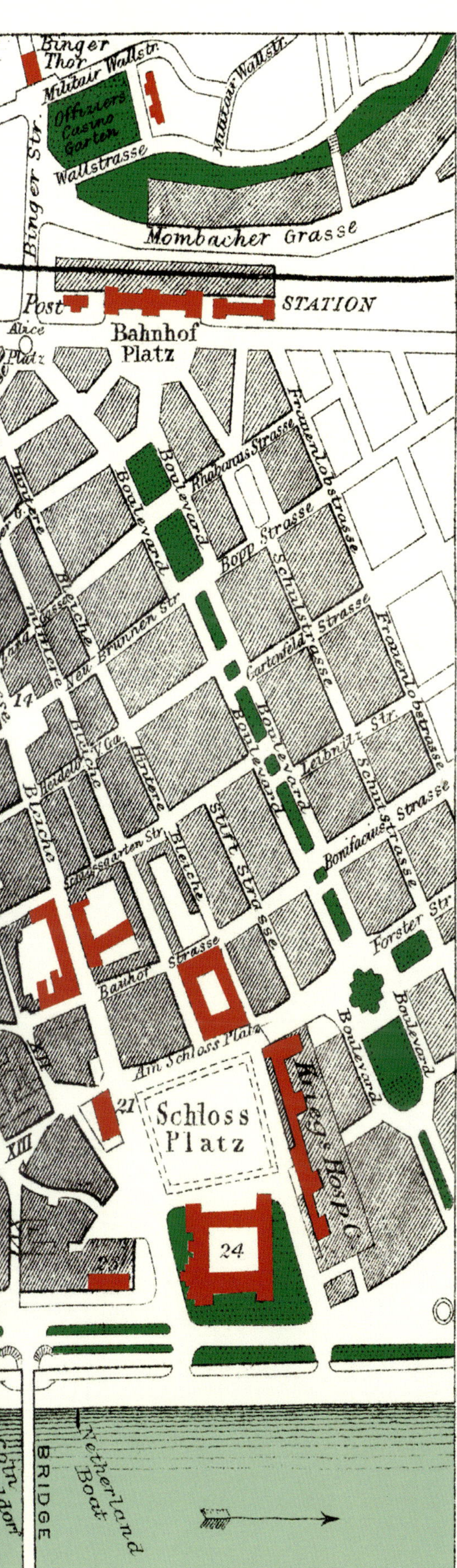

Explanation of the numbers:

1. Board for the Administrat.ⁿ of the Fortress — Festungs Gouvernement
2. S.ᵗ Stephans Church — Stephans Kirche
3. Government Palace — Regierungs Pallast
4. Commandant of the Fortress — Festungs Commandant
5. Poor-house — Armenhaus
6. Corn Exchange — Fruchthalle
7. Gymnasium — Gymnasium
8. S.ᵗ Emmeram — S. Emmeram
9. S.ᵗ John's Church — Johannes Kirche
10. Gutten berg-place & Monument — Gutenbergs Platz u. Monum.ᵗ
11. Theatre — Theater
12. Town Hall — Stadthaus
13. Hall of Justice & Lockup — Justiz u. Arresthaus
14. Library and Gallery of paintings — Bibliotheck u. Gallerie
15. S. Ignatius — S.ᵗ Ignatz
16. House of Correction — Correctionshaus
17. Cathedral — Dom
18. S.ᵗ Quentin's Ch.ʰ — S.ᵗ Quintin
19. S.ᵗ Christopher's Ch.ʰ — S.ᵗ Christoph
20. Gottenberg Court (Casino) — Hof zum Gottenberg (Casino)
21. S.ᵗ Peter's Ch.ʰ — Peters Kirche
22. S.ᵗ Christopher's Ch.ʰ — Kirche S.ᵗ Christoph
23. Teutonic House (Residence of the Governor) — Deutsche Haus (Wohnung des Gouverneurs)
24. Castle (now Bonding Wareh.ᵗ) — Schloss jetzt Lagerhaus
25. Post Office — Postamt (drey Kronen)
+. Barracks — Casernen

I Gau Gasse	XVI Zeuchaus Gasse
II Münster Gasse	XVII Bauern Gasse
III Hohl	XVIII Schuster Gasse
IV Ballplatz	XIX Das Höfchen
V Thiermarkt	XX Der Speisemarkt
VI Gymnasiums Gasse	XXI Liebfrau Platz und Heumarkt
VII Emerams Gasse	
VIII Welschnonen Gasse	XXII Auf dem Brand
IX Obere u. Untere Langgasse	XXIII Rheinstrasse
X Rosen Gasse	XXIV Obere u. Unt Lohr Gasse
XI Juden Gasse	XXV Neuthor Strasse
XII Petersgasse	XXVI Augustiner Gasse
XIII Die Mitternacht	XXVII Gräber Gasse
XIV Der Flachsmarkt	XXVIII Kapuziner Gasse
XV Carmeliter Platz	XXIX Quintins Gasse

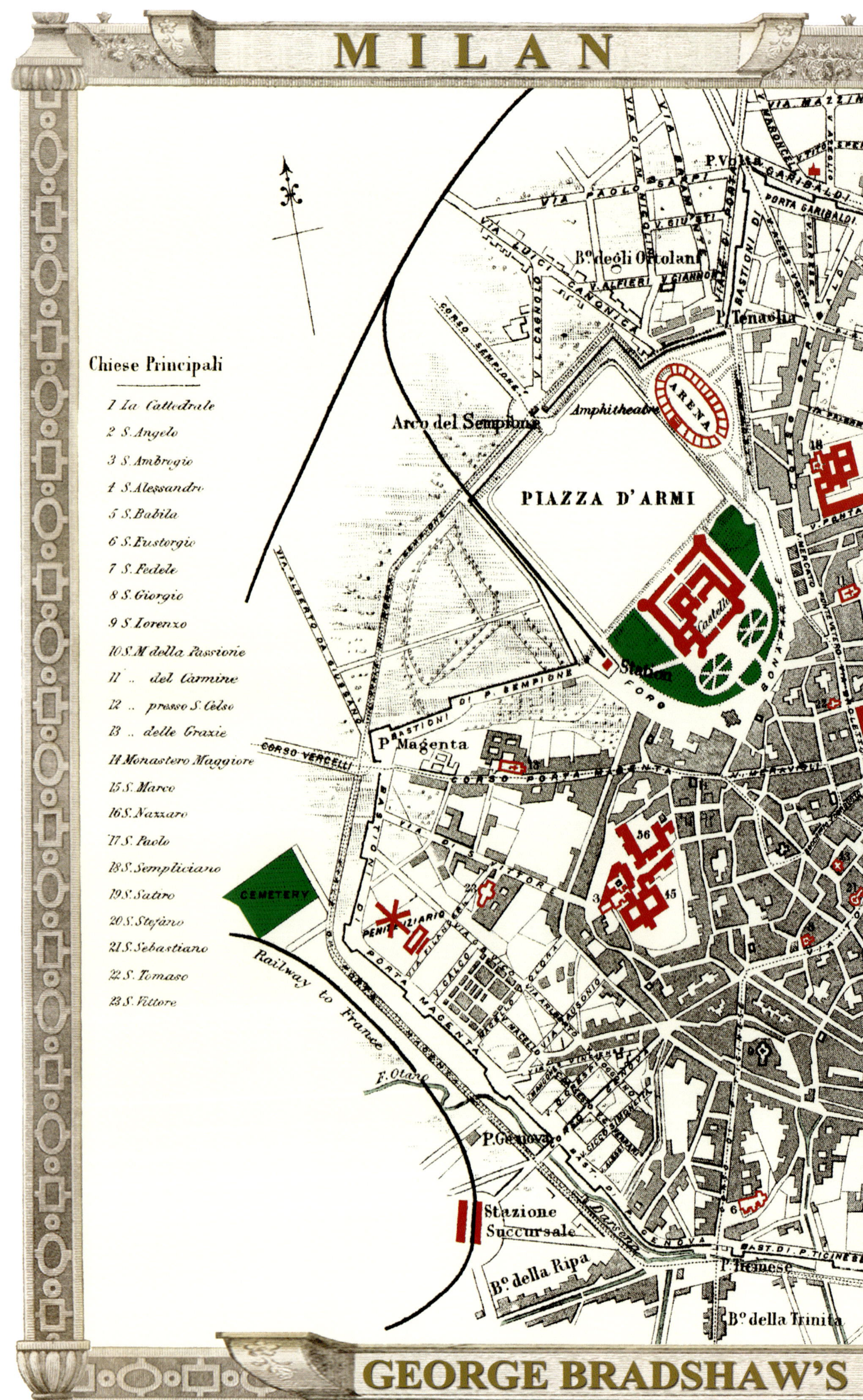
Chiese Principali

1 La Cattedrale
2 S. Angelo
3 S. Ambrogio
4 S. Alessandro
5 S. Babila
6 S. Eustorgio
7 S. Fedele
8 S. Giorgio
9 S. Lorenzo
10 S. M. della Passione
11 .. del Carmine
12 .. presso S. Celso
13 .. delle Grazie
14 Monastero Maggiore
15 S. Marco
16 S. Nazzaro
17 S. Paolo
18 S. Sempliciano
19 S. Satiro
20 S. Stefano
21 S. Sebastiano
22 S. Tomaso
23 S. Vittore

P. Volta
B.º degli Ortolani
P. Tenaglia
ARENA
Amphitheatre
Arco del Sempione
PIAZZA D'ARMI
Castello
FORO
Station
P. Magenta
CORSO VERCELLI
CORSO PORTA MAGENTA
BASTIONI
CEMETERY
PENITENZIARIO
PORTA MAGENTA
Railway to France
F. Olona
P. Genova
Stazione Succursale
B.º della Ripa
P. Ticinese
B.º della Trinita

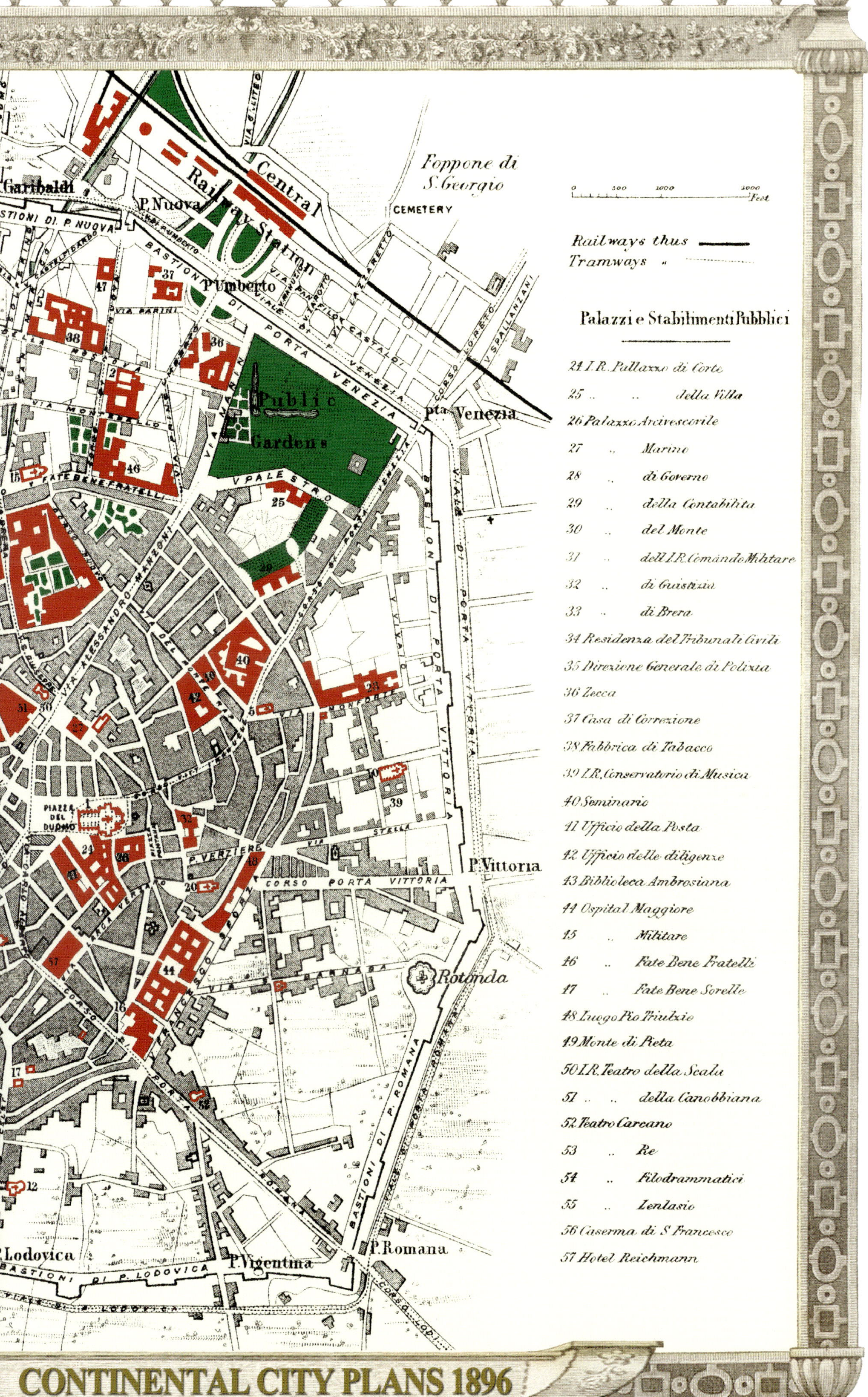

Garibaldi
Foppone di S. Georgio
CEMETERY
P. Nuova
Railway Station
Central
BASTIONI DI P. NUOVA
P. Umberto
VIA PARINI
VIA PANTANO
VIA FIORI
VIA MONFORTE
Public Gardens
pta Venezia
PORTA VENEZIA
V. PALESTRO
BASTIONI DI PORTA VITTORIA
VIALE DI PORTA VITTORIA
P. Vittoria
CORSO PORTA VITTORIA
Rotonda
PIAZZA DEL DUOMO
P. VERZIERE
VIA STRETTA
CORSO DI PORTA ROMANA
VIALE DI PORTA ROMANA
BASTIONI DI PORTA ROMANA
P. Romana
P. Lodovica
P. Vigentina
BASTIONI DI P. LODOVICA

Railways thus ——
Tramways „

0   500   1000   1500 Feet

Palazzi e Stabilimenti Pubblici

24 I.R. Pallazzo di Corte
25 ..   ..   della Villa
26 Palazzo Arcivescovile
27 ..   Marino
28 ..   di Governo
29 ..   della Contabilità
30 ..   del Monte
31 ..   dell'I.R. Comando Militare
32 ..   di Giustizia
33 ..   di Brera
34 Residenza del Tribunali Civili
35 Direzione Generale di Polizia
36 Zecca
37 Casa di Correzione
38 Fabbrica di Tabacco
39 I.R. Conservatorio di Musica
40 Seminario
41 Ufficio della Posta
42 Ufficio delle diligenze
43 Biblioteca Ambrosiana
44 Ospital Maggiore
45 ..   Militare
46 ..   Fate Bene Fratelli
47 ..   Fate Bene Sorelle
48 Luogo Pio Triulzio
49 Monte di Pietà
50 I.R. Teatro della Scala
51 ..   ..   della Canobbiana
52 Teatro Carcano
53 ..   Re
54 ..   Filodrammatici
55 ..   Lentasio
56 Caserma di S. Francesco
57 Hotel Reichmann

A   B   C   D   E

1	Isarthor	G5
2	Siegesthor	G1
3	Ludwigs Brucke	H6
4	Ludwigstrasse	G2
5	Carol Platz Obelisk	E2
6	Maximilians Platz	E3
7	Maxim Joseph Platz	F4
8	Promenade Platz	E4
9	Schrannen Platz	F5
10	Universitats Platz	G1
11	Wittelsbacher Platz	F3

Kirchen u Paläste:

12	Allerheil Hof Capelle	G4
13	Bonifaciuskirche	D2
14	Frauenkirche	E4
15	S. Johanniskirche	E5
16	Kreuzkirche	D5
17	Ludwigskirche	G1
18	Maria Hilfkirche in der Vorstadt Au	H7
19	Michaelis Hofkirche	E4
20	S Peterskirche	F5
21	Protestantische Kirche	D4
22	Theatinerkirche	F3
23	Synagoge	E5
24	Der allgem Kirchhof	D7
25	Die alte Residenz	F3
26	Der neue Königsbau	F4
27	Der neue Saalbau	G3
28	Palast des Herzogs von Leuchtenberg	F3
29	Palast des Herzogs Max in Bayern	F2

Andere öffentliche Gebäude:

30	Acad d bild Kunste	E4
31	Allgem Krankenhaus	C6
32	Arcad d Hofgartens	F3
33	Bergwerks und Salinen Administrat Gebaude	G1
34	Bibliothek	G1
35	Blinden Institut	G1
36	Botanischer Garten	D3
37	Die konigl Erzgiesserei Nymphenburgerstrasse verlangerte Briennerstrasse	B1

F G H I
58 Frohnveste E 6
59 Gewehrkammer
40 Industrie Schule D1
41 Glyptothek D2
42 Kriegsministerium G2
43 Kunstausstellungs-
baude D2
44 Kunstverein F3
45 Odeon F3
46 Pinakothek E1
47 Postgebäude F4
48 Rathhaus F5
49 Reitbahn G4
50 Theater G4
51 Universität G1
52 Vereinigte Samml. G3
54 Hofgarten G3
55 Englischer Garten H2
56 Artillerie Kas. H3
57 Alter Hof F4
Hofgarten
ISAR VOR STADT
ISAR
Haidhausen
Markt
58 Bezirksg. G. E 4
59 H. Geist F 5
60 Joseph Sp. D 5
61 Ob. Appell. E 2
62 Polizei F 4
63 Propylän D 2
64 Servitt. Kl. D 4
65 Volkstheater F 6

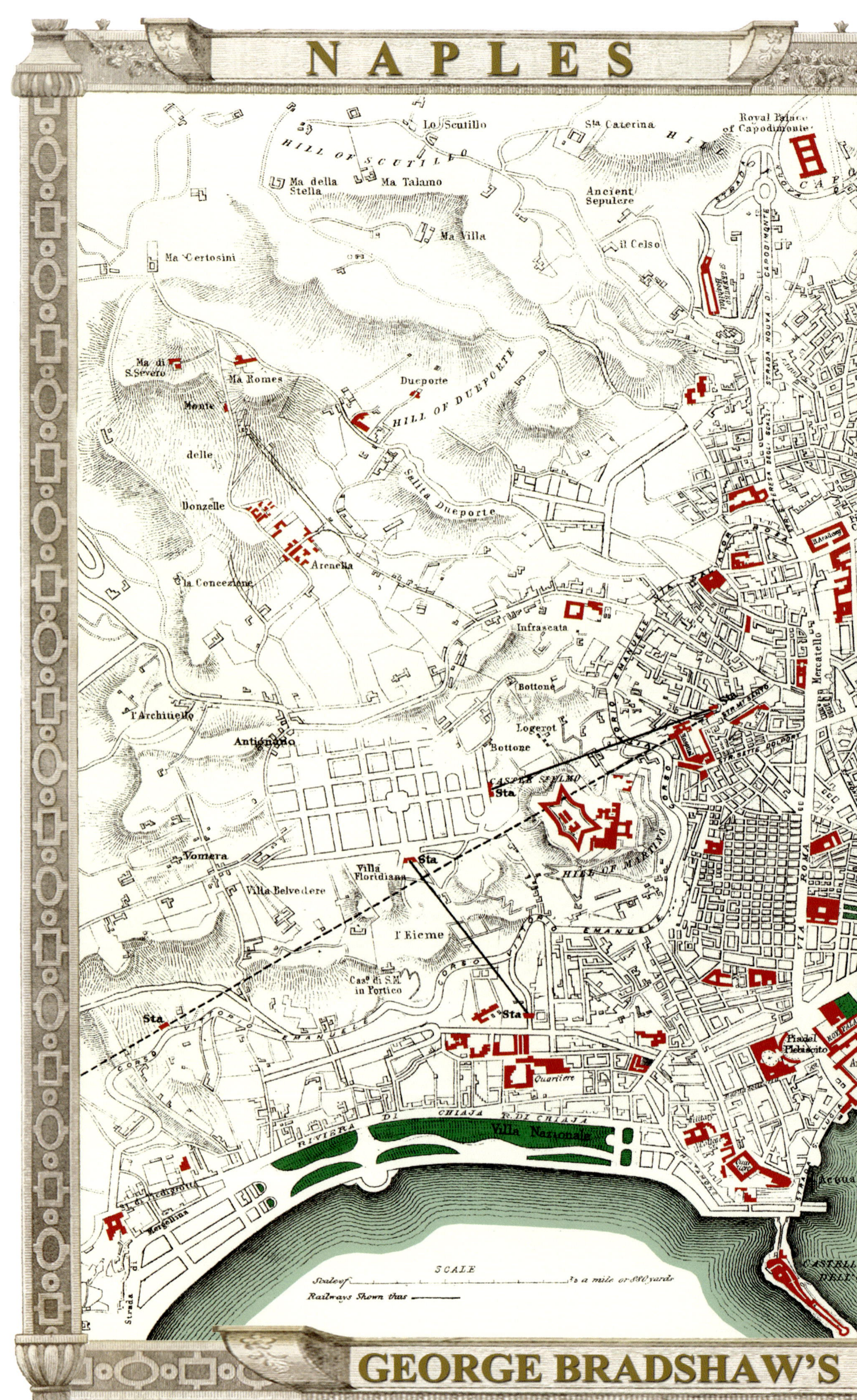

NAPLES
Lo Scutillo
Sta Caterina
Royal Palace of Capodimonte
HILL OF SCUTILLO
Ma della Stella
Ma Talamo
Ancient Sepulcre
Ma Villa
il Celso
Ma Certosini
Ma di S. Severo
Ma Romes
Dueporte
Monte
HILL OF DUEPORTE
delle
Salita Dueporte
Donzelle
Arenella
la Concezione
Infrascata
l'Archiuello
Bottone
Antignano
Logerot
Bottone
ASPER S. ELMO
Sta.
HILL OF MARTINO
Vomera
Sta
Villa Floridiana
Villa Belvedere
l'Eieme
Cas. di S.M. in Portico
Sta
Sta
Sta
Quartiere
Piazza Plebiscito
ROYAL PALACE
RIVIERA DI CHIAJA
R. DI CHIAJA
Villa Nazionale
Acqua
Mergellina
CASTELLO DELL'O
SCALE
Scale of   ¼ a mile or 880 yards
Railways Shown thus

GEORGE BRADSHAW'S

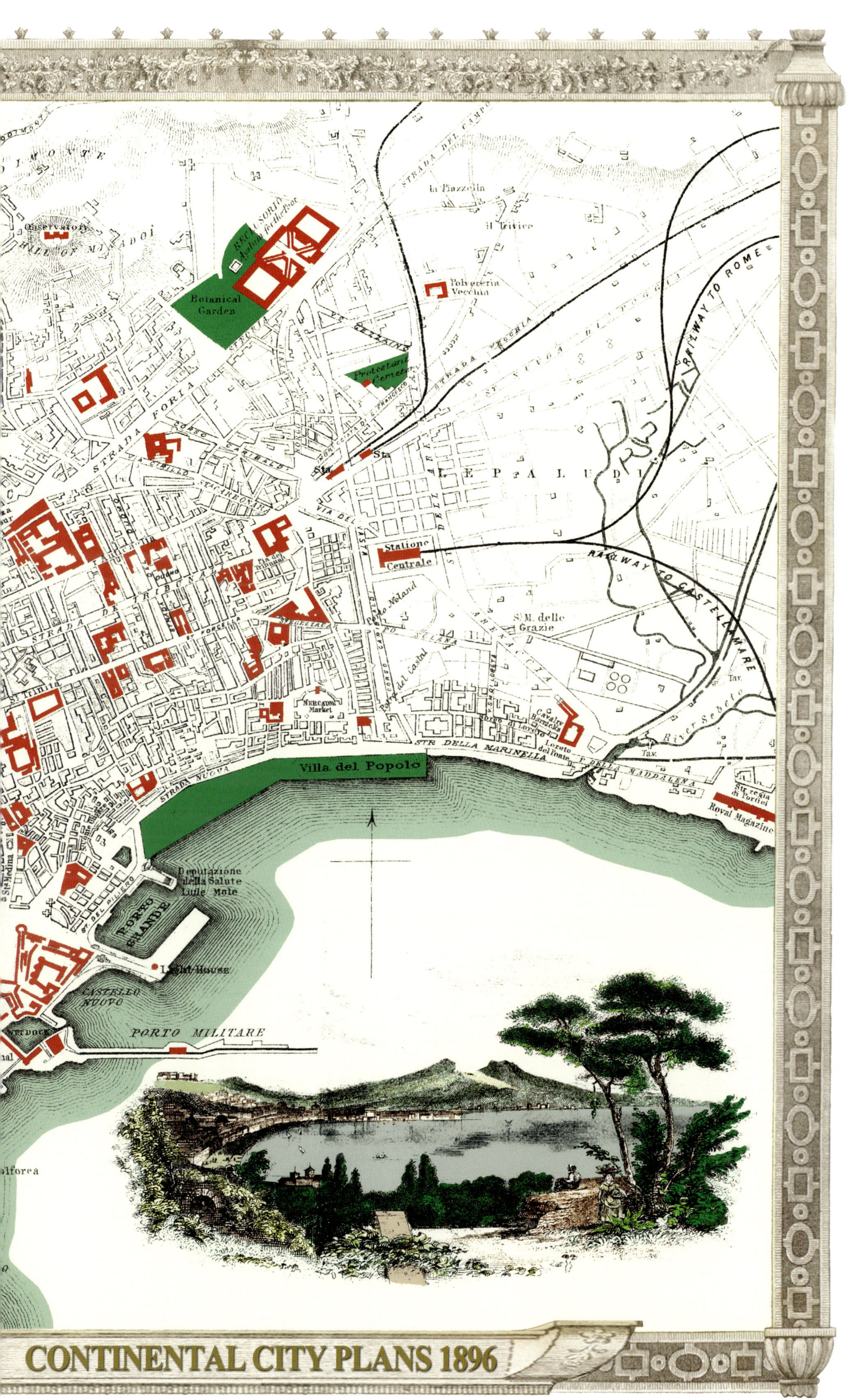

Botanical Garden
Observatory
HILL OF MIRADOI
STRADA FORIA
PORTO CARBELLO
Protestant Cemetery
S. FRANCESCO
Polveriera Vecchia
STRADA DEL CAMPO
la Piazzella
il Trivice
STRADA VECCHIA
RAILWAY TO ROME
LE PALUDI
RAILWAY TO CASTELLAMARE
Stazione Centrale
S. M. delle Grazie
Cavalry Barracks
Loreto del Fonte
River Sebeto
F. DELLA MADDALENA
STR. DELLA MARINELLA
Villa del Popolo
Mercato Market
Royal Magazine
Str. regia di Portici
Deputazione della Salute
Little Mole
PORTO GRANDE
Light House
CASTELLO NUOVO
PORTO MILITARE
Sta Medina

CHÉNAL
ESTACADE D'EST
ESTACADE D'OUEST
BAINS
BAINS
Steam Packet Wf.
New Basin
AVA
BOULEVARD DES
DIGUE DE MER
R. BUCHAREST
RUE DES JARDINS
QUAI LONGUE
RUE DES BATELLERS
RUE DES PECHEURS
RUE ST FRANCOIS
R. DE FLEUVES
QUAI DU CERCLE
RUE LONGUE
RUE DES CAPUCINS
RUE LOUISE
MARCHÉ AUX HERBES
RUE NEUVE
RUE ST PAUL
QUAI DE L'EST
BD. DES SŒURS BLANCHES
RUE DE L'EGLISE
RUE DE FLANDRE
BOULEVARD DU NORD
PLACE D'ARMES
RUE CHRISTINE
RUE DU CERI
RUE LONGUE
RUE D'OUEST
RUE ST SEBASTIEN
RUE DES SŒURS
RUE DE LA CHAPPELLE
RUE ST JOSEPH
RUE ALBERT
RUE DU CARENAGE
PLACE DU THEATRE
AVENUE LEOPOLD
RUE DE NIEUPORT
CHAUSSÉE DE NIEUPORT
PARC
KURSAAL
RUE DE BERLIN
BOULEVARD DE PARIS
RUE DU NORD
RUE DE PETERSBOURG
RUE DE CONST
RUE DE VIENNE
BOUL DE L'OUE
BOUL DU

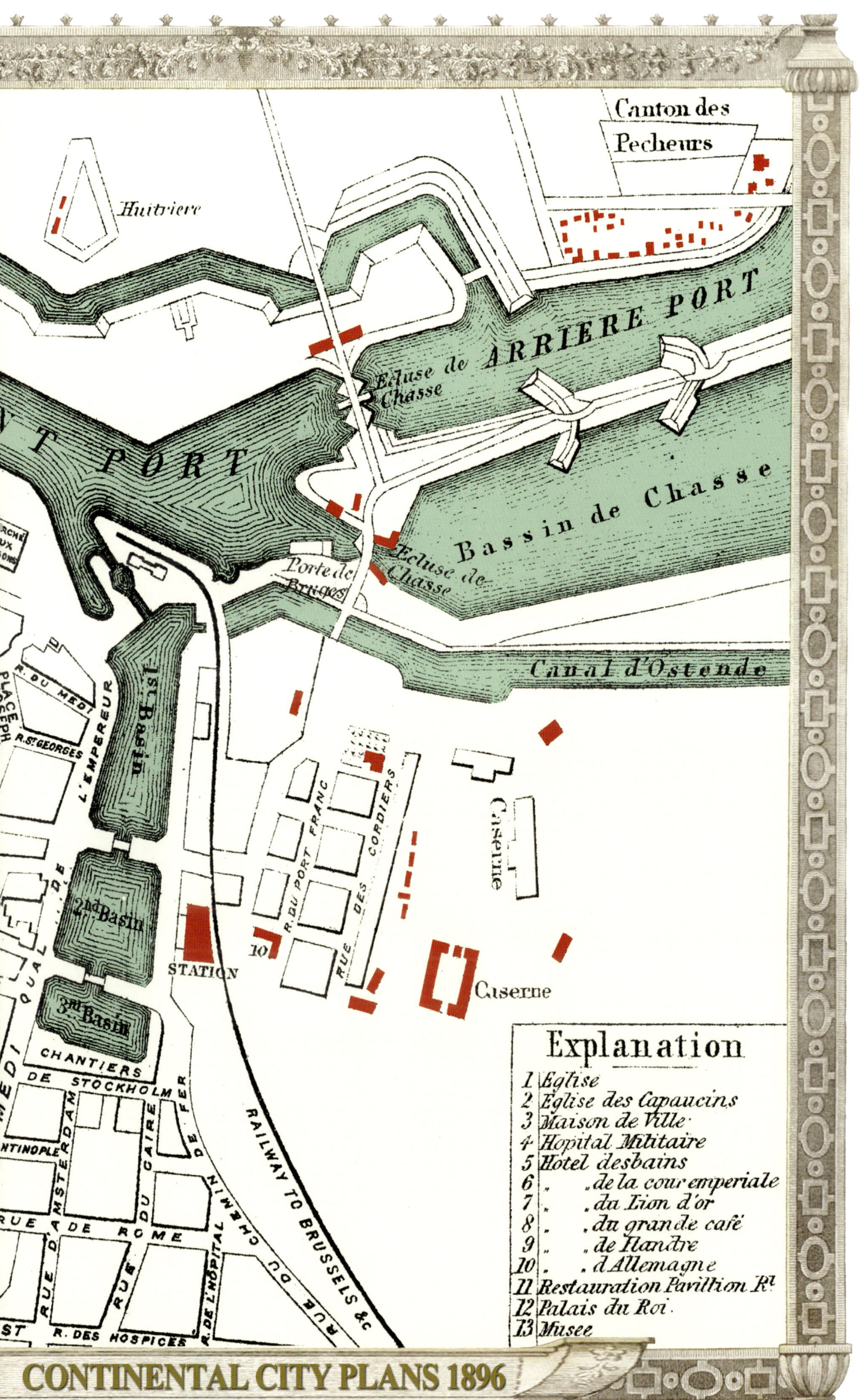

Canton des Pecheurs
Huitriere
ARRIERE PORT
Ecluse de Chasse
Bassin de Chasse
VT PORT
Ecluse de Chasse
Porte de Bruges
Canal d'Ostende
R. DU MEDI
PLACE JOSEPH
R. ST GEORGES
L'EMPEREUR
1st Basin
QUAI DE
2nd Basin
STATION
3rd Basin
CHANTIERS
DE STOCKHOLM
R. DU PORT FRANC
RUE DES CORDIERS
10
Caserne
Caserne
MEDI
NTINOPLE
RUE D'AMSTERDAM
RUE DE ROME
RUE DU CAIRE
R. DE L'HOPITAL
CHEMIN DE FER
RAILWAY TO BRUSSELS &c
RUE DU
ST
R. DES HOSPICES
Explanation
1 Eglise
2 Eglise des Capaucins
3 Maison de Ville
4 Hopital Militaire
5 Hotel desbains
6   „   de la cour emperiale
7   „   „ du Lion d'or
8   „   „ du grande café
9   „   „ de Flandre
10   „   „ d'Allemagne
11 Restauration Pavillion Rl
12 Palais du Roi
13 Musee

Giardini del Prin
cipe di Villa
franca
PORT
Molo
Pta S Giorgio
S. Francesco de Paola
S. Filippo Neri
Strada Macqueda
Pta Carini
14
15
Pta Ossuna
CORSO VITTORIO EMANUELE
Fontana
7
STRADA MACQUEDA
P. Nuova
Piazza Reale
Alberge de
Poveri
Pta Castro
S. Teresa
Pta di Vicari di S.
Francesco
di Sales
P. Montalto

Castello a Mare
Forte Galita
Porta Felice
CALA
FORO ITALICO
Piazza Marina
Pta. dei Greci
LA Strade FLORA
LA BOTTANICA
Pta. Termini
Mte S. Erasmo

Chiese e Stabilimenti Pubblici

1 Palazzo Reale
2 Ospital Grande
3 Cattedrale
4 Collegio di Gesuiti
5 Statua di S Carlo
6 L'Università
7 Pallazzo del Senato
8 Uffizio della Posta e Teatro
   Carolino
9 Pallazzo Gravina
10 Teatro S. Cecilia
11   „   Ferdinando
12 Pallazzo de Forremussa
13   „   del Duca d'Anjou
14 Fonderia Reale
15 Fontana di Garoffello
16 Ospitale dello Spirito Santo
17 Monastero delle Stimmate

WITH THE LATEST IMPROVEMENTS
Railways & Stations
Shown thus
COURBEVOIE
CLICHY LA GARENNE
BATIGNOLLES MONCEAUX
NEUILLY
PUTEAUX
ÉLYSÉE
SURESNES
LOUVRE
PASSY
CHAMP DE MARS
PALAIS BOURBON
St CLOUD
AUTEUIL
GRENELLE
BOULOGNE
QUARTIER DE PLAISANCE
VAUGIRARD
OBSERVATOIRE
SÈVRES
ISSY
VANVES
MONTROUGE
MEUDON
COMMUNE DE CLAMART
COMMUNE DE CHATILLON

BUTTE MONTMARTRE
LA VILLETTE
LA CHAPELLE
PANTIN
ROMAINVILLE
FORT D'AUBERVILLIERS
FORT DE ROMAINVILLE
PETITE VILLETTE
LE PRÉ ST GERVAIS
BUTTES CHAUMONT
ENCLOS ST LAURENT
BELLEVILLE
LA COURTILLE
LE PETIT ROMAINVILLE
BOURSE
MÉNILMONTANT
BAGNOLET
TEMPLE
MÉNILMONTANT
CHARONNE
MONTREUIL
MARAIS DE VILLIERS
POPINCOURT
HÔTEL DE VILLE
FONTARABIE
PETIT CHARONNE
REUILLY
Place de la Nation
VINCENNES
PANTHÉON
BERCY
ST MANDÉ
Esplanade
COBELINS
LA GARE
AUSTERLITZ
CHARENTON
LA MAISON BLANCHE
ST MAURICE
PARC DE VINCENNES
PETIT IVRY
LE KREMLIN
BICÊTRE
IVRY
FORT DE BICÊTRE
FORT DE CHARENTON
FORT D'IVRY
DE VITRY

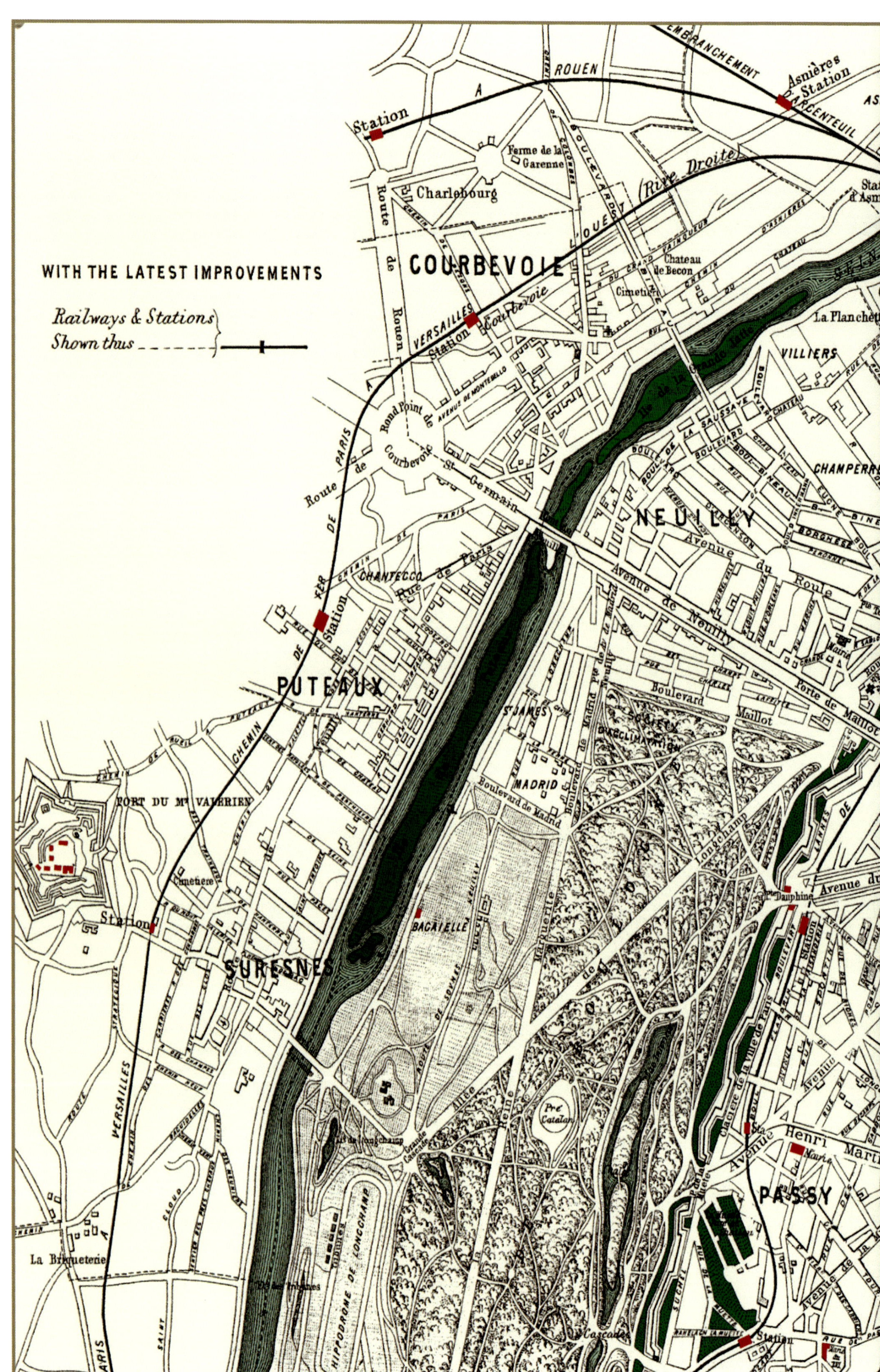

WITH THE LATEST IMPROVEMENTS
Railways & Stations
Shown thus
EMBRANCHEMENT
ROUEN
A
Asnières Station
D'ARGENTEUIL
ASN
Station
Stat.
d'Asm
Ferme de la Garenne
Charlebourg
Chateau de Becon
La Planchett
COURBEVOIE
Cimetiere
VILLIERS
(Rive Droite)
CHAMPERRE
Station de Courbevoie
VERSAILLES
LA SAUSSAYE
NEUILLY
Rond Point de
Avenue de Montebello
Avenue du Roule
Route PARIS de
Courbevoie
St. Germain
Rue de Paris
Avenue de Neuilly
CHEMIN
CHANTECCO
Station
Porte de Maillot
PUTEAUX
St JAMES
Boulevard
Maillot
CHEMIN
ACCLIMATION
MADRID
FORT DU Mt VALERIEN
Boulevard de Madrid
Cimetiere
BACATELLE
Dauphine
Avenue du
Station
SURESNES
Pré Catalan
PASSY
Henri Marti
Maria
La Briqueterie
HIPPODROME DE LONGCHAMP
Cascade
Station

CLICHY LA CARENNE
Fabrique de Sel Ammoniac
CLICHY
Gare de St Ouen
Pte de St Ouen
CEMETERY LA CARENNE
Station
LA VERSAILLES RAILWAY
LEVALLOIS
Courcelles
Porte de Asnieres
Station de Courcelles D'AUTEUIL
BATIGNOLLES MONCEAUX
Entrepôt du Chemin de Fer Rouen de
CHEMIN DE
Boulevard des Batignolles
VILLIERS
LES TERNES
Courcelles
Boulevard
MONCEAUX
PARIS
Route des Ternes
Station
Place de l'Etoile
Bois de Boulogne
Avenue de la Gde Armée
Hoche
Friedland
BOULEVARD HAUSSMANN
PEPINIERE
ELYSÉE
Avenue
Kleber
AVENUE D'IENA
AVENUE D'ALMA
du Trocadero
Hippodrome
Rond Point des Champs Elysées
Champs Elysées
Avenue Montaigne
Avenue d'Antin
Quai de la Conference
Railway
SEINE FLEUVE
d'Orsay
LOUVRE
Quai des Tuileries
Quai d'Orsay
M. des Militaire
M. des Tabacs
l'Université
Esplanade des Invalides
Quai Voltaire
HOTEL DES INVALIDES
BOULEVARD B-DE-LA-HAUBOURG
GRENELLE
Baths Restaurant

Glacière
de St Ouen
BUTTE
NTMARTRE
LA VILLETTE
LA CHAPELLE
BUTTES CHAUMONT
PARC DES CHAUMONT
ENCLOS ST LAURENT
BELL
LA COURTIL
RA
BOURSE
TEMPLE
REPUBLIQUE
POPINCOURT
Louvre
CHEMIN DE FER DU NORD
Boul de Rochechouart
BOULEVARD ST MARTIN

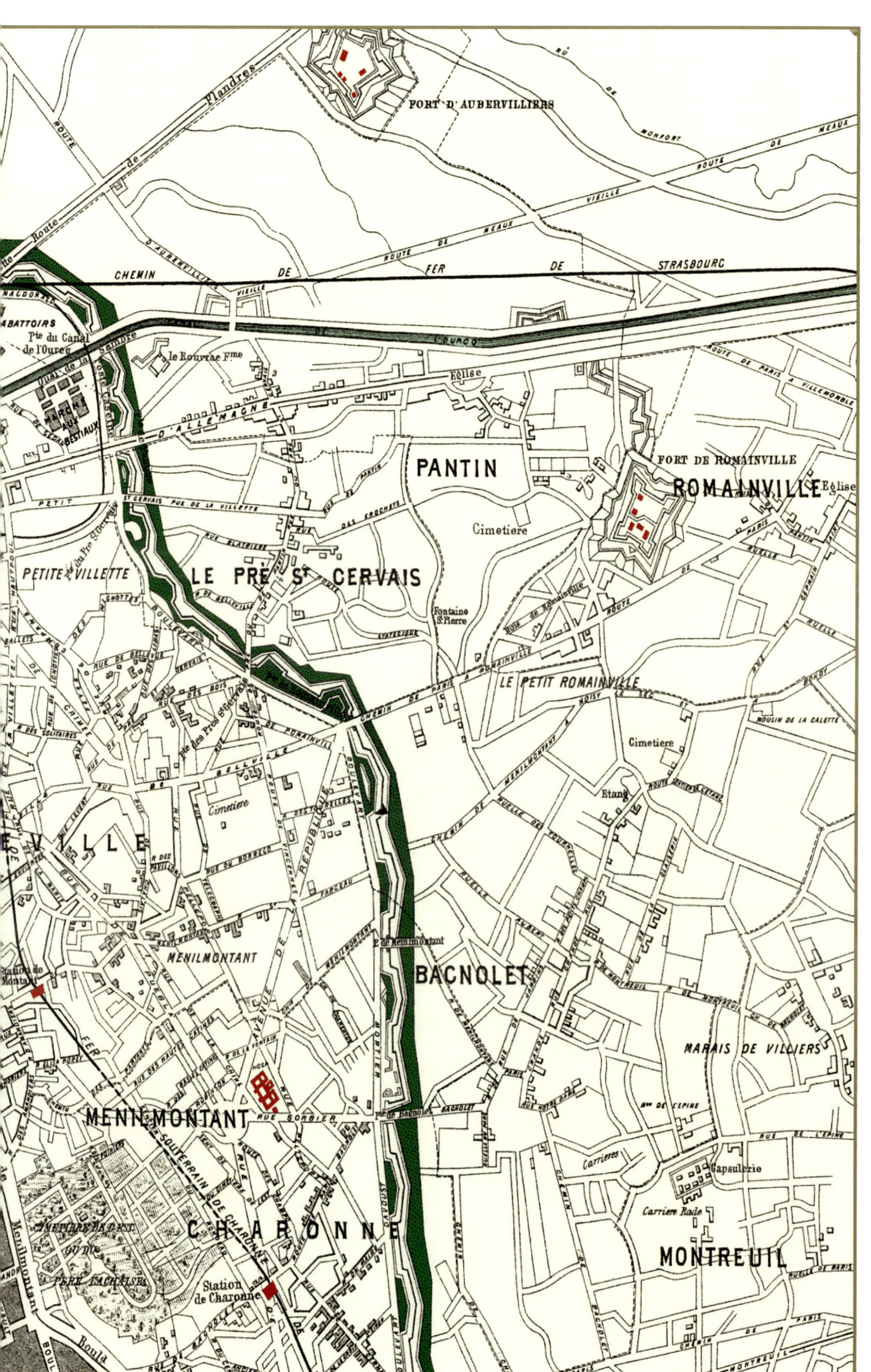

Flandres
PORT D'AUBERVILLIERS
ROUTE DE MEAUX
MONFORT
DE MEAUX
VIEILLE
CHEMIN DE FER DE STRASBOURG
L'OURCQ
ROUTE DE PARIS A VILLEMONBLE
ABATTOIRS
Pte du Canal de l'Ourcq
Le Rouvrae Fme
Église
FORT DE ROMAINVILLE
ROMAINVILLE
Église
MARCHÉ AUX BESTIAUX
D'ALLEMAGNE
PANTIN
Cimetiere
PETITE VILLETTE
LE PRÉ St GERVAIS
Fontaine St Pierre
ROUTE DE ROMAINVILLE
LE PETIT ROMAINVILLE
MOULIN DE LA CALETTE
Cimetiere
VILLE
Cimetiere
Etang
MENILMONTANT
BAGNOLET
MARAIS DE VILLIERS
MENILMONTANT
RUE SORBIER
Pte de Bagnolet
Carrieres
Capsulerie
CIMETIERE DE L'EST
Carriere Rade
ou du
PERE LACHAISE
CHARONNE
MONTREUIL
Station de Charonne
Boul.

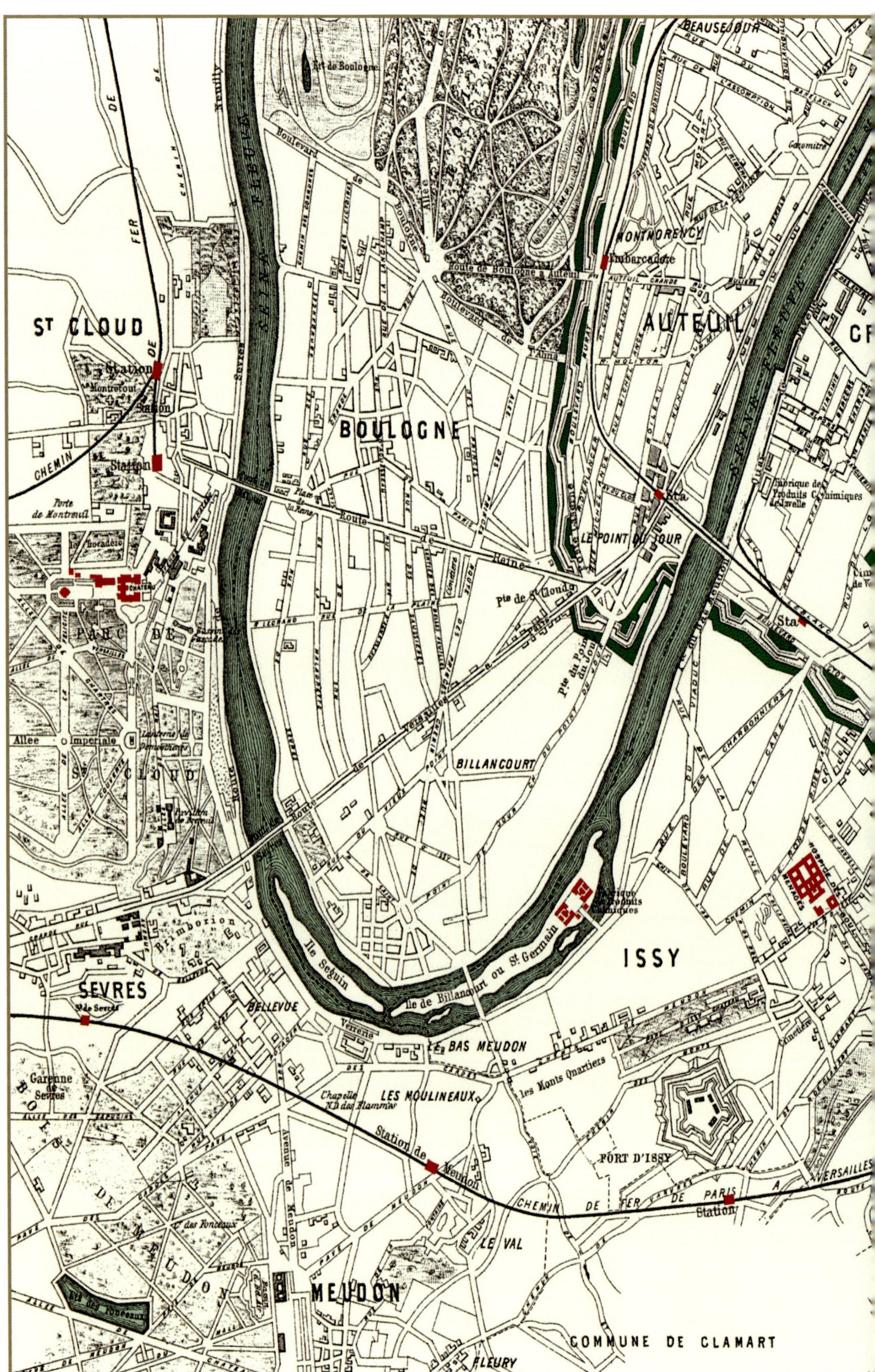

BEAUSEJOUR
ST CLOUD
Montretout
Station
Station
Station
CHEMIN
Porte de Montreuil
Trocadero
CHATEAU
PARC DE
Bassin des Cascades
Allee Imperiale
Lanterne de Demosthene
St CLOUD
Pavillon de Breteuil
Brimborion
SEVRES
R. de Sevres
BELLEVUE
Ile Seguin
Venenie
Garenne de Sevres
BOIS DE MEUDON
Chapelle N.D des Flammes
LES MOULINEAUX
Avenue de Meudon
C. des Fonceaux
Ile des Tonneaux
MEUDON
BOULOGNE
Bois de Boulogne
Route de Boulogne a Auteuil
MONTMORENCY
Embarcadere
AUTEUIL
AUTEUIL GRANDE RUE
Place de la Reine
Route
Seine
LE POINT DU JOUR
P.te de St Cloud
P.te du Point du Jour
BILLANCOURT
Ile de Billancourt ou St Germain
BAS MEUDON
Les Monts Quartiers
Station de Meudon
LE VAL
FLEURY
AUTEUIL
Sta
Fabrique de Produits Chimiques de Javelle
Sta
Fabrique de Produits Chimiques
ISSY
PORT D'ISSY
CHEMIN DE FER DE PARIS
Station
A VERSAILLES
COMMUNE DE CLAMART

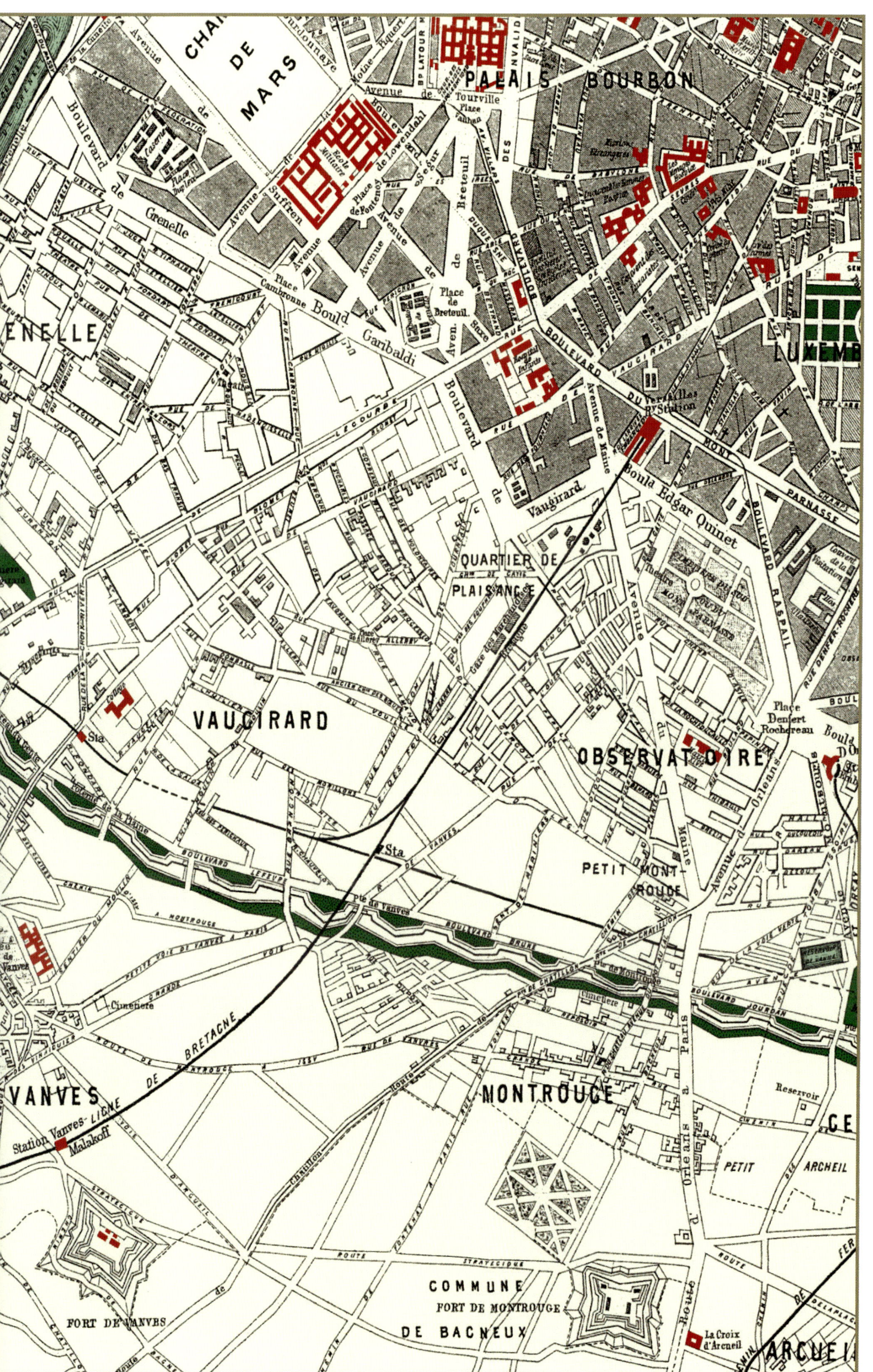

CHAMP DE MARS
PALAIS BOURBON
GRENELLE
LUXEMBOURG
QUARTIER DE PLAISANCE
VAUGIRARD
OBSERVATOIRE
Boulevard de Grenelle
Avenue de Suffren
Avenue de la Bourdonnaye
Ecole Militaire
Place de Fontenoy
Place de Breteuil
Boulevard Garibaldi
Place Cambronne
Avenue de Lowendahl
Avenue de Tourville
Place Tourville
Avenue de Breteuil
Boulevard des Invalides
Boulevard de Vaugirard
Boulevard de Port Royal
Versailles Ry Station
Avenue du Maine
Boulevard Edgar Quinet
Boulevard Raspail
Boulevard Montparnasse
Place Denfert Rochereau
Boulevard d'Orleans
Avenue d'Orleans
PETIT MONTROUGE
VANVES
Station Vanves-Malakoff
MONTROUGE
FORT DE VANVES
COMMUNE DE BAGNEUX
FORT DE MONTROUGE
La Croix d'Arcueil
ARCUEIL
PETIT ARCUEIL
Reservoir
Cimetière
BOULEVARD LEFEVRE
ROUTE STRATEGIQUE

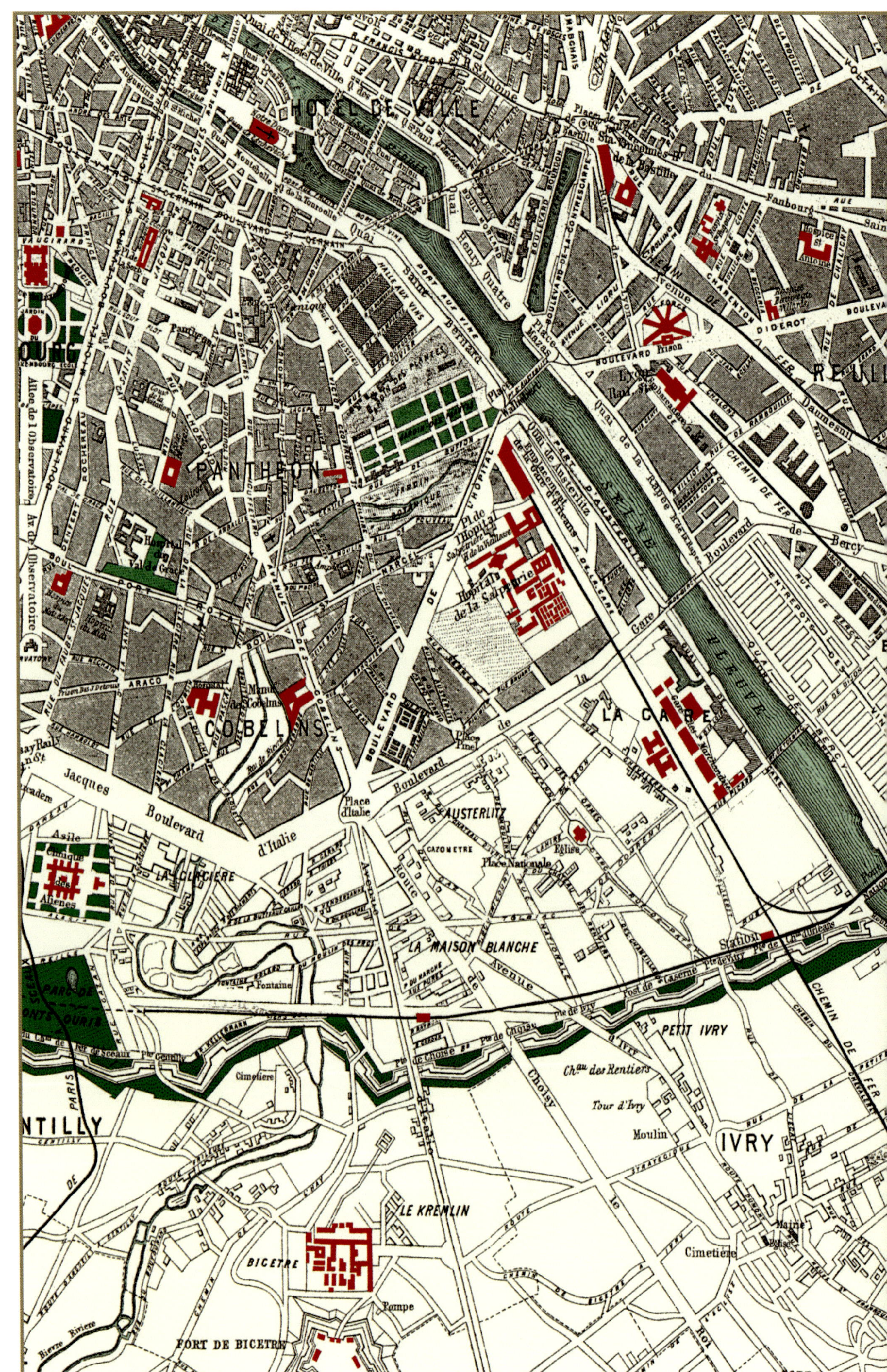

HOTEL DE VILLE
PANTHEON
GOBELINS
LA CURCIERE
BICETRE
LE KREMLIN
FORT DE BICETRE
IVRY
PETIT IVRY
LA MAISON BLANCHE
AUSTERLITZ
Place d'Italie
Place Nationale
LA GARE
REUILLY
Hôpital de la Salpêtrière
Place Pinel
Boulevard d'Italie
Boulevard de Bercy
Tour d'Ivry
Moulin
Cimetière
Fontaine
PARC DE MONTSOURIS
Boulevard Jacques
Asile clinique des Aliénés
GENTILLY
SEINE
ENTREPOT
FORT D'IVRY
Pompe
Chau des Rentiers

FONTARABIE
PETIT CHARONNE
PETIT CHARONNE
Place du la Nation
Antoine
DIDEROT
Borne Avenue du Trone
Sta
Pte de Vincennes
Vincennes
Cimetiere
VINCENNES
Station de Vincennes
Grande Rue de Paris
Avenue de St Mande
Hospice St Michel
CHATEAU DE VINCENNES
Hopital Militaire
Daumesnil
VINCENNES
Rond du Bel Air
Station Du Bel Air
Station de St Mande
St Mande Bel Air
ST MANDE
Esplanade
Boulevard Daumesnil Reuilly
Ecole de Pyrotechnie
LA CDE PINTE
BERCY
Pte de Picpns
Route
Cimetiere
PARC DE VINCENNES
Station de Bercy
Station
Paris
le Polygone
CHARENTON
Charenton
Hosp des Invalides Civils
ST MAURICE
CONFLANS
SEINE
Maison de Sante
Station de Charenton
MARNE
Chau Gaillard
Chateau de St Frambourg
FORT DE CHARENTON

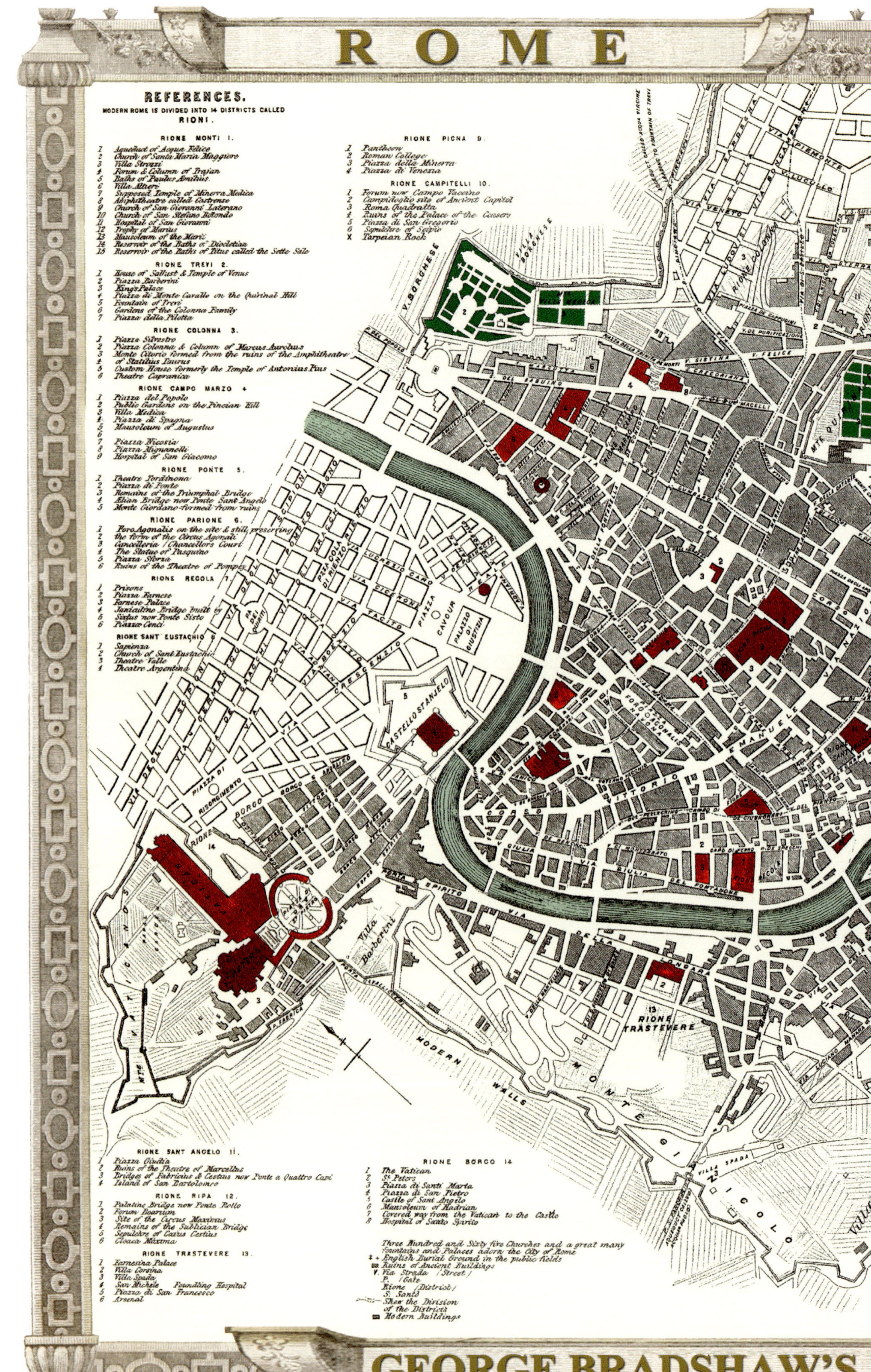

REFERENCES.
MODERN ROME IS DIVIDED INTO 14 DISTRICTS CALLED RIONI.

RIONE MONTI 1.
1 Aqueduct of Acqua Felice
2 Church of Santa Maria Maggiore
3 Villa Strozzi
4 Forum & Column of Trajan
5 Baths of Paulus Æmilius
6 Villa Altieri
7 Supposed Temple of Minerva Medica
8 Amphitheatre called Costrense
9 Church of San Giovanni Laterano
10 Church of San Stefano Rotondo
11 Hospital of San Giovanni
12 Trophy of Marius
13 Mausoleum of the Marii
14 Reservoir of the Baths of Diocletian
15 Reservoir of the Baths of Titus called the Sette Sale

RIONE TREVI 2.
1 House of Sallust & Temple of Venus
2 Piazza Barberini
3 King's Palace
4 Piazza di Monte Cavallo on the Quirinal Hill
5 Fountain of Trevi
6 Gardens of the Colonna Family
7 Piazza della Pilotta

RIONE COLONNA 3.
1 Piazza Silvestro
2 Piazza Colonna & Column of Marcus Aurelius
3 Monte Citorio formed from the ruins of the Amphitheatre
4 of Statilius Taurus
5 Custom House formerly the Temple of Antonius Pius
6 Theatre Capranica

RIONE CAMPO MARZO 4.
1 Piazza del Popolo
2 Public Gardens on the Pincian Hill
3 Villa Medica
4 Piazza di Spagna
5 Mausoleum of Augustus
6
7 Piazza Nicosia
8 Piazza Mignanelli
9 Hospital of San Giacomo

RIONE PONTE 5.
1 Theatre Tordinona
2 Piazza di Ponte
3 Remains of the Triumphal Bridge
4 Elian Bridge now Ponte Sant Angelo
5 Monte Giordano formed from ruins

RIONE PARIONE 6.
1 Foro Agonalis on the site & still preserving
2 the form of the Circus Agonali
3 Cancelleria (Chancellor's Court)
4 The Statue of Pasquino
5 Piazza Sforza
6 Ruins of the Theatre of Pompey

RIONE REGOLA 7.
1 Prisons
2 Piazza Farnese
3 Farnese Palace
4 Janiculine Bridge built by
5 Sixtus now Ponte Sisto
6 Piazza Cenci

RIONE SANT EUSTACHIO 8
1 Sapienza
2 Church of Sant Eustachio
3 Theatre Valle
4 Theatre Argentina

RIONE PICNA 9.
1 Pantheon
2 Roman College
3 Piazza della Minerva
4 Piazza di Venezia

RIONE CAMPITELLI 10.
1 Forum now Campo Vaccino
2 Campidoglio site of Ancient Capitol
3 Roma Quadratta
4 Ruins of the Palace of the Cæsars
5 Piazza di San Gregorio
6 Sepulchre of Scipio
X Tarpeian Rock

RIONE SANT ANGELO 11.
1 Piazza Giudea
2 Ruins of the Theatre of Marcellus
3 Bridge of Fabricius & Cestius now Ponte a Quattro Capi
4 Island of San Bartolomeo

RIONE RIPA 12.
1 Palatine Bridge now Ponte Rotto
2 Forum Boarium
3 Site of the Circus Maximus
4 Remains of the Sublician Bridge
5 Sepulchre of Caius Cestius
6 Cloaca Maxima

RIONE TRASTEVERE 13.
1 Farnesina Palace
2 Villa Corsina
3 Villa Spada
4 San Michele Foundling Hospital
5 Piazza di San Francesco
6 Arsenal

RIONE BORGO 14.
1 The Vatican
2 St Peters
3 Piazza di Santi Marta
4 Piazza di San Pietro
5 Castle of Sant Angelo
6 Mausoleum of Hadrian
7 Covered way from the Vatican to the Castle
8 Hospital of Santo Spirito

Three Hundred and Sixty Five Churches and a great many
Fountains and Palaces adorn the City of Rome
+ English Burial Ground in the public fields
Ruins of Ancient Buildings
V. Via Strada (Street)
P. Gate
Rione (District)
S. Santi
Shew the Division of the Districts
Modern Buildings

Station
BATHS OF DIOCLETIAN
PIAZZA DELLA TERME
Piazza Vittorio Emanuele
S.M.Maggiore
Piazza Manfredo Fanti
VIA DI PORTA S. LORENZO
VIA VOLTURNO
VIA MAGENTA
VIALE PRINCIPESSA MARGHERITA
VIA CARLO ALBERTO
PRINCIPE EUGENIO
VILLA ALTIERI
Scala Santa
Basilica di S.Giovanni in Laterano
COLOSSEO
Arch of Constantine
ROMAN FORUM
RIONE CAMPITELLI
S. STEFANO ROTONDO
V. CASALI
VIA DI PORTA S. SEBASTIANO
SITE OF THE CIRCUS MAXIMUS
BATHS OF CARACALLA
RIONE RIPA
VIA DELLA MARMORATA
Station
To Naples
Railways thus

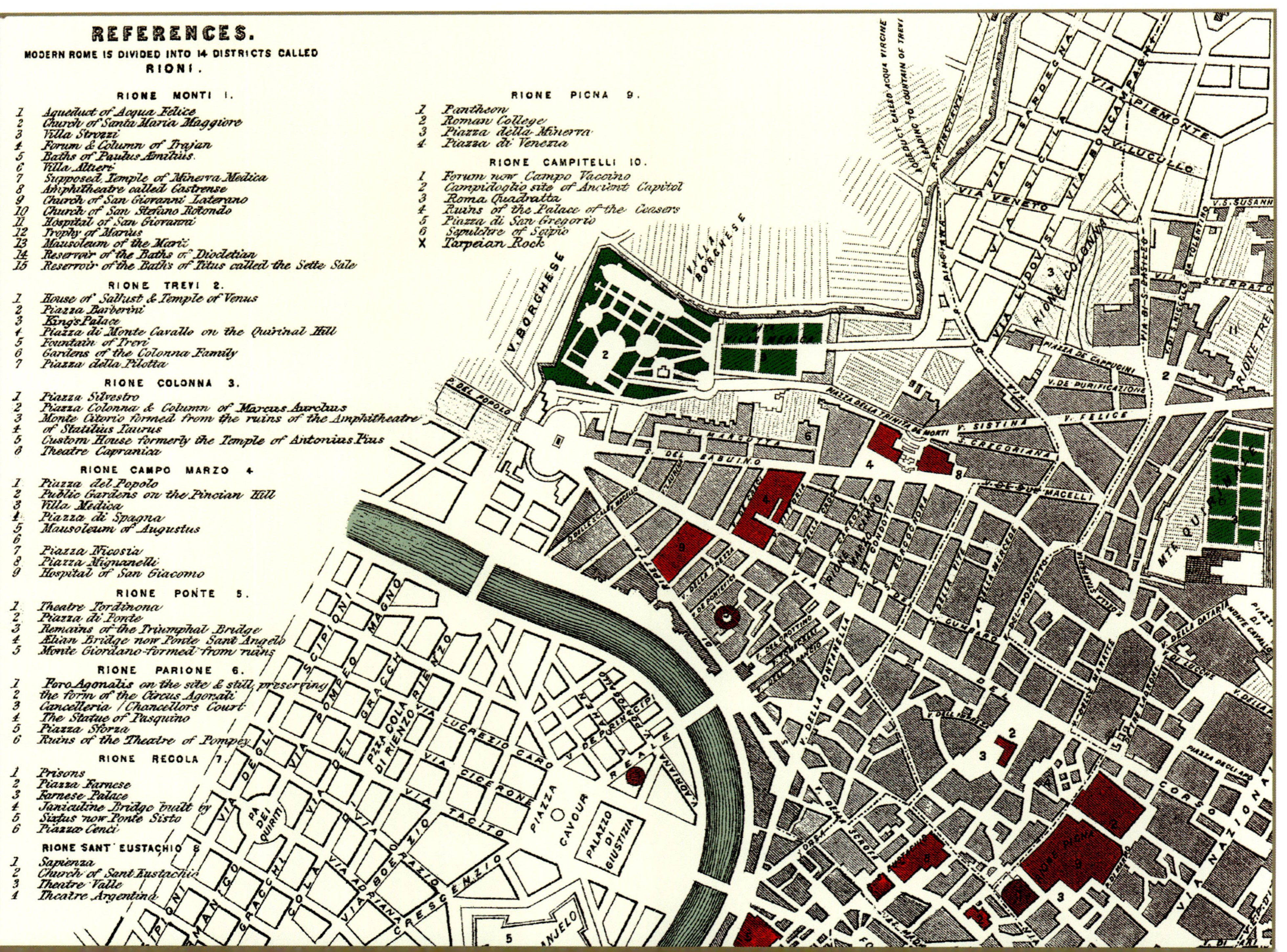

REFERENCES.
MODERN ROME IS DIVIDED INTO 14 DISTRICTS CALLED
RIONI.

RIONE MONTI 1.
1 Aqueduct of Acqua Felice
2 Church of Santa Maria Maggiore
3 Villa Strozzi
4 Forum & Column of Trajan
5 Baths of Paulus Æmilius
6 Villa Altieri
7 Supposed Temple of Minerva Medica
8 Amphitheatre called Castrense
9 Church of San Giovanni Laterano
10 Church of San Stefano Rotondo
11 Hospital of San Giovanni
12 Trophy of Marius
13 Mausoleum of the Marii
14 Reservoir of the Baths of Diocletian
15 Reservoir of the Baths of Titus called the Sette Sale

RIONE TREVI 2.
1 House of Sallust & Temple of Venus
2 Piazza Barberini
3 King's Palace
4 Piazza di Monte Cavallo on the Quirinal Hill
5 Fountain of Trevi
6 Gardens of the Colonna Family
7 Piazza della Pilotta

RIONE COLONNA 3.
1 Piazza Silvestro
2 Piazza Colonna & Column of Marcus Aurelius
3 Monte Citorio formed from the ruins of the Amphitheatre
4 of Statilius Taurus
5 Custom House formerly the Temple of Antonius Pius
6 Theatre Capranica

RIONE CAMPO MARZO 4.
1 Piazza del Popolo
2 Public Gardens on the Pincian Hill
3 Villa Medica
4 Piazza di Spagna
5 Mausoleum of Augustus
6
7 Piazza Nicosia
8 Piazza Mignanelli
9 Hospital of San Giacomo

RIONE PONTE 5.
1 Theatre Tordinona
2 Piazza di Ponte
3 Remains of the Triumphal Bridge
4 Elian Bridge now Ponte Sant Angelo
5 Monte Giordano formed from ruins

RIONE PARIONE 6.
1 Foro Agonalis on the site & still preserving
   the form of the Circus Agonali
2 Cancelleria / Chancellors Court
3 The Statue of Pasquino
4
5 Piazza Sforza
6 Ruins of the Theatre of Pompey

RIONE REGOLA 7.
1 Prisons
2 Piazza Farnese
3 Farnese Palace
4 Janiculine Bridge built by
5 Sixtus now Ponte Sisto
6 Piazza Cenci

RIONE SANT' EUSTACHIO 8
1 Sapienza
2 Church of Sant Eustachio
3 Theatre Valle
4 Theatre Argentina

RIONE PICNA 9.
1 Pantheon
2 Roman College
3 Piazza della Minerva
4 Piazza di Venezia

RIONE CAMPITELLI 10.
1 Forum now Campo Vaccino
2 Campidoglio site of Ancient Capitol
3 Roma Quadratta
4 Ruins of the Palace of the Ceasers
5 Piazza di San Gregorio
6 Sepulchre of Scipio
X Tarpeian Rock

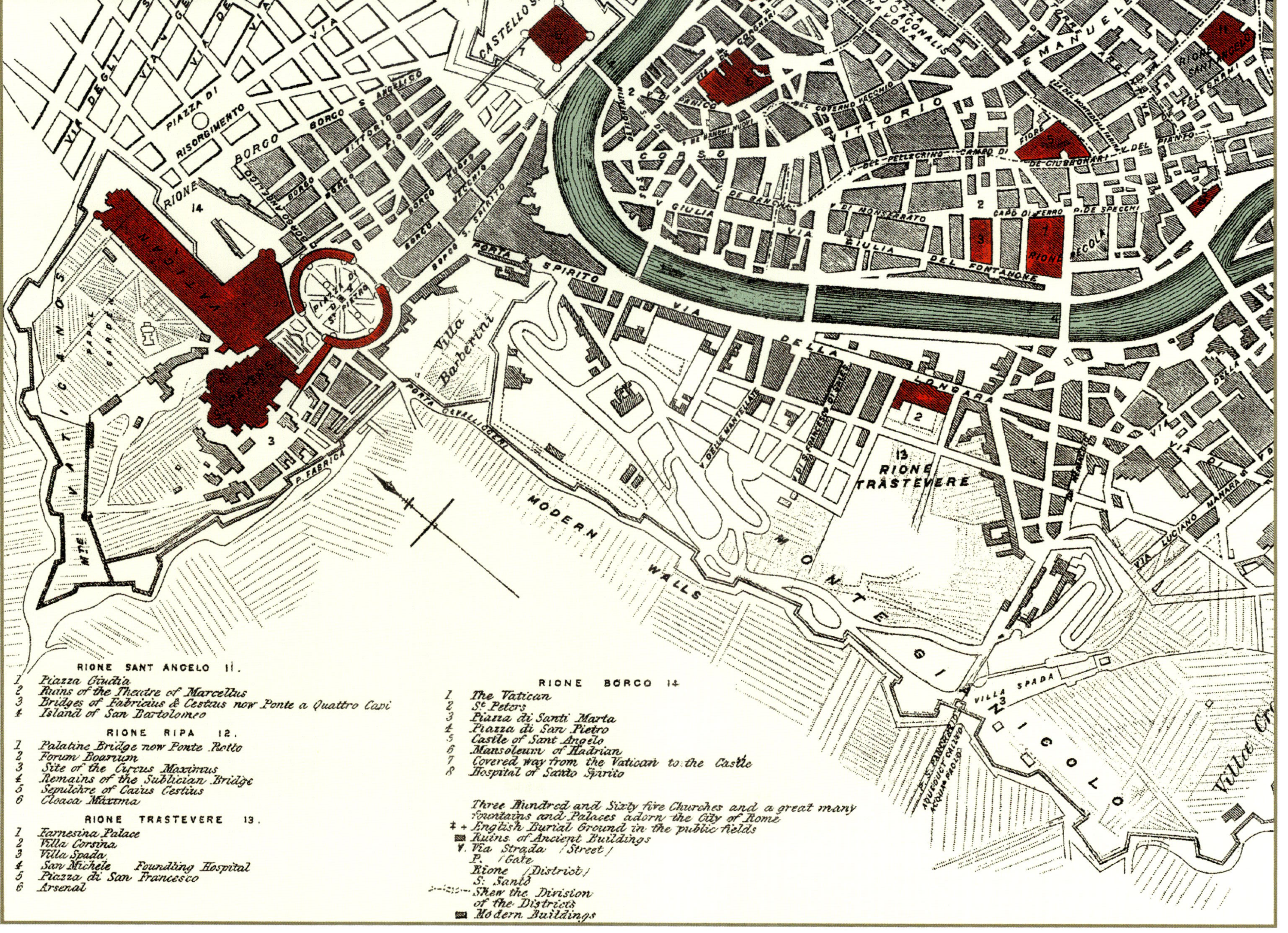

RIONE SANT ANGELO 11.
1 Piazza Giudia
2 Ruins of the Theatre of Marcellus
3 Bridges of Fabricius & Cestius now Ponte a Quattro Capi
4 Island of San Bartolomeo

RIONE RIPA 12.
1 Palatine Bridge now Ponte Rotto
2 Forum Boarium
3 Site of the Circus Maximus
4 Remains of the Sublician Bridge
5 Sepulchre of Caius Cestius
6 Cloaca Maxima

RIONE TRASTEVERE 13.
1 Farnesina Palace
2 Villa Corsina
3 Villa Spada
4 San Michele   Foundling Hospital
5 Piazza di San Francesco
6 Arsenal

RIONE BORGO 14.
1 The Vatican
2 St Peters
3 Piazza di Santi Marta
4 Piazza di San Pietro
5 Castle of Sant Angelo
6 Mausoleum of Hadrian
7 Covered way from the Vatican to the Castle
8 Hospital of Santo Spirito

Three Hundred and Sixty five Churches and a great many
fountains and Palaces adorn the City of Rome
+ English Burial Ground in the public fields
Ruins of Ancient Buildings
V. Via   Strada   (Street)
P.   (Gate)
Rione   (District)
S: Santo
Shew the Division of the Districts
Modern Buildings

RIONE BORGO
RIONE TRASTEVERE
MONTE GIANICOLO
MODERN WALLS
Villa Barberini
Villa Spada
PIAZZA DI RISORGIMENTO
PORTA SPIRITO

VENTE SETEMBRE
MINISTRY OF FINANCE
VIA VOLTURNO
VIA MAGENTA
VIA DI PORTA S. LORENZO
P. S. LORENZO
BUOVA PORTA
To Foligno Ancona
To Naples
Station
PIAZZA CINQUECENTO
BATHS OF DIOCLETIAN
PIAZZA DELLA TERME
MINISTRY OF WAR
VIA QUIRINALE
VIA NAZIONALE
MTE VIMINALE
3. ONE MONTE
VIALE PRINCIPESSA MARGHERITA
VIA D'AZEGLIO
VIA CAVOUR
VIA GIOBERTI
VIA PRINCIPE
VIA MAMIANI
VIA MANZINI
PIAZZA MANFREDI FANTI
VIA RATTAZZI
VIA CAPPELLINI
UMBERTO
VIA RICASOLI
VIA EMANORA
VIA MAMIANI
BIXIO
GARROL
VIA MANZONI
VIA PRINCIPE EUGENIO
P. MAGGIORE
VIA CONTE VERDE GIA CROCE
SANTA CROCE IN GERUSALEMME
B
V. NAPOLENE
V. FARINI
S. M. Maggiore
VIA CARLO ALBERTO
V. STATUTO
Piazza Vittorio Emanuele
Piazza Dante
VIA BUONARROTI
VIA FERRUGGIO
VIA GUISTI
VIA MACHIAVELLI
VIA MERULANA
VIA ARIOSTO
VIA TASSO
VIA EMANUELE FILIBERTO
VILLA ALTIERI
LABIGANA
Neroniano
Acquedotto
Scala Santa
Basilica di S. Giovanni in Laterano
P. S. GIOVANNI
VIA AGOSTINO DEPRETIS
VIA MILANO
MTE ESQUILINO
V. DI S. MARTINO
V. POLVERIERA
V. DELLE SETTE SALE
VIA LABICANA
V. DI S. GIOVANNI
VIA S. STEFANO
V. DEI PUBLICO
V. DEL COLOSSEO
COLOSSEUM
Basilica di Constantine
Arch of Constantine
ROMAN FORUM
V. CASALI
S. STEFANO ROTONDO
VIA DELLA FERRATELLA
ACQUA MARANNA FORMERLY AQUA CHIARA
NARTRONIA
2
10

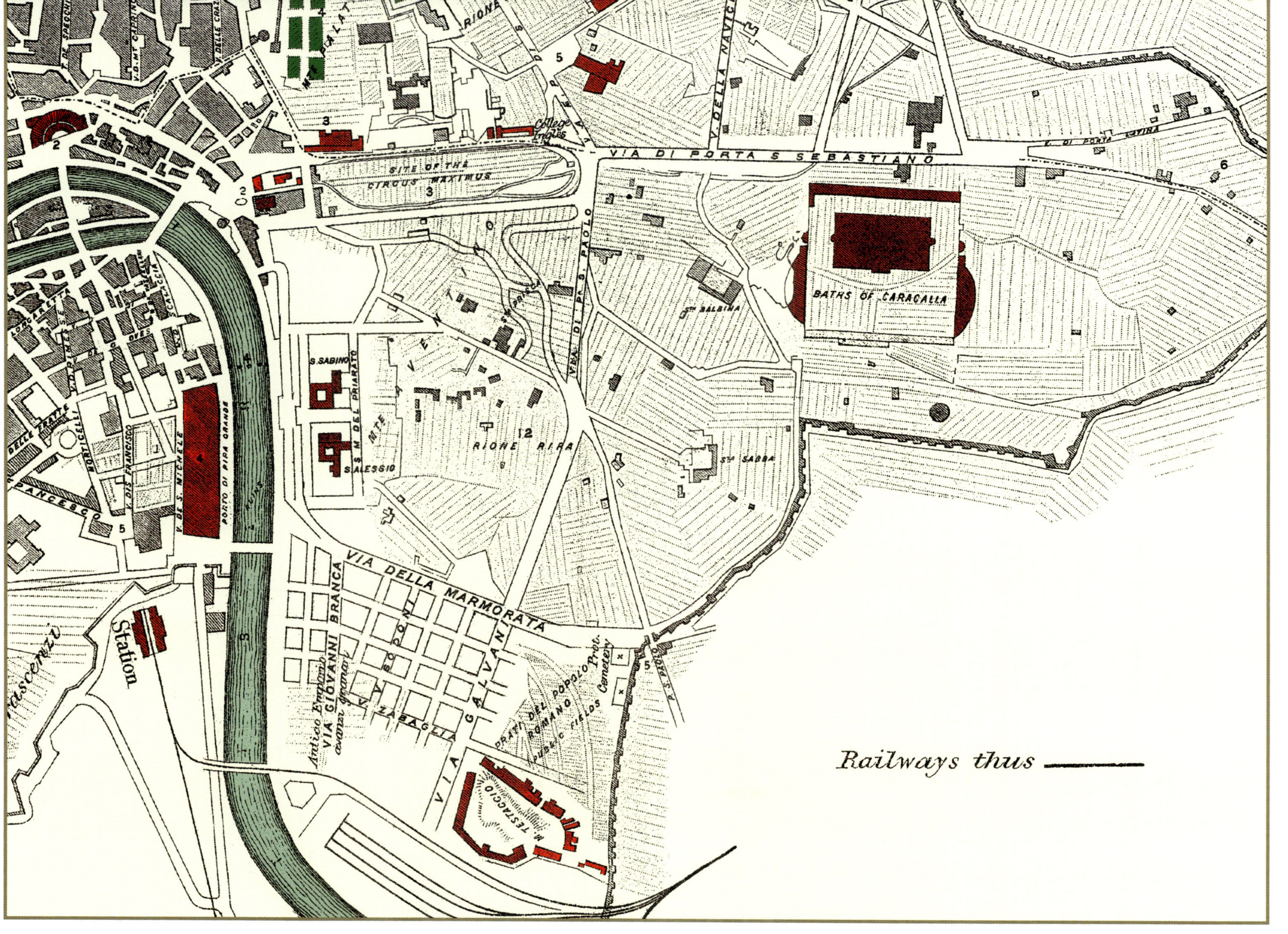

Railways thus
VIA DI PORTA S. SEBASTIANO
BATHS OF CARACALLA
V. DELLA NAVIC
P. DI PORTA CAPINA
College Inglese
SITE OF THE CIRCUS MAXIMUS
RIONE
S.ta BALBINA
VN. DI P.ta S. PAOLO
RIONE RIPA
S.ta SABBA
MONTE
S. SABINO
S. M. DEL PRIARATO
S. ALESSIO
VIA DELLA MARMORATA
VIA GALVANI
VIA GIOVANNI BRANCA
Antico Emporio
cavani granai
V. BODONI
V. ZABAGLIA
M. TESTACCIO
PRATI DEL POPOLO ROMANO
Public Fields
Prot. Cemetery
PORTO DI RIPA GRANDE
V. DE S. MICHELE
V. DI S. FRANCESCO
Station
Pascenzi
DELLE FRATE
MONTICELLI
PANCESCO
VIA CATACCIA

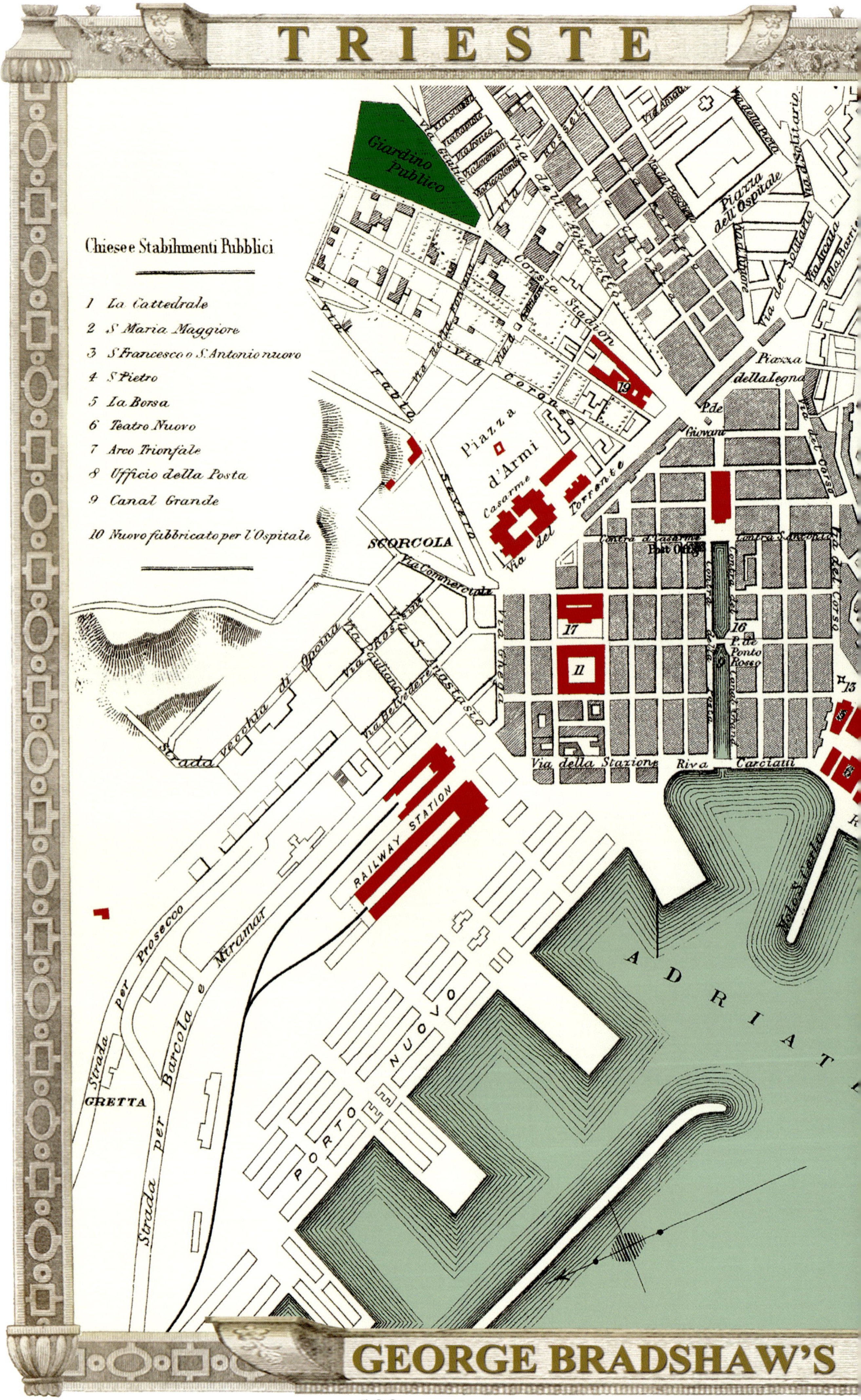

Giardino Pubblico

Chiese e Stabilimenti Pubblici

1 La Cattedrale
2 S. Maria Maggiore
3 S. Francesco o S. Antonio nuovo
4 S. Pietro
5 La Borsa
6 Teatro Nuovo
7 Arco Trionfale
8 Ufficio della Posta
9 Canal Grande

10 Nuovo fabbricato per l'Ospitale

Piazza dell'Ospitale
Piazza della Legna
P. de Giovani
Piazza d'Armi
Casarme
SCORCOLA
Via Commerciale
Via del Torrente
Contra d'Casarme
Post Office
P. de Ponto Rosso
Via della Stazione
Riva Carciatti
RAILWAY STATION
Strada Vecchia di Opcina
Via Coroneo
Strada per Prosecco
Strada per Barcola e Miramar
GRETTA
PORTO NUOVO
ADRIATIC

CHIARBOLA SUPERIORE
S. Giacomo
Bosco Pontini
ai Navali
Castric
Cattedrale S. Giusto
Museum
Sansa
S. Vito
Piazze Edifici pubblici ecc.
11 Dogana nuova
12 Piazza Grande
13   "   della Borsa
14   "   del Squero vecchio
15   "   di Lipsia
16   "   del Ponte Rosso
17   "   della Dogana
18 Edificio della Sanità
19 Anfiteatro Maurone
CHIARBOLA INFERIORE
Vicolo d'officina
Via Tiger
Via Massimiliana
del Mandracchio
Lazzaretto vecchio
Stazione S. Andrea
Molo S. Teresa
Faro
Via Murat
Passeggio di S. Andrea
SEA

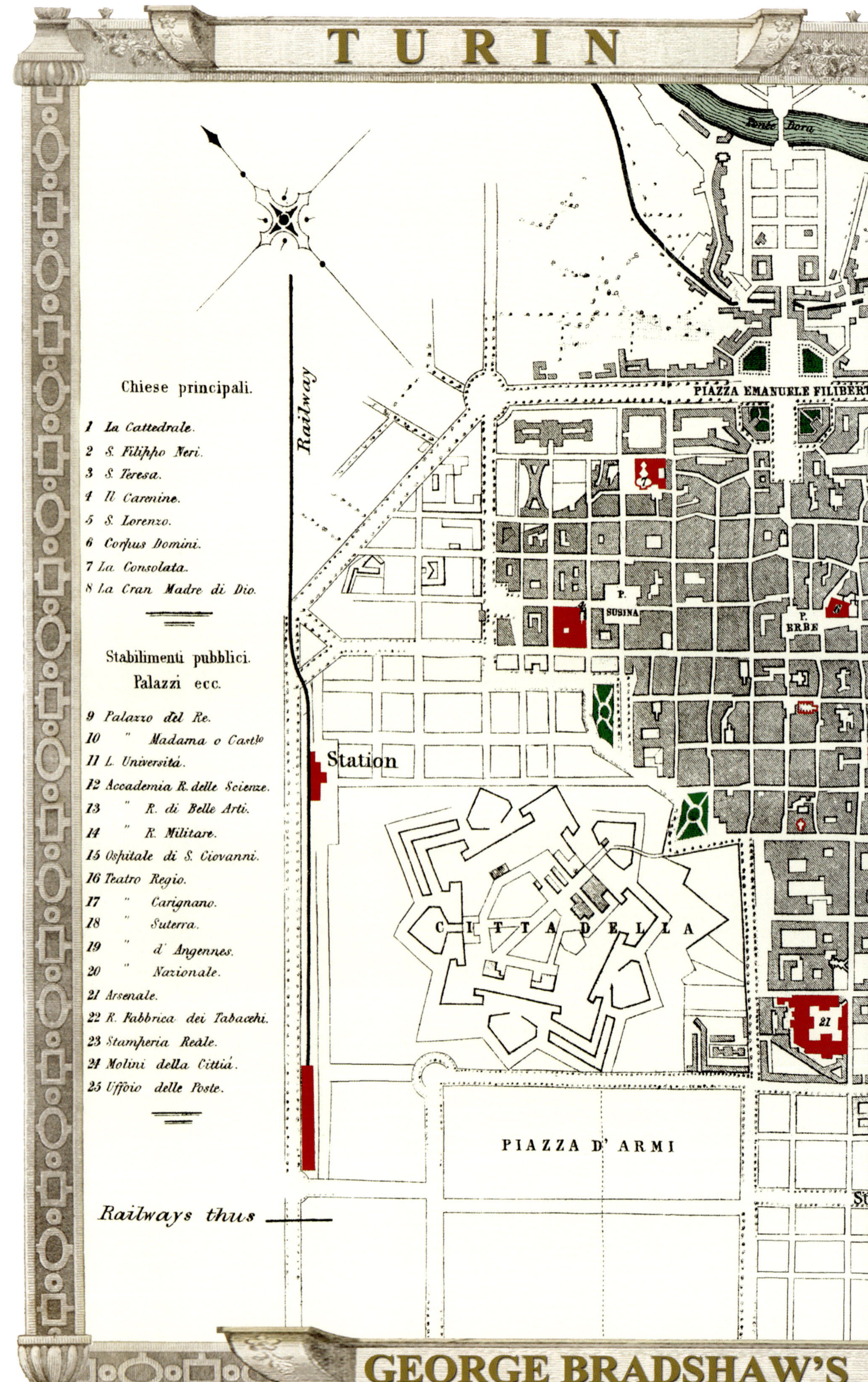
Chiese principali.

1 La Cattedrale.
2 S. Filippo Neri.
3 S. Teresa.
4 Il Carmine.
5 S. Lorenzo.
6 Corpus Domini.
7 La Consolata.
8 La Gran Madre di Dio.

Stabilimenti pubblici.
Palazzi ecc.

9 Palazzo del Re.
10 " Madama o Casto
11 L. Università.
12 Accademia R. delle Scienze.
13 " R. di Belle Arti.
14 " R. Militare.
15 Ospitale di S. Giovanni.
16 Teatro Regio.
17 " Carignano.
18 " Suterra.
19 " d' Angennes.
20 " Nazionale.
21 Arsenale.
22 R. Fabbrica dei Tabacchi.
23 Stamperia Reale.
24 Molini della Cittià.
25 Uffoio delle Poste.

Railways thus

Railway
Station
PIAZZA EMANUELE FILIBERT
Ponte Dora
P. SUSINA
P. ERBE
CITTADELLA
PIAZZA D' ARMI
St

Scale
100 200 300 400 40 Yds 1/4 of a Mile.
ORA F.
GIARDINO REALE
PIAZZA CASTELLO
PIAZZA VITTORIO EMANUELE
PIAZZA CARLINA
PIAZZA S. CARLO
PORTA NUOVA Felice
zione Centrale
Ponte del Po
Ponte di Ferro
FIUME
PO
Il Monte
1 9 16 14 23 10 11 17 25 13 18 12 2 19 15 20 8

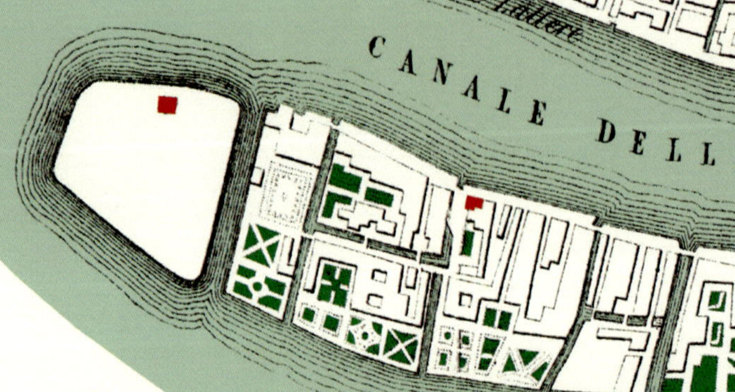

Chiese principali

1 S. Marco
2 S. Giovanni e Paola
3 S. Giorgio Maggiore
4 S. Maria de' Frari
5 S. Maria della Salute
6 Il Redentore
7 S. Salvatore
8 Zaccaria

Palazzi e Stabilimenti
pubblici.

9 Palazzo Ducale
10 Accademia di Belle Arti
11 Pallazzo Manfrin
12 " Grimani a S. Maria
- Formosa.
13 I. R. Ufficio delle Poste
14 Ospitale civile
15 Teatro della Fenice
16 " Gallo
17 " Apollo
18 " Malibran
19 Staz.^a della Str.^a di Ferro per Padova

Railway shown thus ———

Sacco della Misericordia
BACINI
Darsena novissima
ARSENALE
Arsenale nuovo
Isola
S.Pietro di Castello
CANAL DI CASTELLO
Via Garibaldi
Riva de Schiavoni
Piazza S.Marco
GRANDE
Dogana
Isola S.Giorgio
CANALE DI S. MARCO
GIUDECCA
Scale
0   200   400   600   800   880 Yards
a ½ a Mile

Chiese principali

1 Cattedrale

2 S. Anastasia

3 S. Bernardino

4 S. Fermo Maggiore

5 S. Giorgio

6 S. Maria in Organo

7 S. Sebastiano

8 S. Zeno

Stabilimenti Pubblici, Palazzi ecc.

9 Municipalitá

10 Tombe di Scaligeri

11 Posta delle Lettere e Diligenze —
Erariali

12 Ponte di Castel Vecchio

13 .. della Pietra

14 .. Nuovo

15 .. delle Navi

16 Teatro Filarmonico e Museo
Lapidario

17 Tomba di Giulietta

Railways shown thus ___________

pta S Giorgio
Castel S Pietro
P. del Vescovo
Strada per Vicenza
Stazione della
Strada Ferrata per Vince
Piazza Bra
Piazza d'Armi
P.S. Vittoria
Cimitero
Gasometro
Via Pallone
Corso Vittorio Emanuele
Strada Ferrata per Vicenza Station
Stazione Porta Nuova
Station
Nuova
ADIGE

VIENNA
NEUES DONAU BETT
DONAU STADT
PROJECTED
NORTH RAILWAY STATION
NORTH WEST STATION
K.K. Augarten
FRANZ JOSEF STATION
Allgemeines Krankenhaus
Infanterie Caserne
RATH HAUS
UNIVERSITAT
PARLAMENT
Votive Kirche
Invaliden Haus
ROSSAUER LANDE
REFERENCE.
1. Innerstadt
2. Leopoldstadt
3. Landstrasse
4. Wieden
5. Margarethen
6. Mariahilf
7. Neuban
8. Josefstadt
9. Alsergrund
SCALES
English
Wien
Railways thus
Tramways
GEORGE BRADSHAW'S

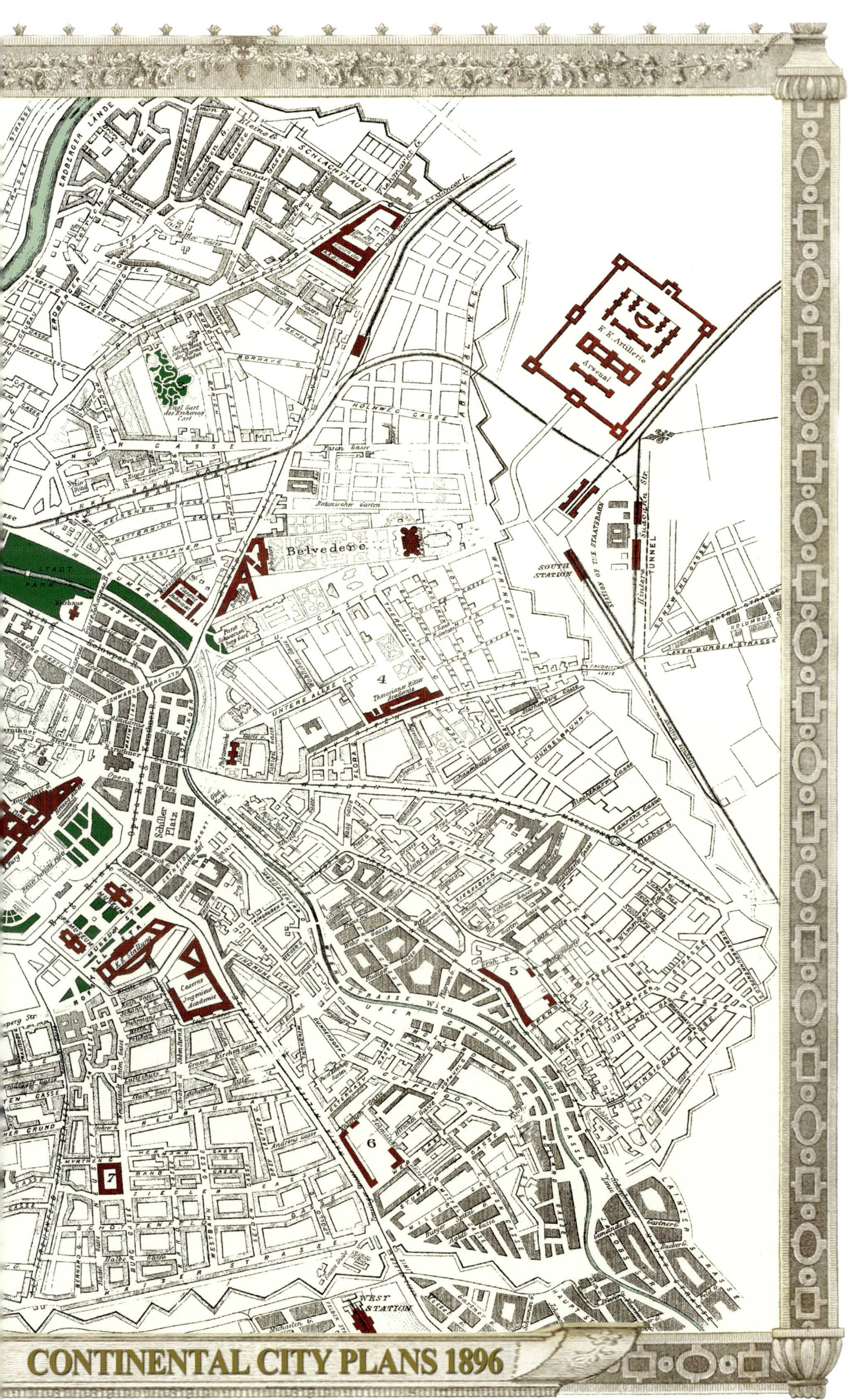

ERDBERGER LÄNDE
SCHLACHTHAUS
K.K. Artillerie
Arsenal
STATION OF THE STAATSBAHN
SOUTH STATION
TUNNEL
Belvedere.
STADT PARK
Schiller Platz
WEST STATION

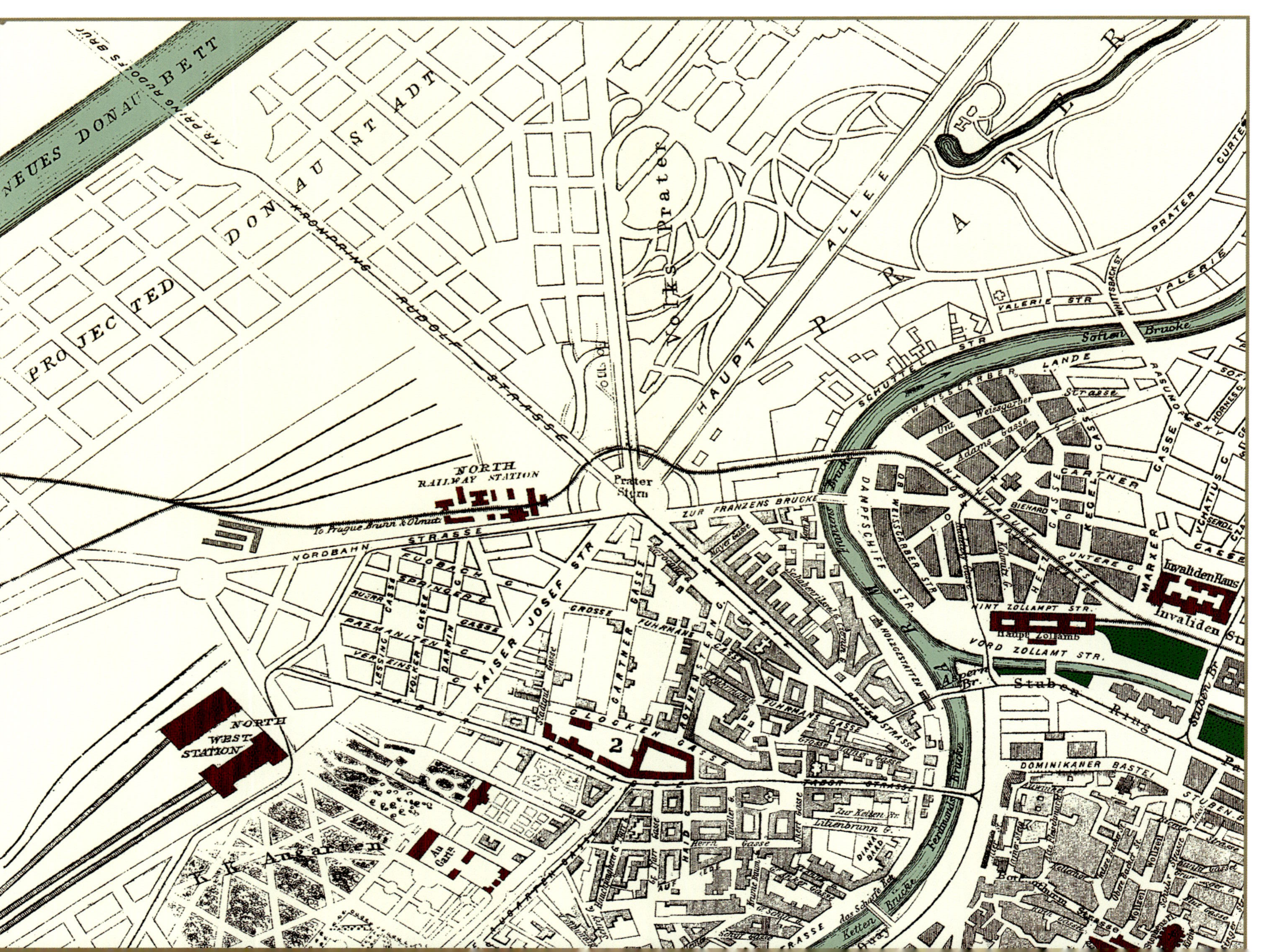

NEUES DONAU BETT
KRONPRING RUDOLFS BRUK
PROJECTED
DONAU STADT
KRONPRING RUDOLF STRASSE
NORTH RAILWAY STATION
NORTH WEST STATION
NORDBAHN STRASSE
To Prague Brunn & Olmut
Prater Stern
VOLKS Prater
HAUPT ALLEE
PRATER
A
CURIE ALLEE
PRATER STR
VALERIE STR
WHITTSBACH ST
VALERIE STR
SCHUTTEL STR
Sollen Brucke
LANDE
WEISSGARBER Strasse
Unt Weissgarber gasse
Adams gasse
OB WEISSGARBER STR
DAMPFSCHIFF STR
BIENARD G
GARTNER GASSE
KEGELN GASSE
MARXER GASSE
GUNTERE G
HIETH GASSE
RASUMOFSKY GASSE
VCHATIUS G
HORNSC
SENDL
CASSE
Invaliden Haus
Invaliden Str
ZUR FRANZENS BRUCKE
HINT ZOLLAMPT STR
VORD ZOLLAMT STR
Haupt Zollamb
A Bern Br
Stuben Ring
DOMINIKANER BASTEI
STUBEN B
KAISER JOSEF STR
GROSSE GASSE
GLOCKEN GASSE
FUHRMANG
FUHRMANS GASSE
GARTNER GASSE
ELOBACH G
SPRINGER G
RUJRR GASSE
PAZMANITEN GASSE
VERSINSKING
LESSINGER
VOLKER GASSE
DARWIN G
2
TABOR STRASSE
BRAZEN STRASSE
Schabenstand G Czernin
Zur Keisen Str
Lilienbrunn G
Herrn gasse
Brunn gasse
Ketten gasse
Ferdinands Brucke
K. K. Augarten
Au Gart

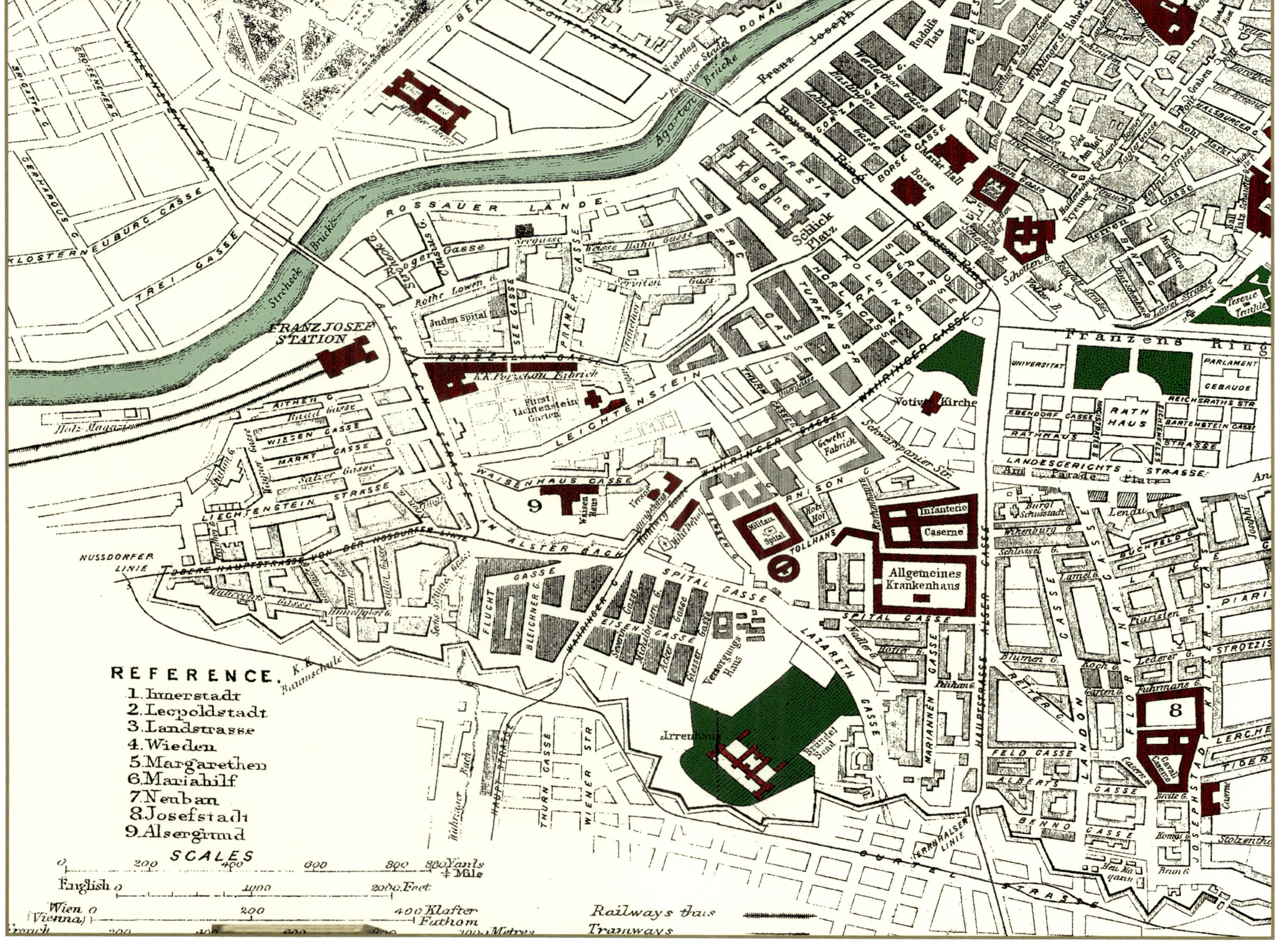

REFERENCE.
1. Innerstadt
2. Leopoldstadt
3. Landstrasse
4. Wieden
5. Margarethen
6. Mariahilf
7. Neuban
8. Josefstadt
9. Alsergrund
SCALES
English
Wien (Vienna)
French
Yards
Mile
Feet
Klafter
Fathom
Metres
Railways thus
Tramways
FRANZ JOSEF STATION
FRANZENS RING
UNIVERSITAT
PARLAMENT GEBAUDE
RATH HAUS
REICHSRATHS STR
LANDESGERICHTS STRASSE
Parade Platz
Votiv Kirche
Infanterie Caserne
Allgemeines Krankenhaus
Militair Spital
Tollhaus
Irrenhaus
Versorgungs Haus
Schick Platz
Rudolfs Platz
Börse
Börse
Market Hall
Juden Spital
Fürst Lichtenstein Garten
K.K. Porzellan Fabrik
Gewehr Fabrik
Waisen Haus
DONAU
ROSSAUER LÄNDE
Franz Joseph
LEICHTENSTEIN
WARINGER GASSE
SPITAL GASSE
LAZARETH GASSE
THERESIA
Kserne
SCHWARZSPANIER STR
WAISENHAUS GASSE
AN ALSTER BACH
LIECHTENSTEIN STRASSE
MARKT GASSE
WIESEN GASSE
SALZER GASSE
NUSSDORFER LINIE
Obere Hauptstrasse von der Nussdorfer Linie
KLOSTERNEUBURG GASSE
GERHARDUS G
FLUCHT GASSE
BLEICHNER G
THURN GASSE
WIENER STR
GURTEL STRASSE
FELD GASSE
FLORIANA GASSE
ALBERTS GASSE
LANDON GASSE
BENNO GASSE
LERCHEN
PIARISTEN GASSE
MARIANNEN GASSE
8
9

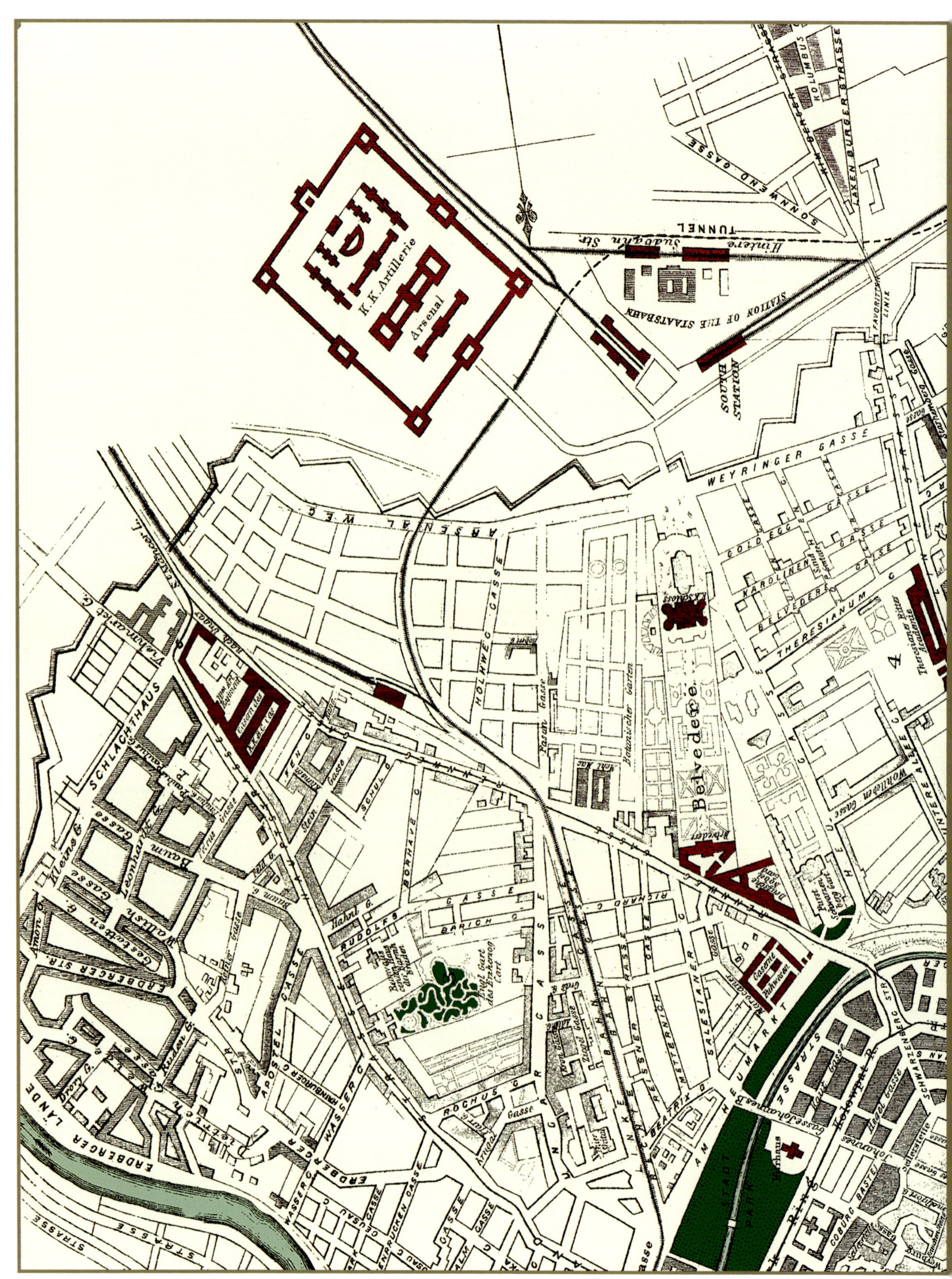
K.K.Artillerie
Arsenal
TUNNEL
Innere
Südbahn Str.
STATION OF THE STAATSBAHN
SÜDBAHN STATION
FAVORITEN LINIK
SONNWEND GASSE
KOLUMBUS GASSE
LAXEN BURGER STRASSE
WEYRINGER GASSE
GOLDEGG GASSE
KAROLINEN GASSE
BELVEDERE GASSE
THERESIANUM
Theresian. Ritter Academie
ARSENAL WEG
KOLHWEG GASSE
Paran Gasse
SCHLOSS
Botanischer Garten
Belvedere
Wollüth Gasse
UNTERE ALLEE
SCHLACHTHAUS
Viehmarkt
Hasenauer
Al. Koh-Tec.
SCHUL G.
BÖRHAVE G.
Hahn G.
BARICH G.
RUDOLFS
Lustgart des Erzherzog Carl
ROCHUS G. GASSE
UNGARGASSE
RICHARD G.
BEATRIX O.
REISSNER G.
METTERNICH G.
SALESIANER G.
AM HEUMARKT
STADT PARK
COBURG BASTEI
SCHWARZENBERG STR.
ERDBERGER STR.
ERDBERGER LÄNDE
STRASSE
WASSER G.
CUSAU GASSE
ENRPRICKEN GASSE
ALM GASSE
Kleine &
Gestettern G.
Baum G.
WALLISH
LINKE

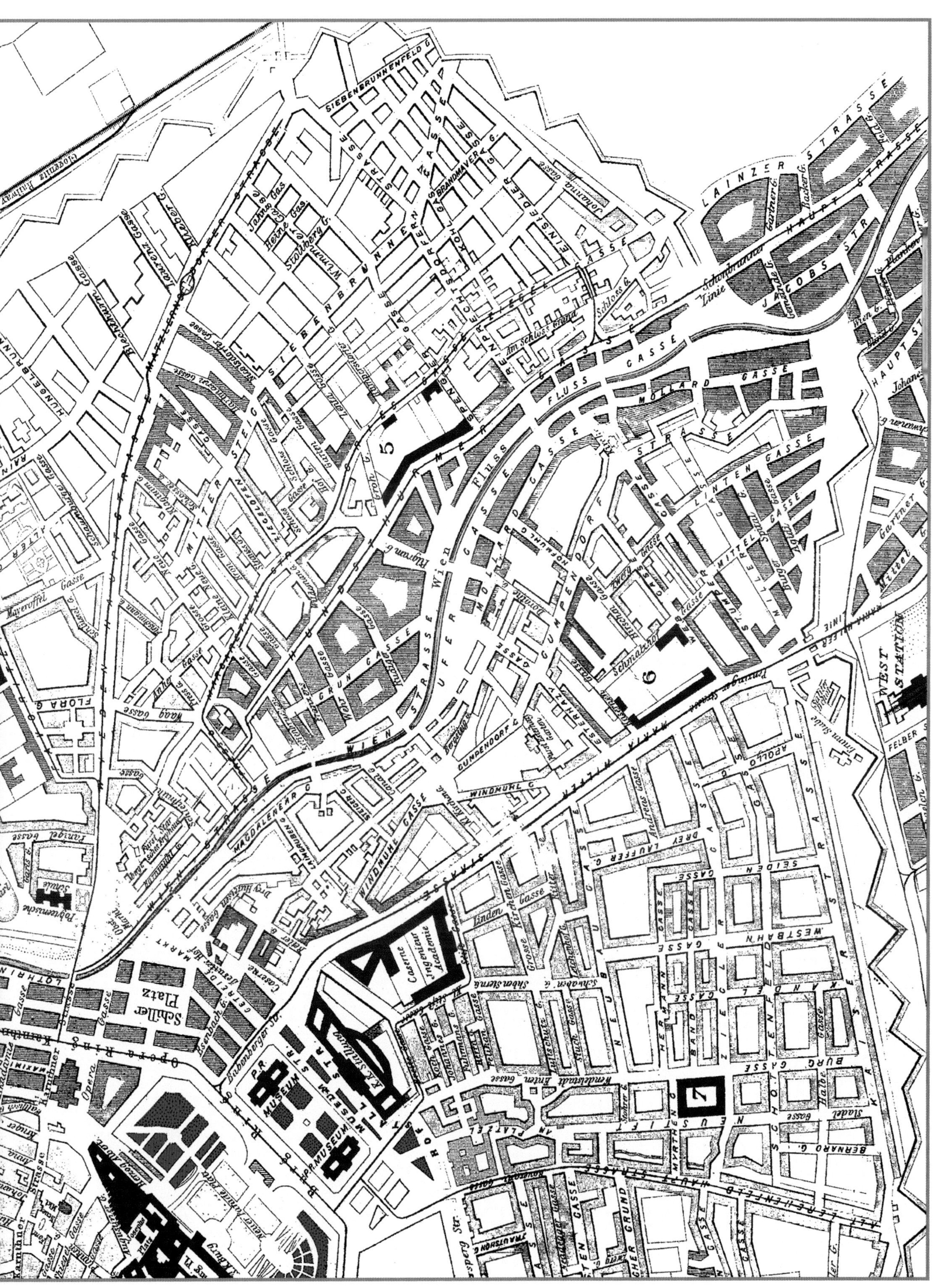

BRADSHAW'S
A MAP OF
Northern & Central Europe
WITH THE
RAILWAYS OPENED & IN PROGRESS
1853
EXPLANATION
Railways in operation Shown thus
do   in course of construction
SKAGERRACK
CATTEGAT
Christiania
Christiansand
Bergen
Holstein
Hamburg
London
Brussels
Paris
Orleans
Stutgard
Munich
Switzerland
Tyrol
Lyons
Besancon
Augsburg
Bordeaux
Perpignan
Montpellier
Turin
Milan
Florence
Tuscany
Piedmont
Rome
CORSICA
GULF OF GENOA
GULF OF LYONS
MEDITERRANEAN SEA
ENGLISH CHANNEL

GULF OF FINLAND
St Petersburg
Esthonia
Revel
Livonia
GULF OF RIGA
Riga
Courland
Vitersk
BALTIC SEA
Stockholm
Upsala
Gottland
Berlin
Dresden
Vienna
Hungary
Galicia
Transylvania
Poland
TURKEY
VENICE OR ADRIATIC SEA

Names of the States and Territories which for
want of space are marked on the Map with Nos

1 The States of the Emperor of Austria.
2 The States of the King of Prussia.
3 The Duchy of Mecklenburg.
4 The Duchy of Oldenburg.
5 The Duchy of Brunswick.
6 Belonging to Hanover.
7 Territories of Prince Lippe.
8 Principality of Waldeck.
9 Electorate of Hessen.
10 Grand-duchy of Hessen Darmstadt.
11 Duchy of Nassau.
12 Duchy of Hessen Homburg.
13 Luxemburg & Limburg.
14 Territories of the principality of Schwarzberg
15 Territories of the Grand-duchy & Duchy of Saxony
16 Territories of the Russian principalities.
17 Territories of the Duchy of Anhalt.
18 Belonging to Bavaria.
19 Grand-Duchy of Baden.
20 Territories of the Prince of Hohenzollern
21 Principality of Leichtenstein.
22 Frankfort a/m.
23 Bremen.
24 Hamburg.
25 Lubeck.
26 Cracow.

The Nos upon the line between two places show the distance from one
place to another in German Miles, without reference to the Countries, as
for example.

Vienna ⊛ —— 8 —— o Hainburg —— or 8 German Miles
Bologna o —— 7 —— o Ferrara —— or 7¾ German Miles
Bern o —— 4 —— o Solothurn —— or 4½ German Miles
Paris ⊛ —— 4 —— o Dammartin —— or 1¾ German Miles

5 German Miles equal to 1 English.

EXPLANATION OF THE MARKS

⊛ Capital Towns
◎ Towns in General.
o Smaller Towns & other places.
o. Forts & Fortified Towns.
~ Springs & Baths.
Steam Navigation upon Seas & Rivers.
Steam Track.
Connexion of the Principal & of the Post Roads

RAILWAYS
Railways opened & travelled upon.
Still being constructed.

Bradshaw & Blacklock 27 Brown St Manchester & 59 Fleet St London

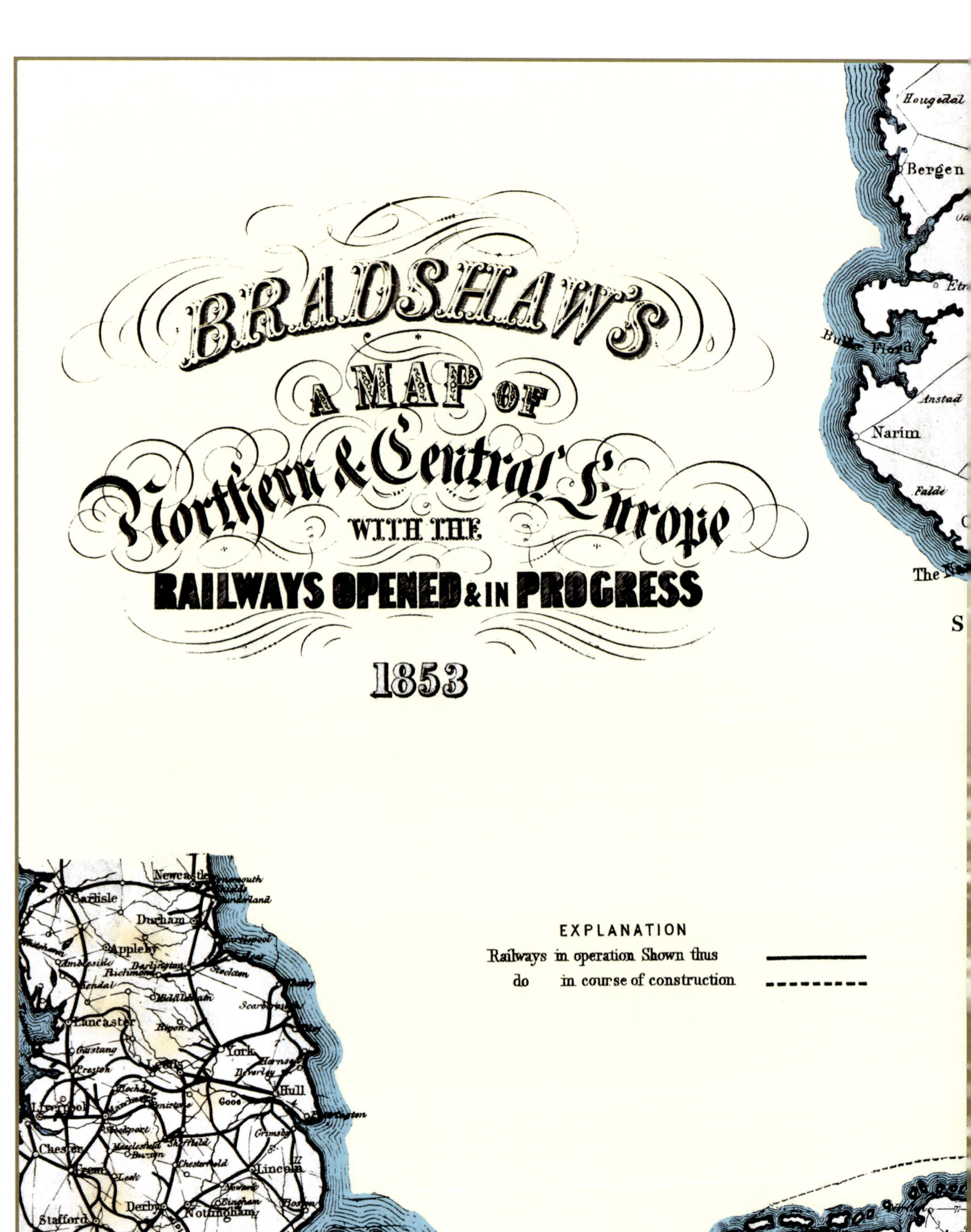

BRADSHAW'S
A MAP OF
Northern & Central Europe
WITH THE
RAILWAYS OPENED & IN PROGRESS
1853
EXPLANATION
Railways in operation Shown thus
do in course of construction
Hougedal
Bergen
Narim
Anstad
Falde
Carlisle
Newcastle
Durham
Appleby
Ambleside
Richmond
Darlington
Kendal
Stockton
Middleham
Scarborough
Lancaster
Garstang
Ripon
Preston
Leeds
York
Hornsea
Beverley
Rochdale
Hull
Liverpool
Penistone
Goole
Chester
Sheffield
Grimsby
Macclesfield
Buxton
Chesterfield
Lincoln
Crewe
Leek
Newark
Stafford
Derby
Bingham
Boston
Nottingham
Shrewsbury
Oakham
Wolverhampton
Stafford
Lynn
Birmingham
Leicester
Peterborough
Dereham
Worcester
Coventry
Norwich
Rugby
England
Yarmouth
Cheltenham
Harleston
Northampton
Newmarket
Lowestoft
Buckingham
Norfolk
Stroud
Cambridge
Bury St Edmonds
Gloucester
Aylesbury
Royston
Ipswich
Oxford
Colchester
Bristol
Bath
Bradford
Reading
Rochester
Devizes
Maidstone
Canterbury
Salisbury
Guildford
Ashford
Winchester
Southampton
London
Groningen
Delfzyl
Leeuwarden
Harlingen
Assen
Alkmaar
Hoorn
Koevoorden
Kampen
Zwolle
Lingen
Amsterdam
Haarlem
Deventer
Holt
Amersfoort
Rhein
Haag
Delft
Utrecht
Arnheim
Rotterdam
Nymwegen
Emmerich
Munster
Dordrecht
Cleve
Wesel
Bergen Zoom
Breda
DenBosch
Hertogen
busch
Hamm
Ostende
Dortmund

Hauge
Ojer
Hanebio
Gelle
n
Ousserangen
Diona
Aal
Hoff
Aaasnæs
Transtrand
Mora
Naas
Fahin
Orange
Grisselhamn
Opdal
Oran
Sala
Lawen
Houg
Nyy
c
Upsala
Deli
Drammen
Konsvinger
Philipstad
Westeras
Previg
Christiania
Fedet
Stockholm
Hvideso
Konsberg
Arrika
Carlstadt
Nora
d
Nylte
Moss
Holmedal
Orebro
Krageroe
Frederikshald
Wiby
Trosa
Osterrisom
Stromstad
Askersund
Nykoping
Arendal
Holm
Mariestadt
Christiansand
Venensborg
Ledkoping
Linkoping
Gusum
KAGERRACK
Falkoping
Gottenburg
Jonkoping
Tornsvalla
Westevick
CATTEGAT
Hongsbacka
Gallstad
Ekesjo
Eladstrand
Borglun
W
Borg
Ammekalla
Hals
Warberg
Lenholm
Aby
Aalborg
Falkenburg
Lenhofda
Mariage
Unnary
Wexio
Wiborg
e
Holstebroe
Randers
Halmstadt
Torsas
Kalmar
Aarhus
Torsas
Hapholme
Lille Hollum
Engelholm
Onsby
Carlscrona
Farum
Horsens
Helsingborg
Sweden
Carlscrona
Varde
Veile
Helsingor
Christianstadt
Carlshamn
Gottland
Friedericia
Holbeck
Zeeland
Copenhagen
Hoppy
Kolding
Ringsted
Malmo
BALTIC S
Rube
Odense
Funen
Cimrisham
Hadersleben
Nyborg
k
Istad
L. Bornholm
Wanerhuus
Tondern
Swendborg
D
Ronno
Swanike
Flensburg
L. Femern
Kerding
Lauenburg
Schleswig
Stolpe
Danzig
Fredericstadt
Kosln
Holstein
Stralsund
Kolberg
Bulow
Rendsburg
Neumunster
Rostock
Greifswald
Cuxhaven
Riebot
Travem
Wismar
Butzow
Wollin
Naugard
Schiefelbein
W
Cuxhaven
Gluckstadt
Lubeck
Schwerin
Gustrow
Stettin
Drin
Alto
Hamburg
Malchin
Dam
Tuchel
Bremervorde
Harburg
Bergedorf
Ludwigslust
Ne Strelitz
Locknitz
Friedland
4
Bremen
Luneburg
Fronzlow
Naugard
Stargard
Oldenburg
Rothenburg
Perleberg
Gransee
Angermunde
Schwelt
Konigsborg
Landsburg
Bromberg Weil
Hanover
Celle
Stendal
Berlin
Posen
Brunswick
Magdeburg
Potsdam
Frankfort
2
Kastrin
Hildesheim
Dessau
Kottbus
Gulben
Lissa
Paderborn
Nordheim

Kumo
Tavastgus
Nistad
Leviza
Fredrikssan
Dransinikeva
Portas
Borgo
St Petersburg
Aho
Salo
Helsingfors
Houty
Pomerania
Eknas
GULF OF FINLAND
Peretschie
Dolgeivka
Arad1
Kagal
Eve
Taranie
Novgarod
Revel
Revel
Esthonia
Ober Palen
Budney
Dago
Ongar
Fellin
Dorpt
Borovitchi
Idefer
Talce Virtzerv
Pernau
Oezel
Pskov
Livonia
Gulben
Ostrov
Kibris
Ragugof
Pasher
GULF OF RIGA
Venden
Launzen
Kokenzfer
R u V i t e r s k
Goldinger
Talzen
Riga
Lieutzin
Luzenpol
Mitan
Agitza
Sebej
Courland
Bartau
Poplelan
Pompieli
Dvinaburg
Chaty
Shavti
Telsze
Szwale
EA
Poniewiesh
Vossiany
Polengen
Rossiana
Wilkomir
Swenzany
Memel
Keydany
Schwarzen
Tauroggen
Nissben
Kowno
Rositten
Wilna
Sartau
Tilsef
Labiau
Stallupohnen
Maryampol
Konigsburg
Insterburg
Kalwary
Pillau
Braunsberg
Goldapp
Dzietzov
Elbing
Angerburg
Olezko
Raszky
Dirschau
Pr Holland
Lyck
Grodno
Marienburg
Cutkstadt
Ayrs
Raygorod
Kaminshka
Ozerode
Willenberg
Solcelka
Monim
Marienwerder
Szzzuzzyn
Witkopisk
Rushana
Graudenz
Neidenburg
Lopica
Bialystok
Strassburg
Mlawa
Ostrotenka
Bielsk
Prushana
Thorn
Stirpe
Nur
Lipno
Pultusk
Drohiczyn
Kobrin
Brzesc
Plock
Drohiczyn
Gombin
Wyszogrod
Warsaw
Brzesc Litewsky
Krasniewice
Sochatzow
Siedlev
Rathe
Czortozere
Olvek
Onurg
Lowicz
Gora
Garwolin
Poland
Warta
Rawa
Kozienicz
Mogilno
Koide
GULF OF

Names of the States and Territories which for
want of space are marked on the Map with Nos
1 The States of the Emperor of Austria.
2 The States of the King of Prussia.
3 The Duchy of Mecklenburg.
4 The Duchy of Oldenburg.
5 The Duchy of Brunswick.
6 Belonging to Hanover.
7 Territories of Prince Lippe.
8 Principality of Waldeck.
9 Electorate of Hessen.
10 Grand-duchy of Hessen Darmstadt.
11 Duchy of Nassau.
12 Duchy of Hessen Homburg.
13 Luxemburg & Limburg.
14 Territories of the principality of Schwarzberg.
15 Territories of the Grand-duchy & Duchy of Saxony.
16 Territories of the Russian principalities.
17 Territories of the Duchy of Anhalt.
18 Belonging to Bavaria.
19 Grand-Duchy of Baden.
20 Territories of the Prince of Hohenzollern.
21 Principality of Leichtenstein.
22 Frankfort o/m.
23 Bremen.
24 Hamburg.
25 Lubeck.
26 Cracow.

ENGLISH CHANNEL
Brussels
Calais
Malines
Namur
Liege
Aix la Chapelle
Bonn
Coblenz
Luxembourg
Trier
Metz
Nancy
Strassburg
Colmar
Freiburg
Paris
Versailles
Rouen
Havre
Caen
Amiens
Rheims
Verdun
Chalons
Troyes
Dijon
Besancon
Bale
Orleans
Tours
Angers
Bourges
Nevers
Macon
Bourg
Geneva
Lausanne
Bern
Lucerne
SWITZ
Poitiers
Limoges
Clermont Ferrand
Lyons
Chambery
Grenoble
Turin
Piedmont
Bordeaux
Perigueux
Cahors
Le Puy
Valence
Montelimart
Novara
Toulouse
Montauban
Auch
Nismes
Avignon
Marseilles
Toulon
Perpignan
Montpellier
Cette
GULF of LYONS
Gerona
Lerida
MEDITERRANEAN S
GULF of

Dresden
Breslau
Vienna
Presburg
Munich
Stutgard
Frankfurt
Darmstad
Carlsruhe
Salzburg
Gratz
Klagenfurt
Villach
Laibach
Agram
Trieste
Fiume
Zara
Milan
Brescia
Verona
Mantua
Padua
Bologna
Ravenna
Florence
Leghorn
Livorno
Sienna
Ancona
Rome
Teramo
Chieti
Aquila
Tyrol
Bohemia
Tuscany
Parma
Modena
GENOA
TURKEY
GULF OF VENICE OR ADRIATIC SEA

EXPLANATION OF THE MARKS

Capital Towns
Towns in General.
Smaller Towns & other places.
Forts & Fortified Towns.
Springs & Baths.
Steam Navigation upon Seas & Rivers.
Steam Track.
Connexion of the Principal & of the Post Roads

RAILWAYS

Railways opened & travelled upon.
Still being constructed.

The Nos upon the line between two places show the distance from one
place to another in German Miles, without reference to the Countries, as
for example.

Vienna   8   Hamburg   — or   8   German Miles
Bologna   7   Ferrara   — or   7¼   German Miles
Bern   4   Solothurn   — or   4½   German Miles
Paris   4   Damstin   — or   1¾   German Miles

5 German Miles equal to 2 English.

Galicia and Lodomir
HUNGARY
Transylvania
TURKEY

Czentochau
Cracow
Lemberg
Przemysl
Sambor
Stanislawow
Czernowitz
Chotim
Jassy
Schemnitz
Waitzen
Ofen
Pesth
Debrezin
Szolnok
Szegedin
Theresiopel
Arad
Gross Wardein
Clausenburg
Karlsburg
Hermanstadt
Cronstadt
Peterwardein
Temesvar

THE WORLD
ON MERCATORS PROJECTION
SWEDEN & NORWAY
ATLANTIC OCEAN
BAY OF BISCAY
NORTH SEA
ENGLISH CHANNEL
MEDITERRANEAN
MOROCCO
ALGERIA
TRIPOLI
BRADSHAW'S
RAILWAY MAP OF EUROPE
BY J. BARTHOLOMEW, F.R.G.S.
Scale of English Miles
Scale of Kilometres
EXPLANATIONS
Main lines of Railways shewn thus
Other lines of Railways shewn thus
Boundaries of Countries shewn thus
The Figures printed thus (25) over the surface of the Map refer to the Pages in the Guide
where the Trains on that particular Line of Railway may be found.
FROM BRADSHAW'S CON
JULY

GULF OF FINLAND
Lake Ladoga
ST PETERSBURG
Wologda
Gulf of Riga
MOSCOW
KÖNIGSBERG
WILNA
WARSAW
Kiev
CASPIAN SEA
Astrahan
Mouths of the Volga
SEA OF AZOV
CRIMEA
CAUCASUS MOUNTAINS
M Elbrus
Tiflis
BLACK SEA
Varna
BUCHAREST
SERVIA
BULGARIA
TURKEY
Adrianople
CONSTANTINOPLE
SEA OF MARMORA
Smyrna
TURKEY IN ASIA
GREECE
Crete or Candia
Cyprus
SEA
BARCA
Mouths of the Nile
ALEXANDRIA
PORT SAID
EGYPT
SUEZ
MEDITERRANEAN SEA
PORT SAID
CAIRO
SUEZ
ISTHMUS OF SUEZ
Arabian Desert
Libyan Desert
ARABIA PETRÆA
GULF OF SUEZ (RED SEA)
Plain of Sinai
ASSIOUT
EGYPT
English Miles

THE WORLD
ON MERCATORS PROJECTION

SWEDEN & NORWAY
English Miles
ATLANTIC OCEAN
NORTH SEA
BALTIC SEA
GULF OF BOTHNIA
Arctic Circle
NORTH CAPE
Tromsö
Lofoden Islands
Mael Strom
LAPLAND
Bodö
Sulitelma
Saltdal
Gellivara
Jockmock
Mo
Vegen
Bronö
Sörsele
Torefors
Haparanda
Tornea
Namsos
Asele
Ratan
Umea R.
Christiansund
Throndhjem
Storlien
Storen
Melhus
Singsaas
Molde
Sundal
Östersund
Ragunda
Bracke
Hernösand
Sundsvall
Aalesund
Roros
Ange
Horningdal
Tonset
Hanestad
Sarna
Ljusdal
Hudiksvall
Christinestad
Förde
Kopping
Rollnas
Söderhamn
Bjorneborg
Sogne Fj.
Lillehammer
Rena
Siljan L.
Ocklebo
Gefle
Vosse
Bergen
Hamar
Innsjön
Borlänge
Fahlun
Aland
Abo
Odde
Randsfjord
Kroderen
Edeback
Sala
Upsala
Hango
Haugesund
Saude
Drammen
Charlottenberg
Herrljunga
Uttersberg
STOCKHOLM
Dagö
Stavanger
Christiania
Kongsverg
Sandvig
Sarpsborg
Christinehamn
Örebro
Nyköping
Ösel
Skien
Eda
Otterbacken
Norrköping
Kragerö
Nandnes
Nsrbo
Egersund
Mariestad
Arendal
Mjölby
Westervik
Gothland
Flekkefjord
Mandal
Christiansand
Uddevalla
Wadstena
Wisby
Farsund
Lindesnes
SKAGER RACK
Skagen
GOTHENBURG
Jönköping
Wexjö
Winngicby
Oscarshamn
Hense
Fredrikshavn
Svenljunga
Multsred
Säfsjöstrom
Kalmar
Liban
Thisted
Warberg
Carlscrona
KATTEGAT
Halmstad
Jyby
Struer
Holstebro
Dolmen Wisland
Karlshamn
Bornholm
Ringkjöbing
Skien
Aarhus
Elsinore
Skanderborg
COPENHAGEN
Christiansstad
Malmö
Fredericia
Kolding
Ribe
Veile
Svendborg
Nexö
Esbjerg
Nykjöbing
Ringsen
Nestved
Trälleborg
Husumedsund
VIENNA
Nuenstadt
INNSBRUCK
AUSTRIA
TYROL
Brenner Pass
Meran
Botzen
Villach
Klagenfurt
Marburg

Lake Ladoga
GULF OF FINLAND
Gulf of Riga
ST PETERSBURG
MOSCOW
WARSAW
POLAND
HUNGARY
ODESSA
BUDA PESTH
CRACOW
Kiev
Kursk
Orel
Smolensk
Witebsk
Riga
Reval
Pskov
Novgorod
Rybinsk
Twer
Klin
Rschewo
Bologoje
Kaluga
Mohilew
Minsk
Pinsk
Brest Litewski
Lemberg
Czernowitz
Balta
Nikolaev
Kherson
Taganrog
Ekaterinoslav
Kremenschug
Poltava
Romney
Sumy
Bjelopolje
Konotop
Tchernigov
Gomel
Starodub
Bobruisk
Mosyr
Rowno
Kowel
Lublin
Radom
Iwangorod
Siedlec
Bialistock
Grodno
Wilna
Kowno
Königsberg
Insterburg
Tilsit
Memel
Libau
Mitau
Dünaburg
Polozk
Swentsiany
Minsk

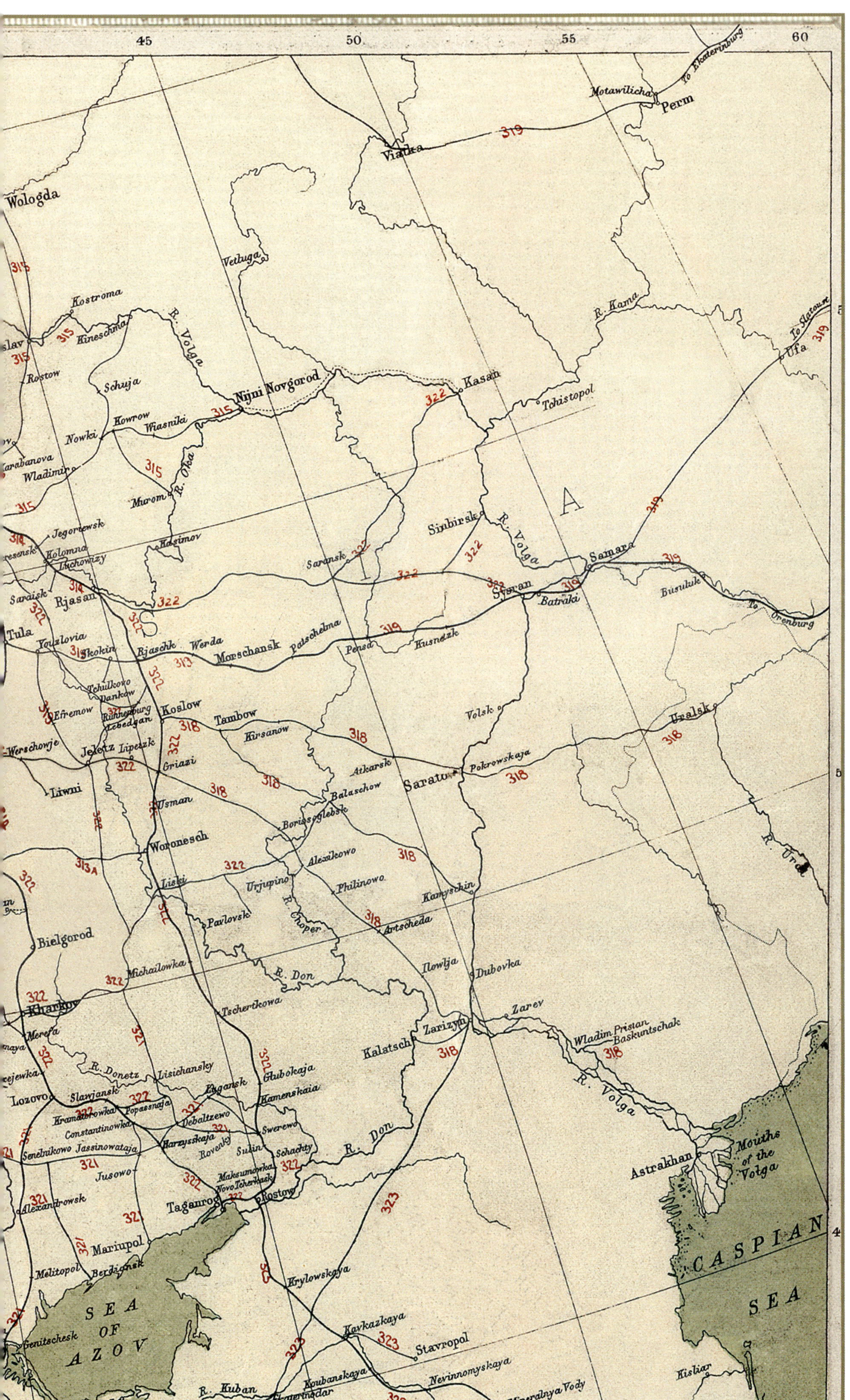

45
50
55
60
Motawilicha
Perm
To Ekaterinburg
319
Viatka
Wologda
Vetluga
R. Kama
To Slatoust
Ufa
319
Kostroma
Kineschma
R. Volga
315
Schuja
Nijni Novgorod
Kasan
322
Tchistopol
slav
315
Rostow
Nowki
Kowrow
Wiasniki
315
A
Karabanova
Wladimir
R. Oka
Murom
315
Sinbirsk
R. Volga
Samara
319
315
Jegorjewsk
Kasimov
Saransk
322
322
319
Kolomna
Tuchowizy
Saransk
322
Sisran
382
To Orenburg
Saraisk
Rjasan
322
Batraki
310
Busuluk
314
Tula
Youzlovia
Rjaschk
Werda
Morschansk
Patschelma
Pensa
Kusnezk
319
Skokin
313
Tchulkowo
Dankow
Volsk
Uralsk
Efremow
Koslow
318
Tambow
318
Ranenburg
Lebedjan
Kirsanow
318
Jeletz
Lipezk
322
Griazi
Atkarsk
Pokrowskaja
318
372
318
Saratow
318
Liwni
Usman
318
Balaschow
Woronesch
Borissoglebsk
322
Alexikowo
318
Liski
Urjupino
Philinowo
Kamyschin
R. Ural
313A
Pawlowsk
R. Choper
318
Artscheda
Bielgorod
R. Don
Ilowlja
Dubovka
322
Michailowka
Zarev
Kharkow
322
Tschertkowa
Zarizyn
Wladim Pristan
Baskuntschak
Merefa
321
Kalatsch
318
321
R. Donetz
Lisichansky
Glubokaja
318
Lozowo
Slawjansk
327
Lugansk
Kamenskaia
R. Volga
Kramatorowka
Popassnaja
Debaltzewo
Swerewo
Constantinowka
321
R. Don
Senelnikowo
Jassinowataja
Harzyskaja
Sulin
Schachty
321
Rowenky
Astrakhan
Mouths
of the
Volga
Jusowo
Maksumowka
322
Novo Tcherkask
Alexandrowsk
Taganrog
Rostow
321
322
Mariupol
323
321
Melitopol
Berdjansk
CASPIAN
Krylowskaja
Genitschesk
SEA
SEA
OF
AZOV
Kavkazkaya
Stavropol
323
323
Nevinnomyskaya
R. Kuban
Koubanskaya
Mineralnya Vody
Kislar
Ekaterinodar
323

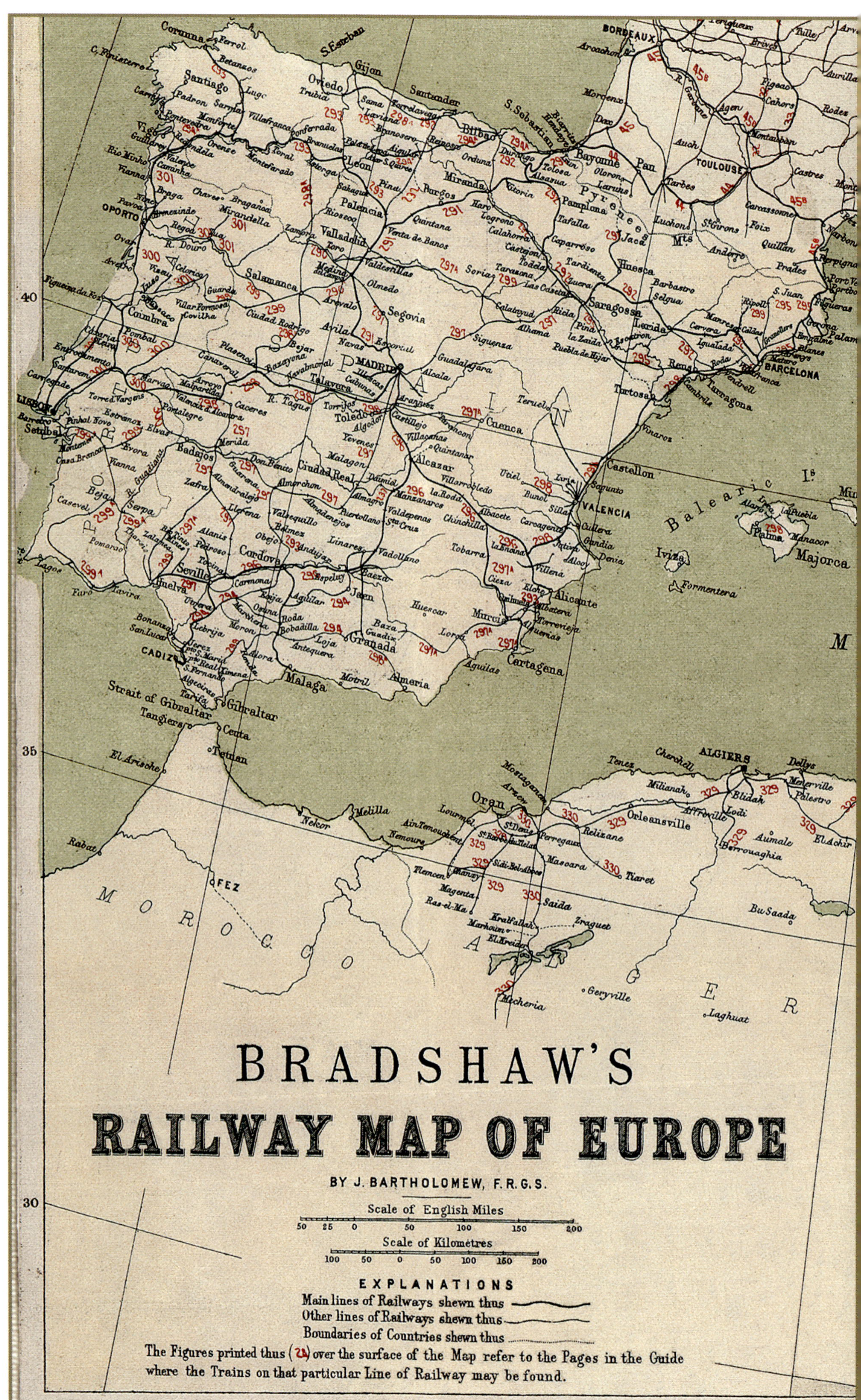

BRADSHAW'S
RAILWAY MAP OF EUROPE
BY J. BARTHOLOMEW, F.R.G.S.
Scale of English Miles
Scale of Kilometres
EXPLANATIONS
Main lines of Railways shewn thus
Other lines of Railways shewn thus
Boundaries of Countries shewn thus
The Figures printed thus (24) over the surface of the Map refer to the Pages in the Guide
where the Trains on that particular Line of Railway may be found.

CRIM
Sebastopol
Balaclava
BLAC
BLACK SEA
Szegedin
Arad
Temesvar
Belgrade
SERVIA
ROUMANIA
BUCHAREST
Galatz
Braila
Tultcha
Mouths of the Danube
Serpents I.
Kronstadt
Hermannstadt
Focsani
Tchernavoda
Silistria
Mangalia
Kustendje
Varna
Balchik
BULGARIA
Shumla
Rustchuck
Giurgevo
Nicopoli
Sistova
Rasgrad
Tirnova
Pravadj
Widin
Rahova
Caracal
Nisch
Pirot
Sofia
Balkan Mts
Slivno
Jamboli
Burgas
MONTENEGRO
Cetinge
Novibasar
Leskowatz
Mitrowica
Pristina
Vranja
Kostendil
Ichtiman
EASTERN ROUMELIA
Eski Saghra
TURKEY
Uskub
Racanik
Saremba
Philippolis
Tirnova
Adrianople
Midia
Bender
Keuprulu
Shtiplic
Mustafa Pacha
Kuleli Bourgas
Little Burgas
Tchorlou
Bosphorus
Demir Kapsu
Demotika
Uzun Keupri
Tchataldje
CONSTANTINOPLE
Scutari
Ismid
Ochrida
Mironce
Seres
Kavala
Bidikli
Rodosto
S. Stephano
Ismid
Ghevgheli
Enos
SEA OF MARMORA
Mudania
Brussa
Monastir
Salonica
Thasos
Gallipoli
Chanak Kalessi
Biledjik
Eskishehr
Durazzo
Valona
Gulf of Salonica
Mt Olympus
Embros
Dardan
Lemnos
Edirmid
Kutaya
Angos
taranto
Kalabak
Janina
Larissa
Trikkala
Volo
Aiwaly
Mitylene
Pergamos
Somali
TURKEY
Alayund Jn.
Akshehr
Tchivri
Dinair
Corfu
Arta
Pharsala
Sporades
Skyros
Chios
SMYRNA
Bournabat
Baindir
Odemish
Seraikeuy
St Maura
GREECE
Missolongi
Lepanto
Mt Parnassus
Euboea
Chalcis
Thiva
Turbali
Tireh
Aidin
Nazli
Cephallonia
Patras
Kiaton
Megara
ATHENS
Andros
Ephesus
Scalanova
Samos
Zante
Corinth
Piraeus
Syra
Hermopolis
Catacolo
MOREA
Naxos
G. of Kos
Adalia
Arcadia
Kalamata
Sparta
Cyclades
Rhodes
Levisi
Navarino
C. Malia
Cerigo
C. Matapan
Karpathos
Cerigotto
Crete or Candia
N
SEA
Cyrene
G. of Bomba
Bengazi
BARCA
G. of Milh
G. of Bousheidah
Mouths of the
Rosetta
Damietta
ALEXANDRIA
of Sidra
Scibinvel
EG

MEDITERRANEAN SEA
CAUCASUS MOUNTAINS
Mt Elbruz
Mt Kasbec
Dariel Pass
Vladikavkas
Petrovsk
Mordon
R. Terek
Prochladnaya
Feodosia
Anapa
Novorossusk
Yalta
Livadia
Simferopol
K SEA
Gagri
Sukum Kale
Poti
Batoum
Sinope
Ineboli
Tereboli
Trebizond
Kutais
Samtredi
Rion
Kvirilla
Suram
Gori
Tiflis
Bejatubam
Akstafa
R. Kur
To Baku
Elisavetopol
Kars
Erivan
Mt Ararat
R. Aras
Erzeroum
N ASIA
Konieh
Adana
Tarsus
Mersina
Alexandretta
(Iskenderun)
Antioch
Latakieh
Cyprus
Levkosia
Famagusta
Larnaca
Tripoli
Mt Lebanon
Beirut
Acre
Jaffa
Jerusalem
Gaza
PORT SAID
El Arish
Kantara
Salahieh
Zagazig
Ismailia
CAIRO
SUEZ
ALEXANDRIA
ABOUKIR
Aboukir Bay
Ramleh
ROSETTA
Rosetta Mouth
Fort Bowler
Lake Bourlos
Damietta Mouth
DAMIETTA
Deirch
PORT SAID
Lake Menzaleh
Beschit
Kafr Cheik
Shirbin
Talka
Mansourah
SUEZ CANAL
Ft Tineh
El Kaufar
DAMANHOUR
Kaliub
Mehallet el Kebir
Samanhood
Tel el Baroud
Mehallet Roh
Abu Shaik
Kantara
Ballah Lakes
Kafr Ousit
TANTA
Sinbalawin
Norbel
Salahieh
ISTHMUS of SUEZ
Zifte
Abu
Kebir
Tericb
Shibin el Com
ZAGAZIG
Mit Gharb
Tel el Kebir
Norishe
L. Timsah
El Tavraneh
Benha
Bordein
ISMAILIA
Arabian Desert
Natron Lakes
Wardan
Shibin-el-Kanater
Bilbès
Faid
Great Bitter Lakes
Gallioub
Abbasiyeh
Geneffe
Boulak-Dakrur
CAIRO
Shalouffa
Gizeh
Turah
Baths of Helvan
SUEZ
Pyramids
Helvan
Port Ibrahim
ARABIA
Bedreshein
Ras Atakeh
PETRÆA
El Matanieh
Birket el Kerun
Tamieh
GULF OF SUEZ (RED SEA)
Abouxa
Medinet el Fayoume
Wasta
Libyan Desert
River Nile
Bemsouef
Bibbe
Feshn
Wady Araba
Melatieh
Plain
of
Senhur
Megaga
Behnesseh
Abu Girgeh
Samalloot
Minieh
Beni Hassan
Dalgeh
Melawi el Arish
Deyrout
Mero
Manfalut
EGYPT
Arab Hatem
ASSIOUT
R. Nile
English Miles

ENVIRONS OF
PARIS
BRADSHAW'S
RAILWAY MAP
OF
CENTRAL EUROPE
BY J. BARTHOLOMEW, F.R.G.S.
Scale of English Miles
Scale of Kilometres
NORTH SEA
ENGLISH CHANNEL
BAY OF
BISCAY
FRANCE
SPAIN
MEDITERRANEAN SEA
PARIS
LONDON
CHERBOURG
REIMS
ORLEANS
NANTES
ANGERS
TOURS
LA ROCHELLE
ROCHEFORT
BORDEAUX
TOULOUSE
LYONS
GENEVA
TURIN
MARSEILLE
TOULON
BARCELONA
CORSICA
AMSTERDAM
ROTTERDAM
UTRECHT
STRASBOURG
SWITZERLAND
FROM BRADSHAW'S CON
JULY

BALTIC SEA
Gulf of Danzig
COPENHAGEN
HAMBURG
BERLIN
HANOVER
MAGDEBURG
LEIPZIG
DRESDEN
BRESLAU
WARSAW
POLAND
RUSSIA
WILNA
KÖNIGSBERG
DANTZIG
G E R M A N Y
MUNICH
VIENNA
BUDA PESTH
A U S T R I A
TYROL
H U N G A R Y
TRIESTE
VENICE
I T A L Y
BOLOGNA
FLORENCE
Apennines
ADRIATIC SEA
BOSNIA
SERVIA
Belgrade
ROME
EXPLANATIONS.
Main lines of Railways shewn thus
Other lines of Railways shewn thus
The Figures printed thus (24) over the surface of the
Map refer to the Pages in the Guide where the trains
on that particular Line of Railway may be found.
Boundaries of Countries shewn thus

PARIS
Scale of Miles
ENGLISH CHANNEL
Bristol Channel
LONDON
PARIS
S. DENIS
VERSAILLES
VINCENNES
CHERBOURG
BREST
Channel Islands

BRADSHAW'S
RAILWAY MAP
OF
CENTRAL EUROPE
BY J. BARTHOLOMEW, F.R.G.S.
Scale of English Miles
Scale of Kilometres
NORTH SEA
AMSTERDAM
ROTTERDAM
The Hague
Hoek van Holland
Haarlem
Leyden
Gouda
UTRECHT
Arnheim
Groningen
Leeuwarden
Zwolle
Oldenburg
Osnabruck
Munster
Cuxhaven
Heligoland
Cologne
Dusseldorf
Bonn
Coblenz
FRANKFORT
AIX-LA-CHAPELLE
BRUSSELS
ANTWERP
GHENT
Bruges
Ostende
Maastricht
LIEGE
Namur
Mons
Cambrai
Calais
Dunkirk
Dover
LILLE
Valenciennes
Sedan
METZ
Treves
Luxemburg
REIMS
Chalons
Epernay
Soissons
Compiegne
Amiens
Arras
PARIS
Norwich
Yarmouth
Harwich

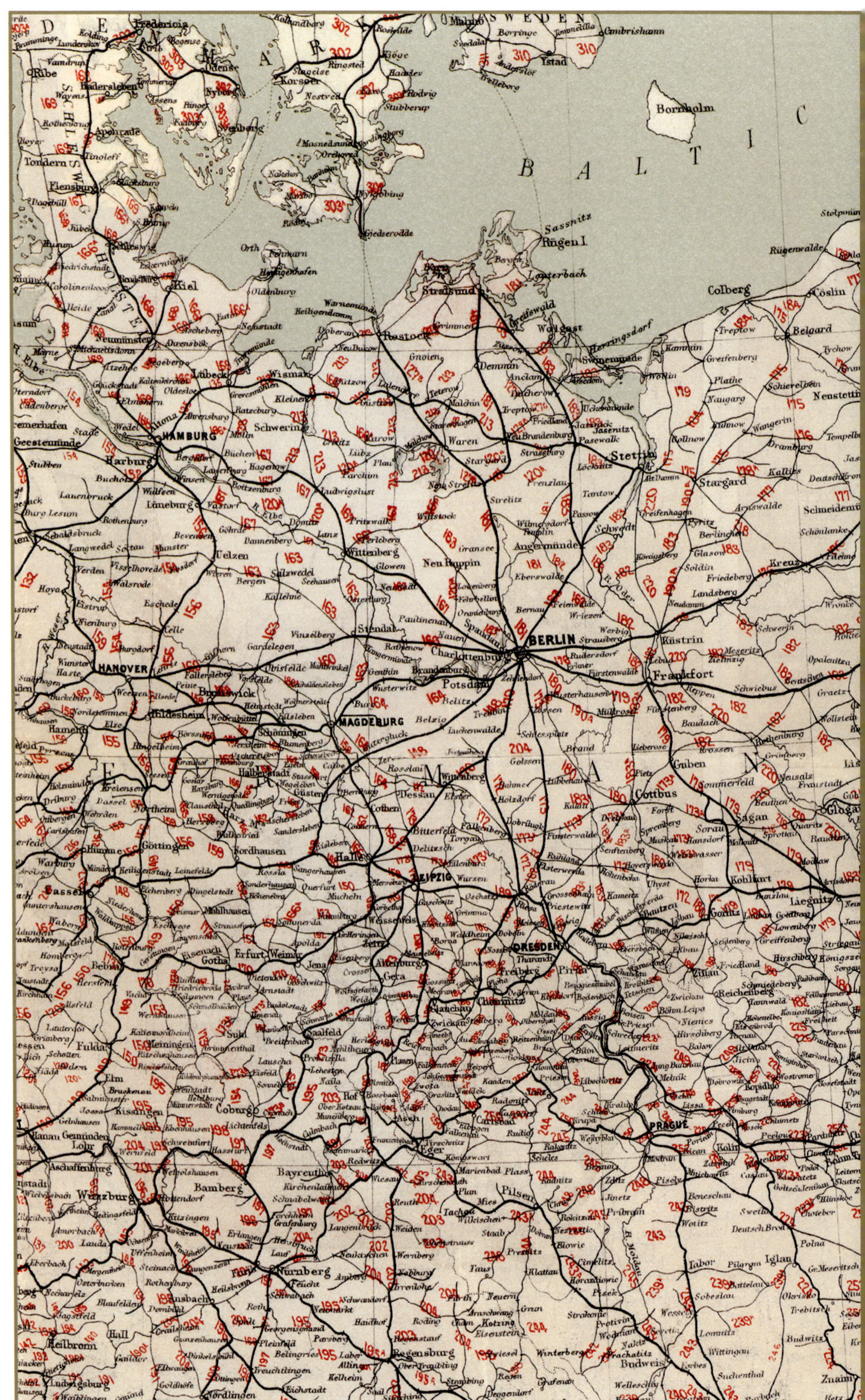

SEA
Gulf of Dantzic
Kurisches Haff
Frisches Haff
R. Niemen
POLAND
RUSSIA
WARSAW
Praga
KÖNIGSBERG
DANTZIC
BRESLAU
CRACOW
Posen
Stolp
Thorn
Bromberg
Grodno
Bialistock
Brest Litewski
Lublin
Chelm
Ivangorod
Radom
Lodz
Przemysl
Tarnow
Kaschau
Ungvar
Munkacs

BAY OF
BISCAY
LARCHELLE
ROCHEFORT
BORDEAUX
Bayonne
Biarritz
Bilbao
S. Sebastian
TOULOUSE
NANTES
LE MANS
ORLEANS
TOURS
ANGERS
Poitiers
Niort
Angouleme
Limoges
Tulle
Brives
Perigueux
Bergerac
Agen
Montauban
Cahors
Rodez
Villefranche
Albi
Castres
Carcassonne
Foix
Andorra
Pamplona
Miranda
Pyrenees
Mts
Pic du Midi
9465
Mt Perdu
10,998
F R A
S P A I N

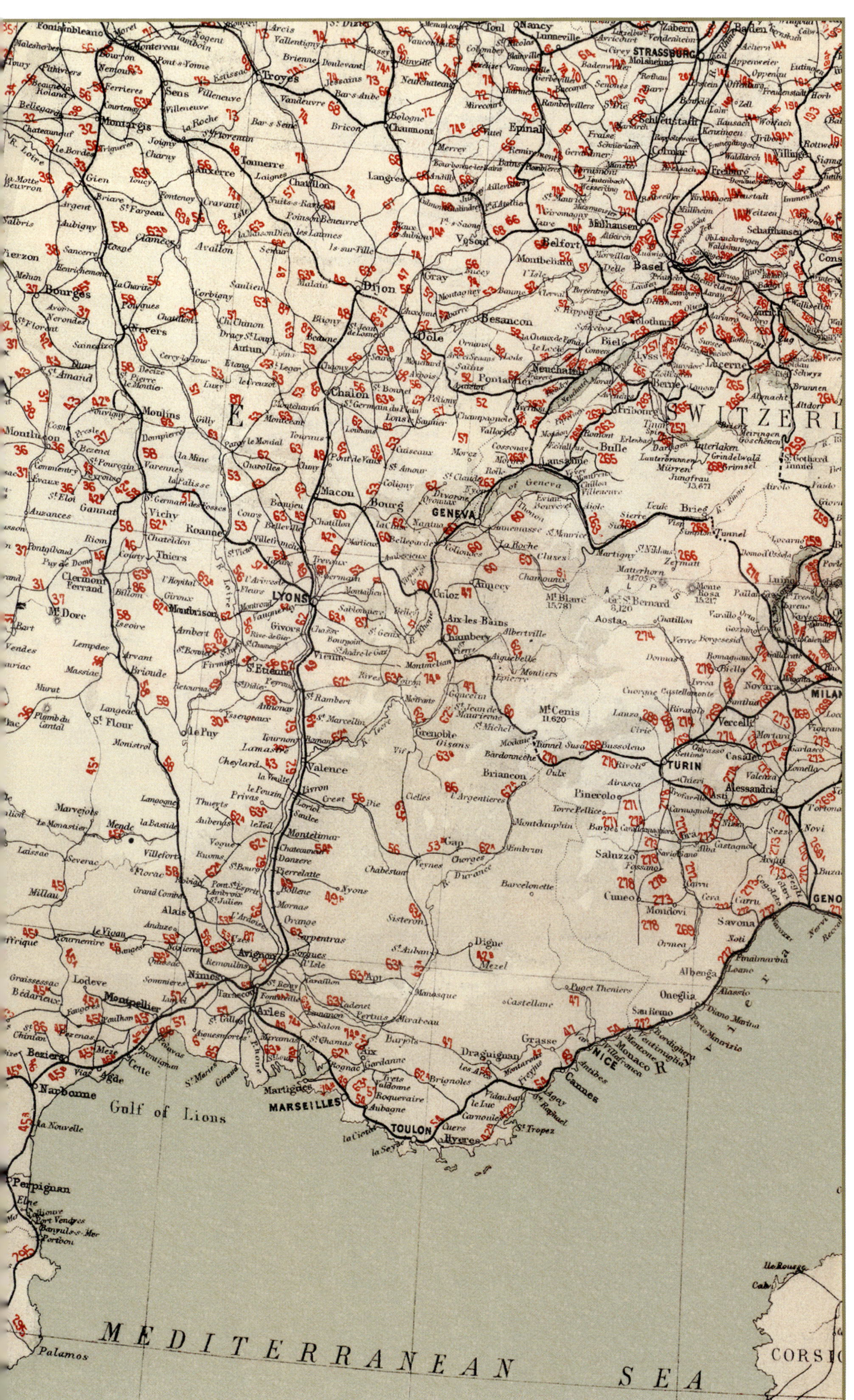

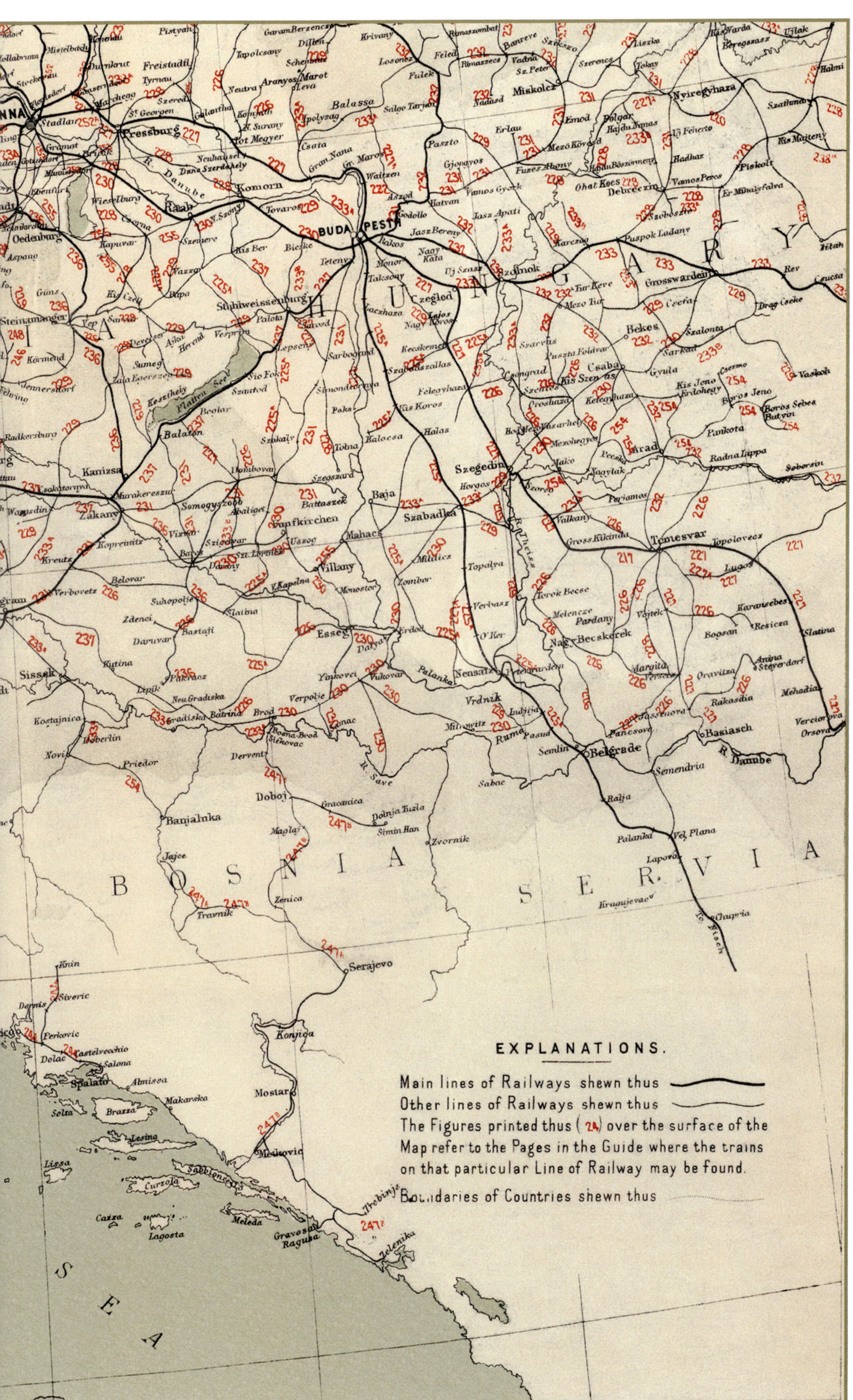
HUNGARY
BOSNIA
SERVIA
BUDA PESTH
Belgrade
Temesvar
Szegedin
Debreczin
Grosswardein
Arad
Miskolc
Nyiregyhaza
Komorn
Raab
Pressburg
Oedenburg
Stuhlweissenburg
Vesprim
Balaton
Platten See
Kanizsa
Zakany
Essegg
Brod
Sissek
Banjaluka
Serajevo
Mostar
Ragusa
Spalato
Semlin
Semendria
Pancsova
Szabadka
Nagy Becskerek
Oravicza
Basiasch
Orsova
S E A

EXPLANATIONS.
Main lines of Railways shewn thus
Other lines of Railways shewn thus
The Figures printed thus (24) over the surface of the
Map refer to the Pages in the Guide where the trains
on that particular Line of Railway may be found.
Boundaries of Countries shewn thus